CARE *and* MANAGEMENT *of the* OLDER HORSE

CARE *and* MANAGEMENT *of the* OLDER HORSE

Heather Scott Parsons

Trafalgar Square Publishing

To Baron
My trusted friend and teacher

© *Heather Scott Parsons 2001*

First published in the United States of America in 2001 by
Trafalgar Square Publishing, North Pomfret, Vermont 05053

Colour separation by Tenon & Polert Colour Scanning Ltd.

Printed in Hong Kong by Dah Hua International Printing Press Co.Ltd.

ISBN 1-57076-213-9

Design by Judy Linard
Illustrations by Maggie Raynor
Edited by Jane Lake

CONTENTS

Amber, a 34-year-old, 13.2 hh New Forest mare, went to live with Jacqui Van Leemputten when she was retired from the local riding school at the age of twenty-four. Now used mainly as a hack, Amber still enjoys the occasional outing to a local show, where she always does well in veteran classes.

ACKNOWLEDGEMENTS

Imust begin by taking this opportunity to offer my sincere thanks to Dr Tina MacGregor BVMS, MRCVS whose pioneering work into the treatment of navicular disease (sponsored by the International League for the Protection of Horses) quite literally saved Baron's life in the mid 1980s, when other veterinary surgeons thought there was no hope for him. Indeed it was Tina's enthusiasm and dedication to equine welfare that inspired in me the same obsession and I suspect that without her influence this book may not have been written.

For their help in more recent years I must also thank the team of veterinary surgeons at Young, Proctor and Wainwright in Northumberland. In particular I must extend my gratitude to Paul Proctor MRCVS, for taking time out of his busy schedule to read the first draft of this book and for offering some invaluable advice on the veterinary aspects.

I would also like to thank Graeme Moran DWCF of North Shields, both for helping to keep Baron sound for many years and for putting up with my endless questions. I must thank equine nutritionist, Teresa Hollands BSc (Hons), MSc from whom I have learnt a great deal, and Andy Foster of A. J. Foster Saddlemakers in Walsall not only for making the most beautiful saddles, but also for his continuing advice and friendship.

I would particularly like to thank my friend Sue Calcutt for her unwavering moral support and shared enthusiasm, and for acting as a sounding board to bounce ideas off. I must also thank Sylvia

When Arlene Sommerville bought Patch in 1995 he already had COPD and arthritis in his hind legs. With appropriate management and plenty of TLC however, Patch, who is now seventeen, shows little evidence of any health problems and is continually placed in coloured cob, veteran, riding club horse, dressage and working hunter classes.

Loch, not just for endeavouring to teach me how to ride with lightness and empathy, but also for her encouragement and generosity of spirit, which once prompted her to make a 700-mile round trip at a moment's notice, simply because she knew I was in need of her help. I feel fortunate indeed to have such good friends.

For help with this book, I offer my thanks to Seven Seas Pet and Animal Health Care, who supplied me with a list of shows holding their Super Solvitax Veteran Classes. I am also grateful to the show secretaries and organisers of many of these events who subsequently forwarded a list of entrants from which I was able to source many of the photographs of elderly horses that have been used throughout this book. Indeed, I must thank every owner who submitted a photograph of their old horse or pony and offer my apologies to those whose pictures we were unable to use owing to space limitations. A special thank you must also go to my friend Johanna Moore for allowing me to use her grey Arab, Saalim, as a model to illustrate certain sections of the text.

I also thank the photographers and companies named below, who were kind enough to give me their permission to use their photographs.

Louise Bruce, page 131; Sue Devereux BA BVSc MRCVS, pages 15, 24, 25, 26, 29 (2), 33, 34 (2), 44, 227 (2), 249, 255, 257; Expo Life, Carlisle, page 233; Rachel Hartley, Lancs., page 1; Phil Jarvis Photography, Herts., page 250; Bob Langrish, page 81; Harry McMillan, Peak Photography, Bathgate, pages 153, 191; MERIEL, Sandringham House, Harlow Business Park, Harlow, Essex, CM19 5TG, pages 41 (2), 42 (2), 43 (2); David Nicholls AWCF, Total Foot Protection, pages 168, 169; Real Time Imaging, Steve Dawe, Tyne and Wear, page 265; Summers Photographic Ltd., pages v, 5; Peter and Marilyn Sweet, Bolton, pages 72, 247; Clive Turner, Tonbridge, page 108; Twin Photographic, London, page 160.

My undying gratitude must also go to Caroline Burt of J. A. Allen for her faith, patience and support throughout this project, and also to my editor Jane Lake for her kindness, encouragement and constructive criticism. Their help and advice has been invaluable.

Last but by no means least, I must thank my husband Keith for his unfailing support, infinite patience and unerring belief in me through thick and thin. Without him so many things in my life may not have been possible.

Author's Notes

For ease of writing, I have throughout this book generally used 'he' whenever I am referring to a horse. In doing so I mean no affront to mares and hope that this will not offend their owners.

Please also note that the opinions expressed within this book, some of which may be considered controversial, are my own and may not necessarily be representative of those individuals named in the Acknowledgements.

Glossary of Terms

Because some of the UK terms differ from those used in the USA, I have provided the following glossary. Some of the terms defined in the glossary also appear in the text for extra clarity.

UK	USA
coarse mix	sweet feed
cubes	pellets
gamgee tissue	gauze
livery yard/yard	boarding stable/barn or farm
napping	refusing to move forward
rasping	floating
rug	blanket
stable/box	stall
veterinary surgeon	veterinarian

Measurements

All the US measurements appear in the text with the UK measurements.

Drug Names

Where applicable, both the UK and the US drug trade names are given in the text together with the generic names.

Part One

GENERAL
CARE *and*
MANAGEMENT

Previous page At twenty
years old, 13.3 hh Jungle
Andante (Jake) can turn
his 'hoof' to anything and
regularly competes in
dressage, cross country
and working hunter
events, winning numerous
championships with his
rider Paula Clinton.

INTRODUCTION

Until fairly recently a horse was considered 'aged' when he reached his tenth birthday and his value would subsequently decline with each passing year as fears about his long-term soundness and ability to work increased. These days, however, owners seldom think of their horses as pensioners until around twenty years of age, even though insurance companies and showing classes for veterans generally categorise horses as old by the time they reach fifteen.

Though the natural lifespan of a horse in the wild will depend on many factors in his environment including the weather, food availability and the presence of predators, it is thought that, on average, wild horses live until around sixteen years of age. Today's domesticated horses commonly live to around twenty-five years of age, though small ponies in particular are known for their longevity and may well remain active well into their thirties or forties. A few have even been known to survive into their fifties, whilst the oldest on record survived until the incredible age of sixty-three.

Such an increase in life expectancy is largely due to a change in the horse's role within Western society from that of a work animal, expected to toil for many hours a day, to one who is cosseted and used mainly for sport and recreation. Now often considered more of a pet than a beast of burden, today's horse owners want their beloved animals to live happy and active lives for as long as possible. This has lead to increasing research and

A rough guide to age comparison	
horse years	human years
15	50
20	60
25	70
30	80
35	90

Though no longer jumped following problems with navicular disease, 19-year-old Dancing Cavalier enjoys showing and dressage with his owner Sophie Neilson, who has found that passive stretching exercises help to keep him supple.

3

Just William, forty-one years young, a 10.3 hh Welsh Mountain pony is a credit to his owner Sue Moorhouse.

advances in veterinary diagnosis and treatment, which along with better nutrition, efficacious vaccines, meticulous worming practices and improved dental care, has resulted in horses living longer than ever before.

Unfortunately, however, society remains ageist and a number of horses are still being unnecessarily written off by the time they reach their mid-teens. Yet an older horse can prove a wonderful schoolmaster (or mistress), capable not only of being a safe and sensible mount for a nervous or novice owner, but also one who is able to teach the more ambitious rider the correct feel for the technicalities of their chosen discipline. Having 'been there and done that' a seasoned campaigner can also provide invaluable competition experience and make a brilliant all-rounder who will look after both himself and his rider when the need arises. That said, it should be noted that, although many elderly horses will be generally easier to handle and less likely to be worried by situations that may send younger ones into a spin, a few who have experienced neglect or indifferent handling by a variety of owners may have developed psychological scars and undesirable behaviour patterns that will take an experienced and sensitive owner to work through. By and large, however, most elderly horses will prove to be trustworthy and reliable friends who will make riding and horse ownership what it should be - pleasurable and fun.

Of course, just like people, as horses grow older, the capacity of their bodily cells to repair and replace themselves begins to decline. As a result, skin will become thinner, losing its resilience and elasticity, meaning that wounds will often take longer to heal and that your horse will lose his ability to maintain an even body temperature, which means that he will feel the cold more in winter and may have difficulty in coping with hot and humid temperatures in summer. Muscle tone may also be lost and tendons and ligaments will weaken. Bones may become more

Kerry Bennett took on 25-year-old Clyde, as a mount for her 5-year-old son. A year later, however, Clyde has exceeded everyone's expectations by having won or been placed every time out with Kerry's daughters in novice/open show jumping, dressage, showing classes etc, and he is now a valued member of the Pony Club team.

fragile and less dense, whilst joint flexibility and dental health will also deteriorate. Eventually the efficiency of the digestive, immune and circulatory systems may also start to decline and hormonal imbalances may become apparent.

There are numerous factors which influence the varying rates at which individuals age. Whilst some may not show any signs of old age until well into their twenties, others may appear to age prematurely in their early teens. In particular, poor conformation, obesity and years of overwork can all increase wear and tear on joints, tendons and ligaments, leading to soundness problems in later life. Similarly, elderly horses who have spent their lives in dusty environments may develop breathing problems, whilst those who have been irregularly wormed may have gut damage which will adversely affect nutrient absorption. In fact, whilst some may just have a weaker constitution than others, the lifespan of the majority of horses is directly influenced by the standard of care they receive throughout their lives.

If buying an elderly horse it is therefore important not only to take into account all the usual prerequisites such as conformation, height, temperament, ability, price etc., but also to find out as much as you can about the horse's previous, as well as current, workload and details of his general management including vaccination and worming history, feed regime etc. Be cautious, for instance, if an old horse appears underweight despite being given large quantities of feed. It may simply be that his diet is inappropriate, but it could also be a sign of liver problems or malabsorption of nutrients due to digestive disfunction. If the horse is not being ridden, consider carefully whether this is really because the owner does not have time, or if it is likely to be because soundness problems only show up when the horse is worked. Regardless of the reasons for him not being ridden, be aware that without regular exercise joints may have stiffened and tendons and ligaments may have weakened, and so he may not be capable of the same amount of work as he would have been had he not been rested.

You must, however, be realistic and accept that whilst few old horses are going to be entirely free of problems, many will still be perfectly capable of general riding club activities that do not demand the same level of fitness expected for other levels of

When buying an elderly horse you can help him settle into his new home by following his previous routine and feed regime as closely as possible for several days before gradually making changes to his diet or daily management.

competition, such as three-day eventing. Nevertheless a prepurchase examination by your veterinary surgeon, paying particular attention to the horse's eyesight, dentition, heart, lungs, soundness and hoof condition, will prove invaluable in identifying and evaluating the severity of any existing health problems which may require specific forms of management to help extend the horse's useful working life.

Irrespective of whether your elderly horse is a new acquisition or has been a member of your family for some time, remember that whilst you cannot turn back the clock or halt the ageing process there is much you can do to help slow the rate of degeneration, prolong your horse's usefulness and improve the quality of his life throughout his pensionable years. Admittedly, an old horse may require a little extra care and attention but there is no secret formula for maintaining an elderly horse's health and condition other than making yourself aware of, and being able to recognise, age-related problems that could arise and knowing how to modify your horse's care accordingly.

Chapter One

GENERAL CARE

I n general, elderly horses benefit from as much turn-out in the field as possible, as this encourages gentle exercise which helps to keep joints supple, aids the process of digestion and assists in the prevention and control of respiratory disease. Whether your old horse lives out or is partially stabled, however, will depend not only on his breeding, but also upon the facilities you have available, the time of year and his individual health and condition. For while there is much to recommend in allowing horses to live out in the field twenty-four hours a day as 'nature intended', we must also realise that nature can be cruel, especially to those who are old or weak. Whilst, therefore, those elderly horses who remain fit and healthy may indeed thrive living out all year round, others will need a little more cosseting if they are to make it from one season to the next.

It is also important to remember that as your horse ages he may become increasingly vulnerable to infection, be more susceptible to extreme weather conditions, and may suffer from digestive problems as well as varying degrees of muscular and skeletal pain due to years of wear and tear. You will, therefore, need to be observant and willing to adapt your horse's management routine to suit his changing needs. For instance, whilst many would assume that a tough old native pony should be able to spend the remainder of his days living out at grass, he may in fact need to be partially stabled if, as a result of worn or missing teeth, he is unable to maintain weight on grass alone. Conversely,

Owned by Janet and Dawn Smith, 32-year-old Cream Puff is still full of energy and regularly ridden. Not surprisingly this sprightly old lady is also a regular winner of veteran horse classes.

9

some elderly thoroughbreds (a breed often considered not hardy enough to live out all year round) may thrive when turned out at grass twenty-four hours a day, provided that is, they have adequate shelter, are given additional feed and supplements and are rugged according to the prevailing weather conditions.

How your individual horse copes with seasonal changes will also play a major factor in determining a management regime that will maximise not only his health and fitness, but also his quality of life. In the winter months for instance, elderly horses may expend as much as 80% of their energy in order to just keep warm. Age-related conditions such as arthritis may also be made much worse by cold wet weather. Many elderly horses may therefore benefit from being kept on a combined system of stable management whereby they are allowed the freedom of the pasture during the day but are brought into the warmth of the stable at night. The combination of gentle exercise, companion-ship of other equines, protection from the elements and a constant supply of food and water, may subsequently not only help increase an old horse's life expectancy, but also the likelihood of his ability to perform for some years to come.

On the other hand, the summer months can present a differ-ent, but nonetheless equally challenging, range of problems. For instance, as the ability to regulate body temperature declines with age, some elderly horses may become prone to heat stress, especially if turned out into a field where no shade or shelter is available. Similarly, swarms of flies and midges may force an old horse to expend a large part of his energy by vigorously nodding his head and galloping around the field in an effort to gain temporary relief from his tormentors, a situation that can cause otherwise unexplained weight loss or lameness. In these circum-stances your elderly horse may be better off if he is turned out overnight and brought into the cool, relatively fly-free sanctuary of a stable or barn during the day.

Sometimes, however, veterinary considerations will override all other factors. If your horse has a severe dust allergy, for example, your veterinary surgeon may advise that, despite the benefits offered by the combined system of stable management, your elderly horse may be better off living out twenty-four hours a day, if his condition appears to be worsening despite the implementation of a clean air regime (*see* Day-to-day Care).

Conversely, an old horse who has lived out all his life, may need to be partially stabled if he becomes prone to laminitis or perhaps develops photosensitization (an adverse reaction to sunlight) as a result of liver disease.

Basic Facilities

From the outset it must be understood that livery yards without all year turn-out facilities are not suitable places to keep old horses. Forcing an elderly horse to stand in his stable for months on end, only to be brought out to be ridden at his owner's convenience will not only make him very miserable, but may also shorten his life expectancy because a lack of movement and fresh air will exacerbate any stiffness in the joints and increase his susceptibility to digestive disorders and infection. It is also hardly surprising that horses deprived of socialising with their own kind are more likely to become difficult to handle and find ways of amusing themselves by, for example, windsucking, crib-biting or weaving: behaviour patterns which are often narrow-mindedly referred to as 'vices'. If you wish your old horse to live a long, happy and active life, then just take a moment to ask yourself how you would cope if you were forced into solitary confinement, locked in the equivalent of a cupboard for months on end, and only allowed out to exercise for an hour or two a day. Even if you were given ample food and water, a comfortable bed and beautiful clothes, would it be surprising if you became bored and lonely, lost your interest in life, and had neither the strength nor stamina to do much work? Whether keeping your elderly horse at home or on a livery yard, therefore, your main priority must be to ensure that you have adequate facilities in order to look after his psychological as well as physical wellbeing.

Field Requirements

Your first priority must be to have access to a field into which your horse can be turned out with others on a daily basis. Ideally, the field should be on gently undulating, well-drained land and be large enough to fulfil the majority of your horse's nutritional requirements. Regrettably this is not always possible as more and more good grazing land is lost to the demands of urbanisation. However, even relatively small fields can be managed successfully providing that your old horse is given supplementary feed and can be partially stabled in winter to prevent the land from becoming a quagmire of deep mud that will place unnecessary strain on tendons and ligaments weakened by age. Hillside fields should be avoided as, though less likely to become badly poached, your elderly horse may become prone to back, hock and stifle strain if forced to constantly brace himself against a steep gradient.

Since even minor injuries can become problematic due to an age-related delay in wound healing, every effort must also be made to reduce the risk of injuries. Care must be taken to ensure that your old horse's field is not overstocked because overcrowding can strain relationships between field companions and increase the risk of squabbling. Similarly, safe, secure and highly visible field boundaries become doubly important. Well-maintained hedges, stone walls, post-and-rail and electric fencing are ideal, but plain wire fencing, which is difficult for horses to see especially if their eyesight is beginning to fail, can be acceptable if topped by a wooden or plastic rail or strand of visibility tape. Barbed wire and sheep netting however are definitely taboo as both have the potential to cause severe, life-threatening injuries. Fences should also circumvent rivers, streams and ponds and be placed a few feet in from the perimeter of any surrounding gardens, as drinking polluted or stagnant water or nibbling at garden plants (many of which are toxic) can cause illness and poisoning from which an ageing digestive system may not be able to recover.

As the effects of age make elderly horses increasingly susceptible to the extremes of both winter and summer weather, they will undoubtedly benefit from free access to a walk-in field shelter if they are expected to live out all year round. Whilst hedges, trees, walls and banks, which can act as good windbreaks and even provide some shade from the sun, may prove sufficient for those who can be partially stabled during the worst weather conditions, they do not offer adequate protection in wet weather for those expected to live out twenty-four hours a day, nor do they provide a refuge from the torment of flies in the heat of summer. Though some owners claim their horses will not use a shelter, in truth this generally signifies that the building is badly situated or appears dark and dingy. Lame or arthritic old horses may also be very wary of entering small shelters where they could be cornered by their more agile field companions. To be inviting, a solidly built shelter must therefore be spacious, light and airy, offer protection from the prevailing winds, have a deep, clean bed and an open-fronted access to allow a quick escape.

Stable Requirements

If your elderly horse's health, a lack of grazing or inadequate shelter determines that he needs to be stabled part of the time, he should be given the largest available stable to enable him to move around easily. The stable must also be well ventilated as research has shown a direct correlation between poorly ventilated stables and high antibody levels in the blood, which indicates that, in such circumstances, a horse's body is constantly fighting against infectious agents. Stale air, dust and mould spores, as well as noxious gasses such as ammonia emanating from urine soaked bedding, can all cause irritation and inflammation of the respiratory tract. Since elderly horses may already have respiratory problems due to years of exposure to such allergens, this will prove increasingly debilitating, especially as the efficiency of their immune system declines with age, making their lungs vulnerable to attack by airborne bacteria and viruses. Louvres or ridge roof ventilation will therefore prove beneficial, as will air outlets on the wall opposite to the stable door. The latter must however be positioned high enough to prevent draughts blowing across your horse's body, otherwise he may develop a chill.

To help reduce the number of airborne pollutants actually entering your horse's stable, you should also ensure that hay and bedding (a major source of dust and fungal spores) are stored in a separate building and that the muck heap is sited downwind of the stable yard. Dusty riding arenas situated close to the stable should also be kept well watered to prevent contamination of your horse's air space and the resulting irritation to his lungs.

Barn Housing

If for various reasons your old horse is unable to live out, and yet suffers from severe arthritis which appears to worsen as a result of stable confinement, housing him in a large barn or indoor school may be a viable alternative, particularly if he can be encouraged to wander around by placing hay at one end of the building and water at the other. If allowed to share the barn or school with other compatible equines, interaction between the group will also encourage gentle movement and may help keep a highly strung horse mentally relaxed. As in the field, however, great care needs to be taken to ensure that the building is not overcrowded and that your old horse is not intimidated by others or prevented from getting his fair share of the hay. Though usually well ventilated, such housing may not be suitable for those with chronic obstructive pulmonary disease (also called COPD or heaves) because, if the surface of an indoor school is dusty, or if bedding in a barn is deep litter, a build up of mould, bacteria and ammonia may impair lung function still further.

Day-to-day Care

Maintaining a Dust-free Environment

In addition to ensuring adequate ventilation for those who are partially stabled, every effort must be made on a daily basis to maintain a 'clean air regime'. This involves taking precautions to ensure that dust and mould spores in your old horse's environment are kept to a minimum, for example by the use of dust-free bedding and the feeding of haylage or soaked hay. Ideally horses in neighbouring boxes should also be maintained on a clean air regime in order to reduce the level of airborne pollutants that may inadvertently contaminate your horse's air space from adjoining stables. Unfortunately not all livery yards insist on such high standards, however, regardless of whether or not you are able to obtain the cooperation of other owners, minimising the levels of respiratory irritants in your own horse's stable will still prove beneficial.

Bedding

As even apparently clean straw can contain more fungal spores than any other type of bedding its use is best avoided. Long straw also has a tendency to become entangled around shuffling, arthritic limbs making it difficult for old horses to move freely around their stables and often results in slippery areas of the floor being exposed as bedding is dragged around the box. These problems can be overcome by using dust-extracted, chopped straw which has been treated with disinfectant to make it distasteful. Alternatively, hemp or dust-extracted shavings can provide a soft, comfortable and generally unpalatable bed that gives safe supportive footing. Shredded or diced paper is also gaining in popularity, particularly for horses suffering from COPD, as it generates fewer airborne pollutants than any other type of bedding.

Various types of rubber matting are also available which, when used alone or with a small amount of bedding in order to encourage the horse to urinate, are certainly labour saving and dust free but, used in this way, rubber matting does not, in my opinion, offer sufficient warmth and comfort for an elderly horse. It will, however, provide a non-slip, insulating layer beneath a *full* bed (though this may be something of a luxury), thereby providing extra cushioning for old joints and helping to reduce the incidence of filled legs, as well as preventing the development of capped hocks, and providing secure footing against which your horse may obtain extra grip when trying to rise to his feet.

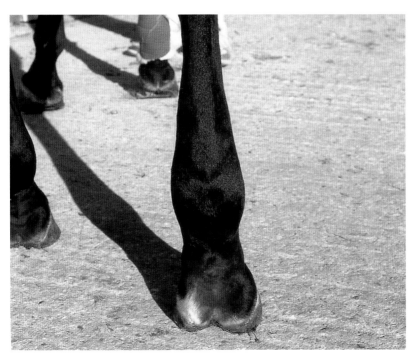

FILLED LEGS
As efficient circulation depends on movement and warmth, inactivity, especially during the cold winter months, can result in a build up of fluid in the lower legs, causing mild swelling without pain or lameness. The condition is most commonly seen in the hind limbs, though all four legs may be affected. With exercise the swelling will invariably disappear and no treatment is needed. Daily turn-out must therefore be provided, though massage and the application of bandages or leg wraps whenever the horse is stabled will help to keep swelling to a minimum. Mild herbal diuretics can also help reduce fluid build up. A 30 g combination of clivers (also known as cleavers) and calendula can be particularly effective.

Note Inadequate dietary fibre can also cause filling of the legs.

Ideally, in order to prevent the build up and inhalation of harmful mould and dust spores, the bed should be mucked-out on a daily basis whilst your old horse is out of his stable. Using deep-litter beds within the small confines of a stable is inadvisable, as over many months this will allow bacteria, mould and ammonia gasses to accumulate which will prove harmful for your elderly horse's lungs and could lead to the development of infections in the feet such as thrush. However, depending upon the severity of any existing respiratory problems, a compromise may be reached by removing droppings from the bed on a daily basis and leaving thorough mucking-out until the weekend, at which time the floor should be cleaned with disinfectant, and any cobwebs, which act as a magnet for dust and bacteria, should be removed from stable walls.

Hay

Hay can also be a major source of dust and should therefore be soaked before feeding. Alternatively, a dust-free vacuum packed hay or haylage may be fed (*see* pages 81–83). No matter what the type of forage on offer, your elderly horse should always be fed from the ground or from a low-level hay manger. This will help to avoid unnecessary strain being placed on his ageing neck and back muscles as a result of being forced to stand in an unnatural position, with the head high and the back hollow, whilst feeding from above head height.

Field Inspections

Out in the field, brief inspections should be made to check for rabbit holes, poisonous plants, broken fencing or litter that may have been thrown over the fence from nearby roadways. Dust-free bedding in field shelters should be regularly mucked-out and droppings should be removed from the field at least twice a week in summer and once a week in winter to prevent the land from becoming heavily contaminated with infective worm larvae, to which elderly horses become increasingly susceptible with age. The removal of droppings will also effectively increase the area of palatable grass available to your horse (by keeping the size of sour 'toilet' areas to a minimum) and will reduce the number of flies attracted to the pasture.

Daily Checks

Regardless of whether he is turned out at grass or partially stabled, your old horse will need visiting at least twice a day, when a hands-on check for, for example, injuries, heat, swelling or loose shoes should be made. You should also look for any more subtle signs of lameness or illness such as an abnormal stance, reduced appetite or a change in the quantity or consistency of droppings etc. Your elderly horse will also need feeding in accordance with his individual needs and you must ensure that clean, fresh water is available at all times (*see* Feeding).

Grooming

Even if your old horse is no longer working and is spending his retirement out at grass, regular grooming will prove beneficial, particularly if he has a long, thick coat as a result of Cushing's syndrome or hypothyroidism (*see* pages 247and 251). Not only will this help to encourage circulation and keep his coat clean, thus reducing the risk of skin infections and parasite infestations, but it will also keep the pores of the skin open, thereby allowing him to regulate his body temperature more easily by ensuring the sweat glands do not become blocked by dirt and mud. Grooming should also be looked upon as an opportunity to build up mutual trust and friendship, and as a way to help your old horse feel wanted, especially if he is no longer ridden.

Grooming can help build a bond of trust and friendship between you and your horse, in just the same way as it does between field companions.

Grooming is, in fact, the simplest form of massage and can help warm up your horse's muscles in preparation for work. Similarly, once your horse has dried off after work, grooming can help relieve muscle spasm and reduce fatigue. Elderly horses who object to being groomed may simply have sensitive skin and may find it more comfortable if softer brushes or cloths are used. Persistent sensitivity could also be a sign of muscle soreness and indicate that a visit from the vet or chiropractor is necessary, or even that a change in work levels or the type and fitting of saddlery is required.

Companionship

By the time they reach old age, many horses will have learned to tolerate spending some of their time alone but it must be remembered that, by nature, horses are gregarious, yet nervous, creatures who will actively seek to band together with others of their own kind for companionship and safety. Stabling an elderly horse where he can see, hear and preferably touch others will go some way to help prevent him from feeling completely isolated but nothing is likely to make him feel happier, safer and keep up his interest in life more than being given the opportunity to interact freely with other horses in a group out in the field.

Unfortunately, some aged stallions who have never been allowed, and thus never learned how, to socialise with other horses, may have to continue to be segregated for the safety of all concerned, though they will frequently accept the company of other animals such as sheep, cattle, or hens. Some old horses cope remarkably well in such situations, especially if they enjoy their work and have developed a deep bond of trust and friend-ship with an owner or rider whom they have known for many years. We would, however, be deluding ourselves if we thought that the two or three hours a person spends with their horse each day, combined with the company of another species, could actually negate the need for the companionship of other equines.

Providing horses with other species of animals for company, is like asking a person to live their whole lives with only a cat or dog as a companion. That animal may be better than nothing, and an emotional attachment will no doubt develop, but after a while that person will still crave human contact and communication. Horses are no different, and even though they will retain any strong bond they have formed with their owner or companion animal, the majority of average horses would still choose to spend some time mingling with other equines if given the choice. Indeed, without the company of other horses, many will soon become lonely, lacklustre, or depending upon temperament, difficult to control.

As turning horses out together can also sometimes result in injury, every precaution should be taken to minimise the occurrence of accidents. Many yards now split mares and geldings into separate grazing paddocks in an effort to avert conflict arising between geldings over in-season mares or, conversely, to avoid the injuries that can be inflicted by unreceptive mares fending off the unwanted attention of the opposite sex. Whilst some experts are horrified by this practice, which they consider sexual deprivation, there seems little evidence of any real detrimental effect. If you are lucky enough to have acres and acres around which the horses may roam, and/or if the mixed sex groups have grown up with each other, then it is certainly feasible to keep them together with the minimum risk of injury. However, the majority of privately owned horses are, rightly or wrongly, kept in relatively small paddocks with other horses with whom they have had no previous connection. Not surprisingly, relationships between them can easily become strained, especially if complicated by issues of sex. It is understandable, therefore, that owners take every possible precaution to try to reduce the incidence of injury which may not only result in expensive veterinary bills, but may also involve a lengthy period of convalescence, particularly in the case of the elderly horse who can prove notoriously slow to recover from injury.

When choosing suitable companionship for your elderly horse, it must be remembered that, just like old people, they too need to retain a sense of importance and dignity throughout their pensionable years and nothing will bring down their self-esteem more than constantly being the underdog. Extra care should therefore be taken to ensure that if an old horse's movement becomes limited, he does not become intimidated by his younger or more agile field companions, as the resulting increase in stress levels could make him prone to illness, cause loss of appetite and

Compatible companionship is vital to ensure your elderly horse's happiness.

poor condition. That said, active elderly horses can prove to be wonderful 'aunts' and 'uncles' to youngsters, teaching them social etiquette that will not only help young horses to integrate with others, but will produce better mannered individuals who will be easier to train. From an older horse's point of view, such a role within the group, can not only help improve their sense of worth, but also provide an interest for those retired to the field.

As long as consideration is given to the temperaments of horses expected to mix together, there should rarely be any serious confrontations or injury once each individual's social status within the group has been sorted out. The risk of confrontations, however, is greatly increased when a new horse is first introduced into an existing group. If fields are divided by solid fencing, such as stone walls, it is recommended that a newcomer is turned into an adjoining field for a few days, where he may greet and sniff his prospective companions whilst protected by a physical barrier. This method of introducing horses must be avoided if dividing fences are constructed from wire or post-and-rail as, should the horses strike out at each other there is a real risk of serious injury should a limb become trapped in the fence itself.

An alternative method of introduction involves taking all the horses out of the field and then turning the newcomer out with a low- or medium-ranking member of the existing group. These two horses should then be allowed to make friends before the other horses are introduced, one by one, preferably in order of their status within the group. Though the risk of injury may still be increased until the new horse finds his place within the established social structure of the group, either method is better than simply expecting an old horse to fend for himself when turned out into a field full of strange horses.

Although it may be tempting to want to take your horse out of the field at the first sign of trouble, it is important to allow horses to be horses and to introduce and take care of themselves as horses do. This may well involve sessions of squealing, striking-out, galloping around and threatening behaviour, all of which is perfectly normal, until the newcomer discovers and settles into his own niche within the group. Obviously you should keep an eye on proceedings throughout the first few days just in case any of the horses are *truly* aggressive towards your horse, in which case you may either decide to try your horse with another group, or segregate the aggressive horse with a few others whose company he finds acceptable. Your old horse should not be turned out overnight, however, until you are absolutely sure that he is getting on well with all his new field companions because, if serious injury should occur, the time lapse between your last visit in the evening and your first visit the next morning could have fatal consequences.

In an ideal world, horses turned out together should have their hind shoes removed, though for various reasons, including hoof condition, workload and owner preference, this may not always be possible to arrange. Whilst initial introductions are being made, therefore, it may be wise for all the horses to wear brushing boots, in order to help protect the vulnerable structures of the lower limbs should an altercation occur. In my experience, boots worn for relatively short periods in such situations can prove invaluable in reducing the severity of an injury and will rarely cause rubbing, especially if lined with fleece to absorb sweat.

It must be accepted that, even when groups have become established, squabbles will arise from time to time and owners must learn not to panic or intervene unnecessarily. Like people, horses will occasionally have disagreements with each other and, whilst they may threaten each other for a few days, such quarrels are often quickly resolved and the horses will either become friends again or perhaps simply decide to keep out of each other's way. Play fighting can also be a cause for concern but, before insisting your horse be moved to another field, consider whether you would take your children away from their friends at school, just because they may sometimes play a little rough and come home with a few bruises? I doubt you would. Being overly protective of your horse can be almost as bad as not caring enough in that you will ruin his happiness and quality of life if you insist that he lives alone.

Seasonal Pointers

Spring and Summer

If your old horse is being turned out onto new pasture in the spring, his time in the paddock should be increased slowly by an hour a day to prevent stress being placed on his digestive system as a result of a sudden change in diet. Indeed, sudden access to lush spring grass which has a high moisture content and is low in fibre can cause diarrhoea. Offering an additional source of fibre (i.e. hay or oat or barley straw) will, therefore, prove beneficial in supporting the functioning of your old horse's gut, especially if droppings become loose.

Since excess fat can put extra strain on the heart, lungs and limbs of elderly horses, access to good quality grazing may need to be restricted throughout the spring and summer if your horse is prone to weight gain or laminitis. Concentrate feed will also need to be reduced, though it is important to ensure that vitamin and mineral levels are maintained (*see* pages 76–80). Conversely, in the height of the summer, when low rainfall may inhibit grass growth, elderly horses may need extra hay and concentrates in order to prevent weight loss, ensure efficient functioning of the gut and avert the temptation to eat any poisonous plants which may have grown unnoticed.

Insects

Dry, hot weather will also result in hard ground and an increase in the population of insects. If an elderly horse is forced to remain constantly on the move in an attempt to escape from the torment of flies, this can lead to brittle, cracked hooves and the extra concussion placed upon the joints will aggravate any arthritic condition. The flies themselves can cause eye and ear infections, and an allergic reaction to midge bites can cause a condition known as sweet itch in susceptible horses. The use of fly repellents and fly hoods or fringes can all prove beneficial, though the provision of adequate shelter is probably the most effective way of reducing associated stress.

Though a long mane and tail can act as natural fly swatters, elasticated fly hoods, which will pull off easily in an emergency, can give your old horse valuable extra protection against insects during the summer months.

23

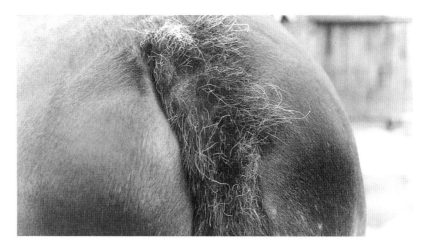

SWEET ITCH
Persistent rubbing, as a result of severe itchiness caused by an allergic reaction to midge bites, can cause hair loss, sores and infection. Eventually the skin in the affected areas (most commonly around the mane and tail) will become thickened and look ridged in appearance. Treatment and prevention involves stabling the horse between the hours of 4 p.m. and 9 a.m., when the midges are at their worst, as well as the use of protective fly screens, rugs, fly repellents and soothing creams. As a last resort corticosteroids may be recommended but must be used with caution as such drugs can have potentially serious side effects, e.g. suppression of the immune system, laminitis, delayed wound healing etc.

Protection from the heat
Shelter will also offer protection from the heat of the sun, which is vital for an elderly horse who may become prone to heat stress as his ability to regulate body temperature declines. Whilst environmental temperatures remain high, great care must also be taken to ensure that your old horse is not overworked as this can commonly lead to electrolyte imbalances and dehydration. Elderly horses suffering from Cushing's syndrome who do not shed their coats in summer may also benefit from a bib or low trace clip, to help prevent them from becoming overheated.

The shade offered by adequate shelter is also essential for those susceptible to sunburn. Indeed, whilst a high factor sun block can help prevent burning of the pink skin behind white markings of the face, muzzle or legs, those elderly horses who have developed a particular sensitivity to ultraviolet (UV) rays as a result of liver problems, may need to be partially stabled or wear a lightweight rug if the effects become more widespread.

Autumn
In the autumn a second spurt of grass growth will again mean that the grazing of those prone to laminitis may need to be restricted. However, as the season progresses and the feed value of grass begins to dwindle, supplementary feed should once again be given before weight loss becomes visible to the naked eye, as any loss of condition will prove particularly hard for an elderly horse to regain over the ensuing winter months. The regular monitoring of your old horse's weight using a weight tape will, therefore, prove beneficial.

Sunburn

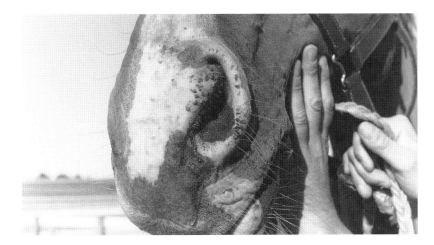

Winter

Winter can be a particularly difficult time for old horses as they tend to feel the cold more easily than younger animals and, as a result, require extra dietary energy (i.e. calories) to help maintain body temperature, just at a time when the nutritional value and availability of grass declines. Though additional concentrate feeds will prove beneficial, it is fibre digestion that produces more internal body heat than any other type of feed. Your elderly horse will therefore need to have free access to hay at all times if he is having trouble maintaining bodyweight. Unfortunately, some elderly horses may continue to loose weight if they are unable to chew and ultimately digest the coarser stems of hay. In this instance an alternative source of fibre must be provided, perhaps in the form of a hay chaff or a sloppy combination of soaked sugar beet, high fibre cubes and alfalfa pellets offered at frequent intervals throughout the day.

Where hay is being fed in the field, it should be put into heaps that are at least sixteen feet apart. This will ensure that an arthritic old horse, who may not be able to move out the way of trouble quickly, has plenty of time and room to manoeuvre should squabbles break out. Putting out at least the same number of hay heaps as there are horses, but preferably two or three more, will also help reduce the risk of your old horse being bullied away from his share of the rations by more dominant field companions. Though feeding hay on the ground will inevitably mean that some will be trampled on and wasted, try to avoid the temptation to hang hay nets or racks along the fence line because

25

LICE
There are two types of louse which infect horses. One survives on skin scurf and debris, whilst the other feeds on the horse's blood and tissue fluids. Old horses in poor condition and those with long, dirty coats are particularly susceptible to infestation, especially during the winter months. Irritation by lice can result in persistent rubbing, self-mutilation and weight loss. Treatment involves an initial application of a delousing preparation to kill the adult lice, followed by a second application two weeks later to kill any larvae that may have hatched from eggs laid in the coat. Treatment with the worming preparation, Ivermectin will also kill blood sucking lice. Lice can be spread by direct contact, therefore an infested horse should be segregated, and all those with whom he has had previous contact should also be deloused as a precaution.

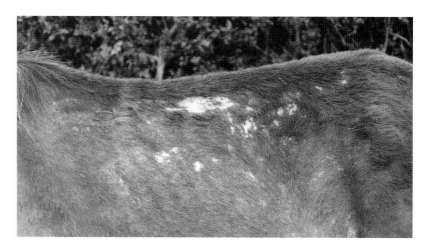

in bad weather, elderly horses may be reluctant to eat from them if it means they must face into the wind and rain.

It must also be remembered that as dry food such as hay forms an ever increasing part of your old horse's diet in winter, his requirement for water will increase. In freezing temperatures, the regular removal of ice from field troughs is essential to reduce the risk of him developing impacted colic. Ideally, heated water troughs should be provided, though for many this may not be a viable option as it will require the routing of underground electricity cables.

Rugs

Despite their advancing years, some fit and stocky native ponies and cobs may cope perfectly well, and indeed be more comfortable, without a rug during the winter months provided they have adequate shelter. But regular checks will have to be made to ensure that their thick, woolly coats do not hide any sudden loss of condition or harbour parasites such as lice or infections such as rain scald.

For the majority of elderly horses, however, the wearing of a rug will prove beneficial in helping them to maintain body condition by reducing the amount of energy they use just to stay warm. Though the natural protection afforded by a horse's coat generally works well in dry, cold conditions, if the hair is saturated and flattened by rain or is disturbed by strong winds, its insulating properties will be lost. As heat dissipates more readily through the less resilient skin of an older horse, this will cause his muscles to shiver, wasting even more energy in an attempt to increase body temperature. In poor weather, therefore, those who need help to maintain weight will undoubtedly benefit from wearing a rug, regardless of whether or not they have been clipped. The extra warmth a rug provides will also encourage circulation and help reduce stiffness, which can prove particularly advantageous to arthritic horses. Indeed, even when partially stabled, such horses may benefit from wearing rugs and leg wraps overnight to keep joints warm and reduce any associated pain. In your efforts to conserve energy, however, you must take great care not to overrug, as creating sauna-like conditions beneath a rug can be responsible for as much weight loss as that caused by plummeting temperatures.

When choosing a rug, the most essential criteria are that it is comfortable and well fitting, as the thinner skin of elderly horses can be very susceptible to rubbing. Outdoors, 'breathable' synthetic waterproof rugs are probably best: when wet, they do not become as heavy or uncomfortable as traditional canvas rugs. Such rugs also allow sweat to escape, which means that if an old horse is experiencing difficulties in regulating temperature on a warm day, sweat can evaporate thus reducing the risk of him becoming chilled through standing in a rug that has become damp from retaining moisture. No matter what the choice of

If your elderly horse needs to wear a rug, choose one that has been made from a breathable material and is designed to sit high up in front of the withers, whilst still having plenty of depth in the neck opening to allow your horse to graze comfortably.

material or design however, particular care must be taken to ensure that a rug does not exert excessive pressure on the prominent withers of an old horse whose back may have begun to sag with age. Choose rugs which are cut well up in front of the withers. If necessary, foam pads sewn inside the rug at either side of the withers will help a little to lift the rug at this point but make sure that the rug does not then become too tight around the shoulders or underside of the neck. Alternatively, a made-to-measure rug that will follow the contours of your old horse's body may prove a worthwhile investment.

Clipping

While the hair of a winter coat is designed to provide warmth and insulation, it does not allow a hot horse to cool down; it inhibits heat loss resulting in stress and tiredness, thus a thick woolly coat may be more of a hindrance than a help to elderly horses who are still being worked. A coat that becomes soaked with sweat may also remain damp for some time increasing the likelihood of the horse developing a chill and losing condition. Winter coats are, therefore, frequently clipped to help working horses to sweat freely and dry more quickly.

The type of clip required should be determined by your old horse's workload and his ability to regulate body temperature, rather than relying on what is currently in vogue on the stable yard. Start off by removing only as much of your old horse's coat as necessary from the areas he sweats most, i.e. the underside of the neck and body where the skin is thinnest. Remember that the more coat you clip off, the more susceptible your horse will be to the cold when he is not working, and he will, therefore, need warmer rugs as well as even more feed and hay if he is to stay warm and maintain condition.

Some old horses with relatively fine coats may not need clipping at all if they are kept fit, in light work and are rugged up early to prevent a full winter coat developing.

Adverse ground and weather conditions

As winter progresses and ground conditions become wet and muddy, regular checks must be made for signs of mud fever and cracked heels to which elderly horses will become increasingly susceptible as their immune system's response to infection

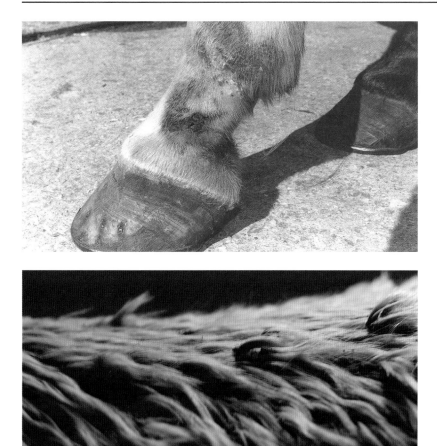

MUD FEVER (*top*), CRACKED HEELS AND RAIN SCALD (*bottom*)
These problems are caused by prolonged saturation and subsequent softening of the skin which allows bacteria to penetrate the weakened tissue thus causing infection. Treatment involves keeping the affected areas clean and dry, the regular removal of scabs, and the topical application of antibiotic ointments. In severe cases, oral antibiotics and anti-inflammatories may also be required. Prevention of mud fever and cracked heels consists of cleaning and thoroughly drying the legs on a daily basis and the application of protective oils or gels to provide a waterproof barrier for the skin. Rain scald, which develops along the back, may be prevented by the use of waterproof turn-out rugs.

becomes less efficient. Foot abscesses may become more common as excessive moisture softens the hoof making it more prone to injury and penetration by foreign objects. Bruised soles may also occur more frequently, either as a result of walking over frozen, rutted ground, or snow and ice balling up in the feet. Indeed, since an elderly horse's stiffening joints may make it more difficult for him to maintain his balance on slippery ground, great care must be taken when walking him out in icy conditions as, should he slip and fall, his less dense and therefore fragile bone structure is more likely to sustain a fracture or break. Where possible, salting pathways or spreading used bedding will help provide extra grip but if conditions become too dangerous, it may be advisable to confine your old horse to his stable for a day or two, remembering to cut down any concentrate feed by at least

> BRUISED SOLES AND FOOT ABSCESSES
>
> Particularly common in those old horses with thin soles and flat feet, bruises are commonly caused by walking over unlevel ground or treading on a stone, whilst abscesses may be caused by penetration of the foot by a sharp object or dirt particle. Both may also occur as a result of concussion or poor trimming and shoeing. Abscesses in particular can cause such sudden and severe pain that the horse is unable to bear weight on the hoof, which often leads owners to believe that their horse has broken his leg. However, the affected foot will often be warmer than the opposite foot, the digital pulse (taken at the back of the fetlock) will be stronger than normal and hoof testers will elicit a painful response. Treatment involves removal of the shoe and, where necessary, the creation of a hole in the foot to allow infection from an abscess to drain away. Depending upon the severity of the condition, tubbing (i.e. soaking the foot in hot water and epsom salts) and poulticing may be recommended, and box rest will generally be advised until the horse becomes sound.

half, whilst giving free access to both soaked hay and water. In such circumstances, allowing him to roam around an indoor or outdoor school for a few hours will help encourage circulation and prevent his joints from becoming stiff but where this is not possible, some passive stretching and massage will prove beneficial.

Though providing your old horse with plenty of gentle daily exercise is essential, common sense must prevail and in extreme weather conditions there is little point in turning him out for long periods if all he is going to do is stand and shiver with cold in a field full of mud where there is little to eat or inadequate shelter. In very bad weather, it will undoubtedly be kinder to turn your old horse out for just a few hours a day, if possible arranging for the time to be split so that he goes out for a short while in the morning and again in the afternoon. No matter how bad the weather however, avoid the temptation to close the top stable door, otherwise in an effort to protect your horse, you may in fact be responsible for damaging his lungs. Without continual changes of air, the atmosphere inside any stable will become damp, causing condensation to form, which will encourage the growth of fungal spores and increase the risk of respiratory problems developing. If you are worried about your old horse becoming cold it is far better to put on an extra rug than to compromise the quality of the air he breathes.

Chapter Two

HEALTH CARE

Know Your Own Horse

Just like old people, elderly horses become prone to infection, disease, digestive disturbances, arthritis etc., as the degenerative changes associated with old age begin to take their toll. Unlike elderly people however, old horses cannot complain verbally about their aching joints, stomach upsets or lack of breath. Instead they rely on their owners' powers of observation to recognise when something is wrong. It is, therefore, up to you to become so familiar with your old horse's normal attitude, appetite, posture and behaviour that it becomes second nature for you to notice any uncharacteristic changes that may signify he is feeling unwell. If for instance your old horse refuses to eat his feed, when normally he would lick his bowl clean, this may indicate that he is feeling quite poorly. However, you may not consider this unusual if you know your horse is a fussy eater who regularly leaves his feeds untouched. Similarly, if your normally sound horse suddenly appears lame when first brought out of the stable, you would probably ask your vet to take a look. If, on the other hand, your horse is known to suffer from arthritis and often appears unlevel following stable confinement, you would be unlikely to worry unduly – provided of course he looked no worse than normal.

Owned by Brandy Goubel, 30-year-old Flicka, a 13.2 hh Welsh cross mare, described as a loyal and trustworthy friend, is now looked after and ridden by 14-year-old Jo Baker, with whom she is regularly placed in show jumping and one-day events, as well as veteran horse and family pony classes!

31

Establishing Your Horse's Normal Health Parameters

Along with careful daily observation, a full veterinary examination of your old horse should be performed once a year. Initially this will help to establish a baseline of normal parameters that will prove invaluable in identifying and subsequently monitoring any health problems, such as a heart murmur, liver disease, lung function, arthritis or cataract formation. Ideally, the examination should include taking a blood test to ascertain your horse's individual blood values against which comparisons can be made should he become ill. This is particularly important if he is to be put on long term phenylbutazone (bute) therapy as the blood can then be monitored for early evidence of bute toxicity (i.e. decreased neutrophils and proteins). It is also important to know that the interpretation of blood tests can sometimes prove difficult because an individual's normal blood parameters can change according to environmental factors, such as exercise, excitement or food. To ensure consistency of data, therefore, repeat blood tests should preferably be performed at the same time of day, under the same circumstances (e.g. when the horse is resting quietly, before being fed or exercised).

You should also ask your vet to show you how to take your horse's temperature, pulse and respiration, as this will often prove useful when trying to decide just how poorly your horse actually is and in some cases may even save his life. If, for instance, your horse is dull and off his feed, but otherwise appears quite normal, you may decide to wait and see how he is later in the day. If, however, you were also able to discover that he had a temperature of over 104 °F, and an increased heart rate of approximately 60 beats per minute, you would know that his condition was more serious than the visible signs would at first indicate, and that your vet should visit as a matter of urgency.

Maintaining a Health File

Once your old horse's normal health parameters have been established, they should be kept on file along with details of his usual habits, feed, weight, exercise programme etc. The dates of any changes you subsequently make to his diet, training or environment (e.g. whether turned out, stabled, taken to a show, mixed with new field companions etc.) should be highlighted, as should any difference in your horse's normal attitude, appetite, condition or performance. Details of any minor injuries such as swelling, lameness, illness, 'off days' and veterinary visits should also be recorded, no matter how insignificant they may appear, together with the type and duration of any medication given and the time taken for recovery. The aim of such a file is not only to ensure that your horse receives appropriate care in your absence or when attended to by a different vet, but also to help reveal any subtle age-related changes or health problems that may otherwise go unnoticed, early recognition of which can, in some cases, quite literally mean the difference between life and death.

In addition, the inclusion in your file of biannual photographs can help show up any gradual physical changes in musculature or hoof conformation that may be worthy of discussion with your vet, trainer and farrier. A calendar will also be of use in helping to remind you to renew your horse's insurance policy and to plan ahead for routine procedures such as yearly health examinations, worming, vaccinations, trimming and shoeing, dental examinations etc., all of which become increasingly important with age.

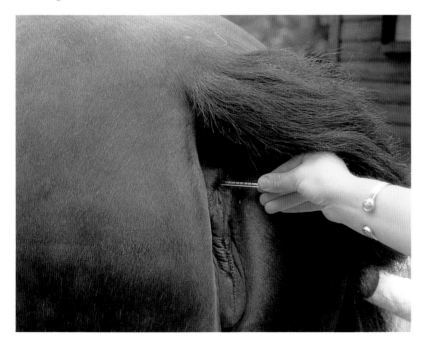

Taking a temperature

Taking a pulse

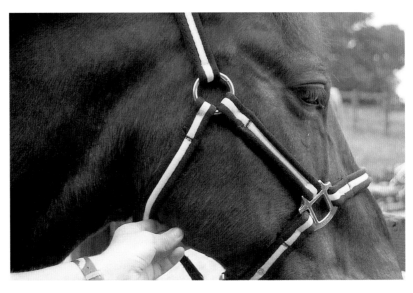

Taking respiration

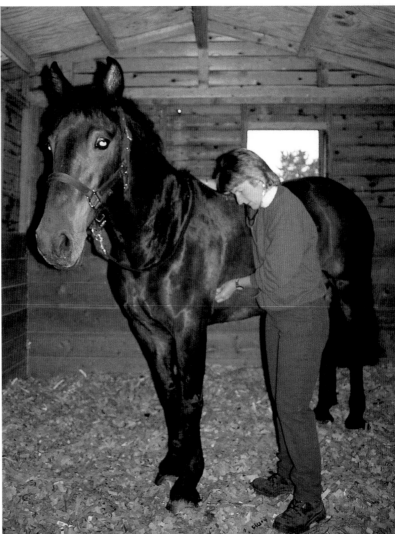

The Signs of Good and Bad Health

	Indicators of Good Health	*Indicators of Ill Health –* *including examples of possible causes*
Temperature (at rest)	100.5 °F + or – 1 °F (38 °C + or – 0.5 °C)	Subnormal temperature is not usually significant if the horse otherwise appears normal. However, possible causes of a drop in temperature include chronic disease, blood loss or shock. If the temperature rises above 102 °F call the vet as this may indicate fever, infection or pain. High temperatures can cause damage to the internal organs and adversely affect gut function. If temperature exceeds 103 °F, treat as a veterinary emergency.
Pulse (at rest)	30–40 beats per minute	Decrease: very rare heart conditions. Increase: pain, stress, infection. **Note** It is normal for pulse rates to rise during exercise or periods of excitement.
Respiration (at rest)	8–16 breaths per minute	Increase: possible infection, allergy, heat stress, severe anaemia, oxygen deprivation. **Note** It is normal for respiration rates to rise during exercise or periods of excitement.
Attitude	Bright and alert. Interested in surroundings.	Dull, uninterested, lethargic: anaemia, infection, pain, hypothyroidism, liver and urinary disorders, heart problems.
Appetite	Normally good, unless horse known to be a fussy feeder. Nerves/stress may also cause some horses to go off feed prior to and following competitions.	Refusal to eat is often one of the first signs of many illnesses including liver disease, hypothyroidism, colic, infection, fever. Normal or increased appetite associated with weight loss: Cushing's syndrome, parasites.
Water consumption	Varies from one individual to another, depending on workload, environmental temperatures etc., but normally approx. 5–10 gallons a day.	Assess your horse's normal water intake and monitor for any changes. A drastic increase in water consumption may, for instance, be a sign of urinary problems or Cushing's syndrome, whilst a decrease may suggest gum disease.

	Indicators of Good Health	*Indicators of Ill Health – including examples of possible causes*
Droppings	Moist, firm balls that break apart when they hit the ground. Greenish/ brown to golden brown in colour depending upon diet. Passed approx. 8–12 times every 24 hrs.	Hard and round: lack of fibre/possible constipation. Sloppy green 'cowpats': sudden access to spring grass. Diarrhoea: digestive disturbances, adverse drug reactions, parasites. Whole grains visible in droppings: teeth problems, digestive disturbances.
Urine	Pale yellow, clear or slightly cloudy. Passed 4–6 times a day, producing between 5–15 litres per day depending upon water intake.	Any change in the frequency, amount or colour of the urine, excessive straining or dribbling: possible Cushing's syndrome, hypothyroidism, urinary problems, azoturia.
Eyes	Bright and clear with salmon pink mucous membranes	Pain, swelling, cloudiness, excessive tearing, thick yellow discharge, light sensitivity: conjunctivitis, periodic ophthalmia, corneal ulcers etc. Abnormal colour of mucous membranes or whites of the eye: redness – inflammation; yellow tinge – liver problems.
Nostrils and mouth	Nostrils clean and dry. Gums salmon pink. Capillary refill time, i.e. if thumb pressure is used to blanch gum, normal colour should return within 1–2 seconds once pressure is released.	Nasal discharge: white – allergy; yellow – infection; foul smelling – sinus problems or fungal infection. Nose bleeds: may or may not be associated with exercise, possible nasal tumour, fungal infection, heart problems. Abnormal colour of mucous membranes: pale – anaemia, shock; yellow – liver disorders; blueish purple – lack of oxygen, heart problems. Coughing/wheezing: infection, allergy, heart problems, choke. Food and water coming from the nostrils: choke. Bad breath, dropping food from mouth: teeth problems. Mouth ulcers: urinary problems, bute toxicity, sharp teeth. Capillary refill time of more than three seconds: circulatory problems, shock.

	Indicators of Good Health	*Indicators of Ill Health –* *including examples of possible causes*
Coat and skin	Coat should be shiny, flat and smooth. Skin elastic and supple. If pinched, skin should spring back into place within 1–2 seconds.	Dull, staring coat: poor condition, parasites, illness. Long, wavy, coarse coat: Cushing's syndrome, hypothyroidism. Excessive itchiness: sweet itch, lice. Lumps beneath the skin: fly bites, allergic reactions, pressure bumps, nodular skin disease. Black brown nodules: melanomas. Wartlike lesions: sarcoids, squamous cell carcinoma. Pinched skin takes 3 seconds or more to spring back into place: dehydration. Raised tufts of hair on the back, lower legs: rain scald, mud fever, cracked heels.
Posture and movement	Weight balanced evenly over all four legs. Free, springy step.	Pointing a toe when resting or landing toe first when moving: pain in heel area, possible navicular. Standing with weight back on heels: possible laminitis. Reluctance to move or bear weight: possible foot abscess, fracture, tendon rupture, laminitis. Persistent tripping/stumbling: possible foot pain, arthritis. Lameness: arthritis, bruising, abscesses, tendon and ligament strain, laminitis.
Limbs and feet	Normally free from heat or swelling.	Heat, pain and swelling: bruise, tendon or ligament strain, infection, acute arthritis. Swelling of lower limb without heat or pain: poor circulation. Stronger than normal digital pulse at the back of the fetlock or pastern indicates pain in the hoof: possible bruising, abscess, laminitis, navicular. Heat in the foot: inflammation, pain. Hoof cracks.
Signs of pain	Not normally present	Sweating, wrinkling of nostril (often on same side as pain), kicking at or looking at belly, excessive rolling, pawing at ground: possible colic, urinary problems. Recumbent for long periods, refusing to rise to feet: possible colic, organ failure, laminitis.

Insurance

In general, horses can be fully insured against vet fees, death or humane destruction, theft or straying and permanent loss of use until they are approximately fifteen to sixteen years old, though some companies have now extended the age limit for existing policy holders to nineteen or twenty years. After this age, the type of cover and financial payouts offered for older horses is severely limited. Invariably, policies for veterans, horses aged between fifteen and thirty years of age, will only cover death or humane destruction if it is the direct result of an accident or theft and do not offer cover against permanent loss of use. Cover against veterinary fees is limited to only accidental injuries, and some companies may even refuse to pay out on internal injuries regardless of whether or not they were the result of an accident. It is therefore vitally important to check the small print of any insurance policy you are considering and to ask for written clarification of any clauses which you feel may be open to interpretation should a claim have to be made.

At the time of writing however, the most important point to note is that veteran policies do not allow claims to be made for veterinary fees incurred as a result of treatment for illnesses such as colic, arthritis, navicular, laminitis etc. Once your horse reaches an age where he can no longer be fully insured, you should therefore consider putting aside regular savings to help pay for treatment should your horse become ill. When you consider that veterinary fees can easily amount to thousands of pounds or dollars should your horse be unfortunate enough to need colic surgery or treatment for severe laminitis, for example, such forward planning could mean the difference between being able to proceed with a life-saving operation, or having to have your old friend put to sleep.

Worming

Over many years, horses can develop a certain level of immunity to intestinal parasites, a fact that leads some owners to believe that they can worm their elderly horses less frequently. It must be noted however that the systemic effects of old age or debilitating disease, can actually reduce the body's response to parasite invasion, making the development of a heavy worm burden more likely. Potentially, this can not only reduce an old horse's ability to digest food and absorb nutrients, causing poor condition and perhaps recurrent or chronic diarrhoea, but it will also increase the likelihood of colic. Ultimately, infestations of certain types of worms may also result in a thickening and narrowing of the arteries, causing a reduction in blood supply to the gut and the formation of blood clots and aneurysms, with potentially fatal consequences.

In an ideal world, all horses would be wormed only when they were known to be carrying a worm burden. This would hopefully mean that horses could be given fewer worming preparations (collectively referred to as anthelmintics) thus reducing the likelihood of worms developing resistances to the drugs currently available. Unfortunately, assessing the number of worm eggs being passed out in the dung (by performing faecal egg counts) only gives an indication of the number of adult egg-laying worms harboured in your horse's gut and does not give any indication of the numbers of immature, migratory or encysted larvae that may be present, which, if left unchecked, could cause massive and irreparable gut damage. Until a more effective diagnostic test can be developed, the majority of veterinary surgeons therefore still recommend the adoption of a vigorous, broad spectrum worming programme in conjunction with good grassland management practices, to ensure that your elderly horse's health is maintained.

For a worming programme to be effective, however, it must take into account the life cycle of the relevant parasites, in order to ensure that the correct wormer is given at the appropriate time, as different wormers are effective against different species of worms, at various stages of their development. The frequency with which a wormer must be administered also varies according to the length of time the drug contained within the product remains effective (known as efficacy rates). It is essential therefore that all horses sharing the same grazing are wormed at the same time, with the same drug, in order to catch worms at a specific stage in their development. Research has shown that if even just one horse goes untreated, it may continue to pass sufficient infective larvae onto the pasture to immediately

Regular worming is a vital part of maintaining your elderly horse's health.

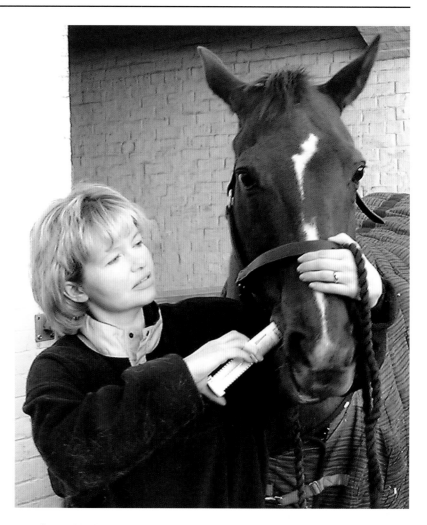

reinfect all the other horses. Similarly, if individual horses are given different drugs, then certain strains or stages of worm may go unchecked, increasing the risk of your elderly horse developing a parasite infestation, despite apparently having been wormed correctly.

Provided you have a basic knowledge of the following major parasites and the drugs which have proved effective in the prevention and treatment of each one, formulating a yearly worming programme for your old horse, is not nearly as complicated as it sounds as, in most cases, control of these parasites will also be sufficient to control other species such as threadworm, onchocerca, stomach worms, lungworms and pinworms.

Large Redworms

Also known as large strongyles. The larvae migrate through the bloodstream causing damage to arteries and blood vessels, before maturing into adults in the large intestine where they can cause colic, a loss of appetite and drastic weight loss, depression, a dull staring coat and anaemia. Control of this parasite is maintained by killing the adult, immature and migratory stages throughout the year using the drug ivermectin at 8–10 week intervals or moxidectin at approximately 13 week intervals. Alternatively pyrantel embonate may be given every 4–6 weeks, however it must be noted that this drug is only effective against the adult stages of the worm.

 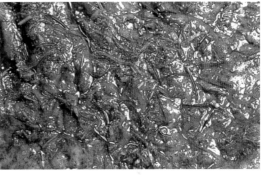

Left Large redworm
Right Small redworm

Small Redworms

Also known as small strongyles and cyathostomes. The larvae burrow into the lining of the large intestine where they can lie dormant in their cysts for a year or more before emerging on mass, most commonly during the winter months. Infestation of these worms can be particularly debilitating as they cause weight loss, severe diarrhoea, oedema of the limbs and ventral abdomen and permanent damage to the gut wall which will reduce an elderly horse's digestive function still further. Effective control of the adult, immature and migratory stages of this worm can be achieved by administering ivermectin every 8–10 weeks or moxidectin at 13 week intervals throughout the year. Pyrantel embonate given at 4–6 week intervals may also be used to help control the egg-laying adult worms, but has no effect on immature or migratory larvae.

To routinely try to kill encysted larvae, a five-day course of fenbendazole or single, standard dose of moxidectin should be given in November and February. In cases where elderly horses are harbouring a particularly heavy burden of small redworm, the sudden death of large numbers of worms may cause acute stress on bodily systems that are already weakened by age. Where this is suspected, advice on which drug to use and the frequency of worming should be sought from your veterinary surgeon prior to administration.

Tapeworms

Also known as *Anoplocephala perfoliata*. Tapeworms can occasionally cause inflammation of the gut, peritonitis and life-threatening impactions. Indeed some researchers have suggested that tapeworms are the cause of up to 20% of colics which require surgery. Effective control of this parasite is achieved if horses who are allowed access to pasture all year round, are wormed twice with a double dose of pyrantel embonate at the beginning and end of the grazing season (usually March/April and September/October).

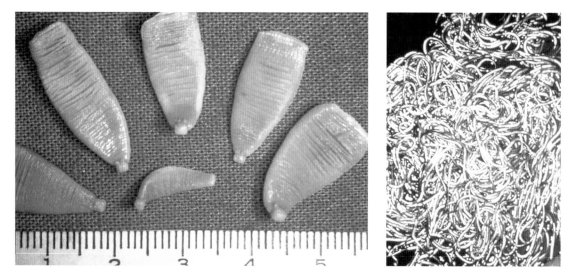

Left Tapeworm
Right Roundworms

Roundworms

Also known as ascarids and *Parascaris equorum*. These worms are most commonly thought of only as a threat to foals and youngsters under the age of two, as it has been shown that mature horses acquire an immunity against such parasites. Unfortunately, however, as the body's immune response may decline due to the systemic effects of old age or disease, there is a risk that geriatric horses may once again become susceptible to roundworm infestation. Migration of roundworm larvae through the bloodstream can cause colic, peritonitis and damage to the lungs which could make an elderly horse even more susceptible to respiratory infections. Regular treatment throughout the year with a broad spectrum wormer such as ivermectin (at 8–10 week intervals), moxidectin (at 13 week intervals), pyrantel embonate (at 4–5 week intervals) or one of the benzimidazole group of drugs (at 5–6 week intervals) will provide effective control.

Bots

The bot fly lays yellow, sticky eggs onto a horse's legs and chest which, when licked off, burrow into the tissues of the mouth before migrating to the stomach, where they can cause ulcers, impactions and even stomach rupture, though such effects are relatively rare. Effective control can be achieved by removal of the eggs from the coat and the administration of either ivermectin or moxidectin in November or December of each year, by which time the first frosts of winter will have killed off the bot fly and the larvae will be vulnerable to attack as they reach the lining of the stomach.

Bots

This pony shows the weight loss and ill thriftiness often associated with a high worm burden.

With this knowledge it should be fairly simple to work out a worming programme that will strategically target various species of worms at a time when they are most vulnerable to attack. However, a worming programme is still best devised in consultation with your veterinary surgeon who will take into account your elderly horse's current state of health and assess his level of exposure to worm larvae. Horses grazed with sheep and cattle on large acreages or those kept in paddocks from which droppings are removed, may, for instance, be able to be wormed less frequently than those turned out in small, overstocked and neglected paddocks. To reduce the risk of the development of drug resistances, your veterinary surgeon will also advise on the annual rotation of the drugs used in your worming programme. (**Note** Small redworms in particular are known to develop resistances to standard doses of the benzimidazole group of worming preparations which in general includes any drug whose chemical name ends in 'azole', e.g. fenbendazole, mebendazole etc.).

For the majority of elderly horses kept in livery yard situations, where paddocks are typically stocked to maximum capacity and/or pasture management is often negligible, a three-year worming programme similar to that shown here will prove appropriate.

Month	Year One Any specifically targeted worms are shown in brackets	Year Two Any specifically targeted worms are shown in brackets	Year Three Any specifically targeted worms are shown in brackets
January			
February	Five-day course of fenbendazole (encysted redworm)	Moxidectin (encysted redworm)	Five-day course of fenbendazole (encysted redworm)
March	Double dose of pyrantel embonate (tapeworm)		Double dose of pyrantel embonate (tapeworm)
April		Double dose of pyrantel embonate (tapeworm)	
May	Standard dose of ivermectin	Moxidectin	Standard dose of pyrantel embonate given every 4-6 weeks throughout the summer months
June			
July	Standard dose of ivermectin		
August		Moxidectin	
September	Double dose of pyrantel embonate (tapeworm)		Double dose of pyrantel embonate (tapeworm)
October		Double dose of pyrantel embonate (tapeworm)	
November	Five-day course of fenbendazole (encysted redworm)	Moxidectin (encysted redworm and bots)	Five-day course of fenbendazole (encysted redworm)
December	Standard dose of ivermectin (bots)		Standard dose of ivermectin (bots)

Any new horse arriving on the yard should be wormed with a five-day course of fenbendazole followed by a double dose of pyrantel embonate, no matter what the time of year, in order to reduce the risk of a sudden increase in infective and perhaps resistant strains of worms being passed out onto the pasture, which could otherwise threaten your elderly horse's welfare.

Though not yet sold in the UK, a feed additive containing small doses of pyrantel tartate is also available in some countries and is quite poular in the USA. Fed on a daily basis this ensures that infective larvae are killed as they are ingested. However, as the drug is not effective against redworm that has already encysted in the gut, treatment using pyrantel tartate should begin in the winter following a five-day course of fenbenda-zole. It must be noted that the drug is also ineffective against bots, therefore a standard dose of ivermectin must also be given prior to commencement of treatment, and repeated in November or December of each year thereafter. Though continuous deworming is more expensive than the strategic use of the anthelmintics described in this section, some owners have reported resultant improvements in their horses' weight and coat condition, as well as a lower incidence of colic. The use of this type of wormer may also be particularly beneficial if your old horse is kept on a yard where owners are not required to follow a specified worming programme. However, the possibility of horses on this regime developing a resistance to the drug is always a real worry, though no obvious problems have so far arisen.

Irrespective of your worming policy, the removal of droppings from the pasture on a daily basis, or at the very least twice a week in summer and once a week in winter will help keep parasite infestation to a minimum. Resting and rotation of grazing areas is also advisable as this will interrupt the life cycle of certain parasites, whilst on large acreages the grazing of cattle and sheep can serve to reduce the equine parasite population because infective larvae passed out in the horses' dung will die if eaten by other animals who are not viable hosts. The harrowing of large fields in hot, dry conditions can also prove useful provided the field can subsequently be rested for at least three weeks until the larvae are killed by the heat of the sun. However, as worm larvae thrive in warm, damp conditions, harrowing in such weather will simply spread infective larvae over a wider area, and is therefore best avoided.

Vaccinations

In the UK, vaccinations are currently recommended against tetanus, equine flu and equine herpes virus. Outside the UK, and particularly in the USA, additional vaccination may also be necessary against botulism, strangles, encephalomyelitis (sleeping sickness), Potomac horse fever, rabies, rotavirus etc., depending upon the prevalence of certain diseases in your old horse's environment.

All old horses must be vaccinated against tetanus as the bacteria are widespread in the environment and can easily invade even tiny wounds, commonly resulting in an agonising death. Vaccination involves two initial injections given one month apart followed by a booster twelve months later. Thereafter, boosters are only required every two years.

Whether or not to vaccinate old horses against viruses is, however, a controversial subject. Owners who favour vaccination say it offers valuable protection at a time in a horse's life when he is increasingly vulnerable to infection due to a decline in the efficiency of the immune system. Those against vaccination say that the vaccines are not efficacious enough to justify administration and that older horses are more likely to suffer from adverse reactions.

For the same reason that doctors recommend that elderly people have yearly flu jabs, many veterinary surgeons are still in favour of vaccination in high-risk situations such as when an old horse is mixing with others at competitions, or on livery yards where the risk of exposure to infection may be increased by the arrival of new horses. But, in low-risk situations, for instance where an old horse is kept at home and is not exposed to the coming and going of other horses, it is felt that vaccination may not be always be necessary. In these circumstances, however, it must be accepted that viral contamination is still possible should airborne particles travel into your horse's airspace from neighbouring yards.

Whilst an elderly horse's antibody response to a vaccine may not be as good as that expected in younger animals, i.e. the vaccine itself may not perhaps prove as effective, studies have shown that the symptoms of any subsequent infection that may occur are generally less severe in vaccinated horses and the time taken to recover from infection is reduced. Even so, it may be worth supplementing your elderly horse's diet with the herb echinacea or 10 g of vitamin C twice a day for a few days either side of an inoculation in an effort to boost the reaction of his immune system to the vaccine.

Though drug companies continually update their vaccines to ensure that vaccination is offered against the most prevelant strains of a virus, it must be noted that any vaccine can only be made against a limited number of viral strains. Therefore if an outbreak of infection involves a new strain of virus, the vaccine may not be totally effective. Similarly, the immunity acquired by vaccinated horses may be overwhelmed if the majority of their stable companions succumb to infection as a result of not having been inoculated. Though in either case the symptoms of infection in vaccinated horses are still likely to be much less severe than in unvaccinated animals.

Though relatively uncommon, adverse reactions to vaccinations do occur, ranging from the development of symptoms of viral infection, to a loss of performance or the formation of an abscess at the site of the injection. Thankfully, where such reactions do occur they are generally fairly minor and due to a combination of factors, rather than simply a result of the vaccination itself. For instance it is known that the administration of a vaccine when, unbeknown to the owner or vet, an elderly horse's immune system is already being challenged by a low grade infection, may be sufficient just to tip the scales in the infection's favour. As a result, if there is any evidence to suggest that your horse, or others on the same yard, may be incubating an infection, your vet may advise the precautionary measure of taking a blood test prior to vaccination in order to minimise the risk of aggravating any pre-existing condition.

In fact, evidence suggests that less than one in 10,000 horses will suffer an adverse reaction which can be proven to be the direct result of vaccine administration. Though it is true that elderly horses can take longer to recover from the effects of an

adverse reaction, no matter how minor they may be, it is important to realise that the protection offered by such vaccines in
high-risk situations often far outweighs the small risk of any side
effects. It is recommended however that in the three or four days
following inoculation, horses should be given only light work,
and that you should discuss vaccine administration with your
veterinary surgeon prior to inoculation if your horse has
any existing health problem or is currently on any form of
medication (eg corticosteroids).

As a result of the criticism levelled at this type of vaccine,
homeopathic alternatives are now frequently being requested
by owners, even though there is currently no proof of their
effectiveness. Whilst arguably, not everything in life can be
scientifically proven, it is worth remembering that despite the
availability of homeopathic remedies long before equine
vaccines were marketed, flu epidemics (which caused a
significant number of equine deaths) were only brought
under control when vaccination programmes were implemented.

The recommended interval between vaccinations will vary
from one country to another, and you should check with your
veterinary surgeon. In the UK, the recommended scheduling for
equine flu vaccination currently consists of two initial injections
four to six weeks apart, followed by a booster 150–215 days later
and subsequent boosters on an annual basis, though these may be
given more frequently if a viral outbreak occurs. A combined flu
and tetanus vaccination is available, however it has been
suggested that for some horses this increases the risk of an
adverse reaction, and that it may be better if the vaccines are
injected into separate sites.

Most recently a new vaccine against flu has been released in
the USA which is administered via a nasal applicator. Recent
trials have suggest that this intranasal vaccine may be more
effective than injectable vaccines and have fewer adverse effects.
In the future it is hoped that vaccines derived from DNA
(deoxiribonucleic acid) will also become available and offer even
better protection against a wider range of viruses.

Vaccination against equine herpes (rhinopneumonitis virus),
which is now thought to be responsible for 70% of viral related
infections of the respiratory tract, currently involves the admin-

istration of two initial injections given at one month intervals. However, boosters are required every six months if a significant level of protection is to be maintained

Dental Care

Unlike humans, horses have evolved with teeth that continue to emerge from the jaw throughout their lives in an effort to compensate for the wear caused by chewing fibrous foods. As the surface of the crown is slowly worn away, the teeth will push up from the root to ensure that the biting surfaces meet directly, thereby enabling the horse to cut and grind his food efficiently. However, as the top jaw is wider than the lower jaw, not all the surfaces of a horse's teeth are in direct contact with each other. This means that, as the grinding surfaces are worn down, the outside edges of the teeth in the upper jaw and the inside edges of the teeth in the lower jaw will become sharp and overgrown, resulting in ulcers and lacerations of the cheeks and tongue if the sharp edges are not removed by your veterinary surgeon or a reputable equine dentist. Additionally, some horses with a conformation defect known as a parrot mouth (where the upper jaw is further forward than the lower jaw) will also develop sharp points on the front edge of their first molars and the back edge of their last molars which, if left unchecked, will cause painful gum abrasions.

By the time your horse reaches twenty years of age, he may only have half an inch of tooth left to erupt and by his late twenties or early thirties, all the hard enamel of the crown will have been worn away. As only the softer root will remain, the chewing of food will therefore become progressively more difficult and the development of gum disease more likely. Older horses are also prone to the development of a 'wave' or 'step' mouth, caused by the loss or uneven wear of a tooth in one jaw, resulting in overgrowth of the tooth in the opposite jaw, which prevents the rest of the teeth from grinding together normally. Age-related decay of the infundibulum in the centre of a tooth, may also cause the outer edges of a tooth to become sharp, whilst the development of root abscesses may

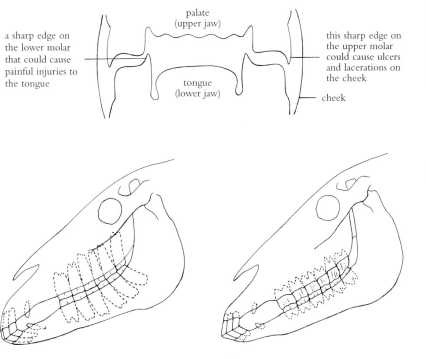

a sharp edge on the lower molar that could cause painful injuries to the tongue

palate (upper jaw)

this sharp edge on the upper molar could cause ulcers and lacerations on the cheek

tongue (lower jaw)

cheek

As the top jaw is wider than the lower jaw, sharp edges will develop on the outside edge of the upper molars and the inside edge of the lower molars.

As your horse ages his teeth will wear away.

5-year-old horse

20-year-old horse

lead to sinus infection, the signs of which include a foul-smelling unilateral nasal discharge and sometimes painful facial swelling.

As a result of inadequate chewing, food particles passed into the digestive tract may be too large for the digestive enzymes and microbes to utilize efficiently. Similarly, insufficient chewing movements will result in reduced saliva production meaning that there is less to smooth the passage of food into the stomach. It is not perhaps surprising, therefore, that many elderly horses become prone to weight loss, are increasingly susceptible to episodes of choke and colic, and may develop neuralgia-like symptoms that will make them reluctant to drink cold water.

Evidence of such dental problems may be manifest by the dropping of small boluses of hay from the mouth whilst eating, bad breath, head shaking and all sorts of resistances to being ridden. By the time any of these problems become apparent, your old horse may have been in incessant pain for

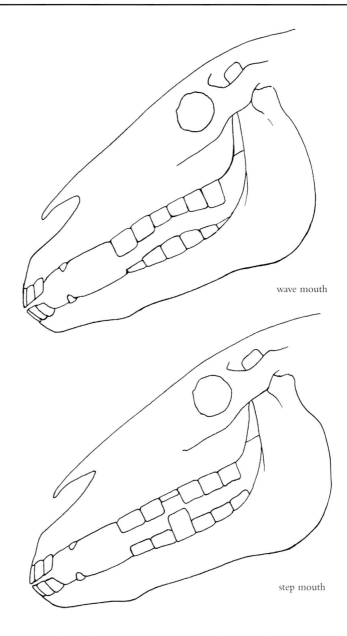

wave mouth

step mouth

some time. Dental examinations should, therefore, be performed by your veterinary surgeon or equine dentist at least every six months, or at any other time pain becomes evident.

Rasping the teeth does not actually hurt your horse as the central portion of the exposed equine tooth does not contain any nerves or blood supply. If there are any loose or broken teeth or any ulcers or cuts within the mouth however, horses

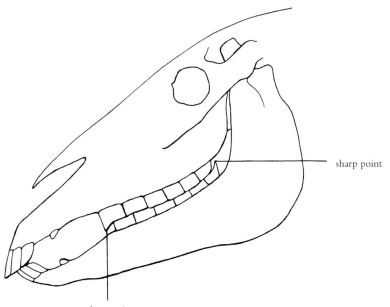

sharp point

sharp point

may indeed show signs of pain because the rasp will almost
inevitably rub against them. Consequently, those horses who
seriously object to having their teeth rasped are generally those
most in need of treatment.

To ensure that even the
very last molars can be
inspected, a speculum
must be fitted to keep the
jaws open.

In many cases vets will insist that dental work be carried out under sedation, as a speculum can cause serious injury to the handler should a horse become fractious. In rare cases a general anaesthetic may be required depending upon the severity of the dental problem. Before a sedative or anaesthetic is administered, your elderly horse should first be given a thorough health examination to identify any other health condition that may lead to the development of complications.

It is worth remembering that research has shown that correct dental care can increase a horse's lifespan by as much as five to ten years and its importance in maintaining your elderly horse's welfare must never be underestimated. However, even elderly horses whose teeth have completely worn away can still be kept fit, healthy and in good condition if careful consideration is given to their diet (*see* Feeding).

Foot Care

Though the condition of a horse's feet can be influenced by genetics, even those with inherently good feet may develop problems in later life as a result of an age-related reduction in circulation and a decline in the efficiency of the digestive system. This can lead to a disruption of the fluid balance within the hoof capsule and the slow growth of poor quality horn due to the inadequate absorption of nutrients, which may result in dry, brittle feet and the development of cracks that allow the infection to work its way in. The sole and hoof wall may also become thinner, making your elderly horse's feet susceptible to bruising and the nailing on of shoes more difficult as the space between the insensitive (external) and sensitive (internal) structures of the foot becomes narrower. As a thin hoof wall is also a weak hoof wall, shoes may also be lost more frequently, which can result in yet further damage to the structure of the hoof.

Correct hoof care must include regular turn-out to encourage circulation to the extremities of the feet and the provision of a diet which will meet all the increased requirements of an elderly horse. Though feeding is discussed in some depth in the next chapter it is worth mentioning here that research has shown that the hoof growth of horses fed fibre ad lib may be increased by as

> HOOF NOTES
> - Ammonia from urine-soaked bedding can prove harmful to your horse's feet, so keep your horse's stable as clean and dry as possible.
> - The overapplication of oil and grease to the hoof can disturb the natural moisture-balancing mechanisms of the foot, seal off oxygen and create ideal conditions for the development of harmful infections. If using a hoof dressing, choose one which allows the foot to breath and apply only when necessary. If, for instance, your horse suffers from brittle feet in the dry summer months, soak his hooves in water for 5–10 minutes each day before applying a hoof dressing. This may help to slow down moisture evaporation and keep the hoof pliable. Conversely, if in the winter months his hooves become cracked as a result of prolonged exposure to wet, muddy conditions, apply a hoof dressing directly to the foot to slow down moisture absorption.
> - In addition to exercise, massage of the coronary band and the application of magnetic hoof boots can help encourage circulation to the foot.

much as 50% in comparison with those on a restricted diet. Without adequate fibre it is also known that the microorganisms in the gut will not be able to manufacture sufficient B vitamins (including biotin) all of which are beneficial to the metabolism and, therefore, hoof growth. As fibre digestion can become more difficult with age, adding a supplementary source of B vitamins (e.g. yeast) can prove beneficial. Similarly, as the hoof wall largely comprises a protein called keratin, diets should contain a good source of all the essential amino acids, and not just the sulphur-containing methionine as is often recommended. Indeed, as protein absorption declines with age, an improvement in hoof condition will often be seen in the spring when protein levels are boosted by the consumption of good grazing. The feeding of diets based on alfalfa, which is a good source of protein and calcium, has also been shown to increase hoof growth whilst the addition of a few tablespoons of an unprocessed vegetable oil or fish oil to the daily diet has been found to help improve hoof condition in elderly horses who may have an increased requirement for essential fatty acids.

It is important to note that it is a combination of adequate energy, protein, vitamins and minerals that will improve both hoof growth and condition, rather than the supplementation of just one or two nutrients that are known to be involved in the formation of healthy hooves. Indeed, there is no evidence that feeding more than the daily requirement of any specific nutrient

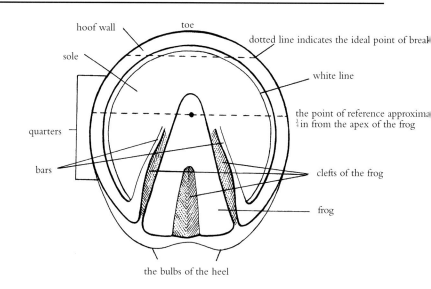

the bulbs of the heel

will have a beneficial effect. On the contrary, if fed to excess, many nutrients are often just excreted and some may have a detrimental effect on the absorption of others. For instance, the excess supplementation of methionine, can adversely affect the absorption of zinc, copper and iron and, rather than promoting good quality horn growth, may actually be a contributory cause to the development of poor quality hooves. If it is to prove effective, any supplement formulated to help hoof growth must, therefore, offer a balanced supply of a wide range of nutrients including essential amino acids, B vitamins, zinc, lysine, copper, iron, vitamin C and vitamin A. This supplementation of the diet may need to be continued for some six to twelve months before any noticeable improvement may be expected in the appearance of the hooves. If, despite adequate nutrition, the feet fail to grow, current research at the University of Edinburgh suggests that this may be due to fungal and/or bacterial infections of the inter-tubular horn (verifiable by the analysis of hoof trimmings) and that the application of a hoof antiseptic may prove beneficial.

Nutrition alone is not sufficient to maintain your old horse's hooves in good condition. Regular trimming every 4–6 weeks is also essential. This will ensure that your horse's feet remain in balance and have a level ground surface, which will help ensure that his body-weight is spread evenly across each foot. Though ideally one front foot should be a mirror image of the other front foot, and one hind foot should mirror the opposite hind foot, it

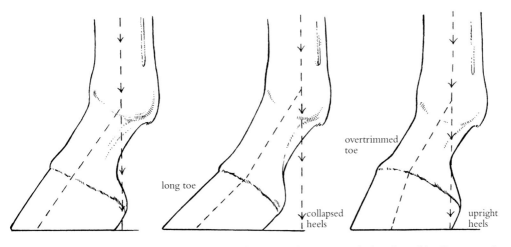

overtrimmed toe

long toe

collapsed heels

upright heels

The ideal hoof/pastern angle   A broken-back hoof/pastern angle   A broken-forward hoof/pastern angle

is quite normal for the front pair of feet to appear slightly rounder and flatter than the hind pair, owing to the increased weight taken on the front legs as a result of the positioning of the head, neck, heart and lungs. Any deviation in the shape of each pair of front feet, or each pair of hind feet, whether as a result of infrequent or poor trimming and shoeing, or even conformational defects, is a sign of possible unlevel load bearing which could lead to an alteration of blood flow within the foot, that may predispose your horse to, or be indicative of, lameness problems.

If, for instance, the toe grows longer as the angle of the hoof wall at the front of the foot becomes shallower than the angle of the pastern, an increasing amount of weight will be transferred to the heels causing them to collapse and predispose the horse to the development of joint problems, tendon strain and navicular syndrome. As the feet grow longer, the point of breakover (i.e. the moment when the foot rolls over onto the toe just before it leaves the ground) will also be delayed, thus placing extra stress on the hoof wall as well as the joints and soft tissues of the limb. If not trimmed back sufficiently, the weight of the horse can also cause the hoof wall to flare outwards resulting in extra pressure being placed on the hoof wall. In the same way that our finger nails would snap and tear if we allowed them to overgrow and then pressed them down on a solid surface, flaring of the hoof wall can cause tearing of the laminae which weakens the attachment of the hoof wall to the inner sensitive structures of the foot, resulting in cracked, brittle feet that will be susceptible to infection. On the other hand, if the foot is overtrimmed so that the angle of the hoof wall becomes steeper than the angle of the pastern and the heels become very upright, concussion on the joints will be increased, hastening the development of arthritis. Foot imbalances can also lead to compensatory muscle use throughout the rest of the body, resulting in the over or underdevelopment of the muscles of the shoulders, chest, back and quarters. Chronic discomfort and muscle spasms in the neck, back or pelvis are not always just a saddle fitting or rider-related problem.

The foot must not, however, be balanced in isolation to the rest of the limb. If, for instance, an elderly horse has over many years been forced to adapt his movement in an effort to compensate for poor conformation, or indeed the pain of arthritis, his weight will no longer be evenly distributed across each foot, resulting in distortion of the hoof capsule. In this case, trying to change the way the horse moves or to alter foot placement in order to create perfect hoof symmetry could prove harmful if it

A wide-web shoe with a rolled toe and adequate length and width at the heels.

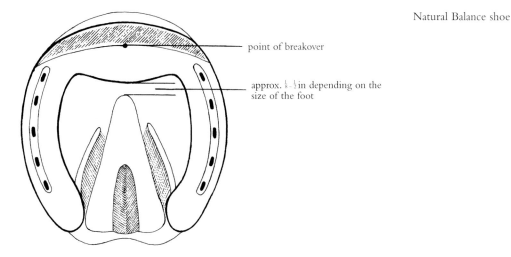

Natural Balance shoe

point of breakover

approx. ⅛–½ in depending on the size of the foot

lead to the hoof capsule deviating from the individual's natural bone alignment. Potentially, this could result in the development of severe lameness by generating torque on the misaligned bones or diseased joints and their supporting ligaments. If your farrier thinks your horse will benefit from corrective trimming, he should, therefore, make changes gradually over a number of visits and carefully monitor your horse's response.

Whilst it is impossible to realign the bones of an aged horse or restore the full functional mobility of a joint, a skilled farrier will be able to help your horse remain sound by applying a shoe that will offer additional support to those areas of the foot which need it most. This may, for example, mean extending the shoe beyond the actual perimeter of the hoof wall, or widening and lengthening the heels, in an effort to reduce wear and increase the weight-bearing area, thus reducing stress on the joints and tissues above, and making the horse more comfortable.

The individual trimming and shoeing requirements of an elderly horse will, therefore, largely be determined by his conformation, workload and how his foot lands upon the ground. If shod, many horses will benefit from a lightweight, wide-web shoe, that has a rolled and/or square toe and plenty of length and width at the heel. This type of shoe will help spread a horse's body-weight over a larger area of each foot, ease breakover and support the heel region, which may come under increasing pressure as the tendons and ligaments of an old horse weaken with age, resulting in a loss of support for the fetlock.

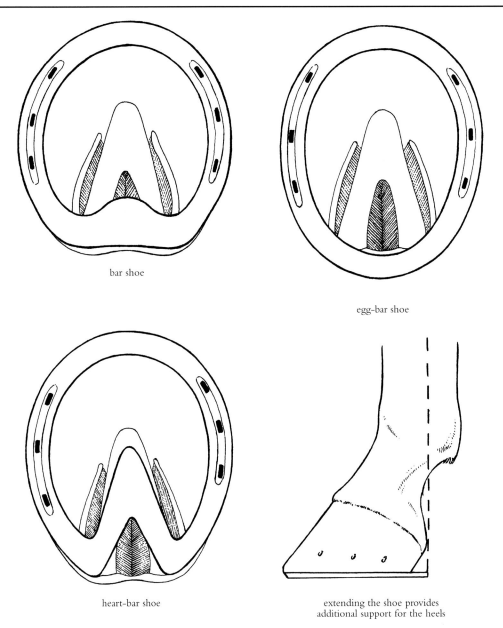

bar shoe

egg-bar shoe

heart-bar shoe

extending the shoe provides
additional support for the heels

Indeed, Natural Balance shoes, which incorporate all of these elements, can make a huge difference to the comfort and soundness of many elderly horses.

Correctly fitted bar shoes, such as the egg-bar or heart-bar may also prove beneficial in helping to stabilize the foot and providing heel support. They are sometimes recommended for those with collapsed heels, quarter cracks, navicular, laminitis etc.

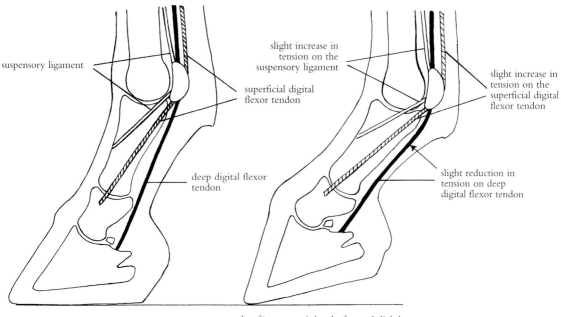

suspensory ligament

slight increase in
tension on the
suspensory ligament

superficial digital
flexor tendon

slight increase in
tension on the
superficial digital
flexor tendon

deep digital flexor
tendon

slight reduction in
tension on deep
digital flexor tendon

hoof/pastern axis breaks forward slightly
increasing concussion on the joints

The effect of
raising the heel by
applying wedges.

Since such shoes protrude behind the heels, it is advisable for
elderly horses shod in this way to wear overreach boots whenever they are turned out in the field, or ridden, in an effort to
prevent the shoe being pulled off. Squaring off the toe of the
hind foot and setting the hind shoe back more towards the heels
may also help reduce loss of the front shoes by reducing the likelihood of the toe of the hind shoe coming into contact with the
heel of the fore shoe.

For horses with long toes and low heels, the use of wedge pads
in an effort to raise the heels and normalise the angle of the foot
is controversial as the compression caused by the wedges can
actually crush the heels still further. Raising the heel also
removes the desirable level footfall, and makes the horse feel as if
he is constantly walking downhill, thus increasing the strain on
other tissues, such as the suspensory ligament. Since raising the
heels also raises the frog and sole further away from the ground,
it is also possible that the frog and soft tissues suspended within
the hoof capsule may prolapse in an effort to make contact with
the ground which could exacerbate existing problems. That said,
compromises sometimes have to be made, and the use of wedges
or graduated bar shoes may prove beneficial in some cases where

A Natural Balance shoe used in conjunction with a pad and 'impression' material to help protect the sole and dissipate body-weight evenly across the foot.

it is also necessary to relieve tension on the deep flexor tendon. The effects of such shoes on the hoof capsule and lower limb must, however, be continually reassessed and, where necessary, additional support for the frog and inner structures of the hoof must also be provided by using sole-packing materials or a pad.

The long-term use of full sole pads to protect the thin-soled, flat-footed horse must be employed with caution as they can actually compound the problem by creating a moist environment in which bacteria and fungi may multiply, causing thrush, and in which the sole will soften and thereby become even more vulnerable to injury when the pad is removed. It is arguable, therefore, whether it is better to simply take extra care in the choice of ground over which a horse is ridden, so as to let the sole harden naturally, in the same way as a human foot would eventually become calloused if a person were to walk barefoot. Most recently however the development of sole-packing materials which dry to a rubber-like consistency that conforms to the shape of the underside of the foot, can, when placed beneath a pad, act like a cushion between the sole and the ground. The risk of the development of thrush has been reduced by the inclusion of antibacterial and antifungal substances within the packing. Often referred to as impression material, such packing can also prove a useful adjunct to the shoeing of laminitic horses as, when placed only over the back two-thirds of the foot, it will provide vital support to the inner structures of the hoof and bony column above, whilst relieving pressure on the most painful areas around the front of the foot.

Of course, not every old horse will need the protection shoes provide. A horse who is only lightly ridden on mainly grassed surfaces, or one who has retired to the field, may do just fine, and be comfortable, going barefoot if he has inherited good quality hooves and conformation. Regular trimming will still be required, however, to remove excessive growth and prevent flaring of the hoof wall, the edge of which should be bevelled to reduce the risk of splitting. In fact, without the constriction of shoes, the feet will be able to expand and contract naturally, which may help increase blood flow within the hoof capsule, and thereby improve the quality and strength of horn.

There is growing support in some countries for the 'natural hoofcare' movement, lead by German veterinary surgeon, Dr Hiltrud Strasser and American farrier, Jaime Jackson. This system involves removing a horse's shoes and frequent trimming of the feet (initially 1–3 times a week) in accordance with the natural wear patterns that develop on the bearing surface of the foot as a result of an individual's most comfortable range of motion. The success of the system also relies on mimicking the natural lifestyle of wild horses as much as possible by providing twenty-four hour turn-out over varied terrain which, for many owners, will necessitate having to create stony areas, mud baths and sand pits within the boundaries of their horse's field. Ridden work is gradually built up as the feet harden and hoof boots (e.g. Equiboots and Easyboots) are used on those occasions where extra foot protection is required. Unfortunately, the demands of urbanisation mean that few owners who keep their horses at livery yards or riding schools will have either sufficient turn-out facilities or the full cooperation of other owners to be able to incorporate all of Dr Strasser's recommendations. They are however still worthy of consideration and her book *A Lifetime of Soundness* (published by Star Ridge Publishing) makes interesting reading, though I would strongly advise against anyone, who has not had thorough training, attempting to trim their own horse's feet.

Dr Strasser also claims that using this method she has had great

Lifting and flexing your horse's legs on a daily basis can help ensure he retains sufficient mobility in his joints to make the trimming and shoeing process easier.

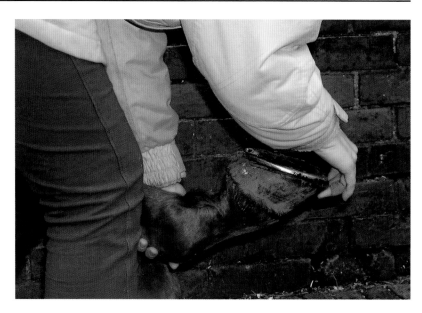

success in treating otherwise seemingly hopeless cases of laminitis, navicular etc. However it is important to note that, using this system, recovery may take up to two years, during which time a horse may experience such prolonged periods of great discomfort as a result of problems such as abscess formation, that some owners and veterinary surgeons may find it difficult to accept, especially since Dr Strasser is also against the use of any form of drug therapy such as pain relievers.

Regardless of whether your horse can go barefoot or needs the protection shoes provide, the importance of regular foot care can never be overemphasised, especially when you consider that up to 90% of all lameness originates in the foot. It is, therefore, important that, even if your old horse finds it difficult to maintain his balance or lift and flex his limbs due to the pain and restriction of arthritis, you must never let this become an excuse for inadequate hoof care. If necessary ask your veterinary surgeon's advice about the possibility of giving (or in some cases increasing) pain relieving drug therapy just before your farrier's visit, and ensure that your farrier is also aware of, and sympathetic to, your horse's problems. Remember, proper foot care will not only save you a small fortune in veterinary fees, but will also increase the longevity, usefulness and quality of your horse's life.

Chapter Three

FEEDING

As a horse gets older, his metabolism starts to slow down. This means that some elderly horses will keep their weight quite easily and may in fact require less energy (calories) to sustain condition than they did in their younger days. Frequently, however, a simultaneous decline in the ability of the digestive system to extract nutrients from the diet (perhaps as a result of previous parasite damage), may mean that an elderly horse's body has to work harder to obtain the level of nutrients required to sustain even the most basic functioning of bodily processes. In order to maintain body-weight, therefore, many old horses may require a high energy feed with elevated levels of nutrients. In particular, research has shown that elderly horses (most commonly those over the age of twenty) who have difficulty in holding condition will have a reduced ability to absorb protein (required to help repair bone and body tissue), phosphorus (involved in the maintenance of a strong, healthy bone structure) and vitamin C (which aids the functioning of the immune system).

Studies have also suggested that fibre becomes more difficult to digest with age, resulting in a decline in both the number and efficiency of microorganisms within the gut. As these microorganisms are responsible for the utilisation and synthesis of certain nutrients, this will have a detrimental effect on an elderly horse's condition and health. In particular, it has been noted that geriatric horses struggle to manufacture sufficient B

In the spring and autumn, access to good grazing may need to be restricted. Twenty-year-old Basildon Fred Flintstone, owned by Nichola Driffield.

vitamins (normally produced in large numbers within the horse's gut), a lack of which will reduce feed utilisation still further and may result in poor appetite, weight loss, muscle weakness, and incoordination, not to mention anaemia, diarrhoea and possibly even increased nervousness.

Stress, whether caused by changes in the environment, weather conditions, illness, chronic pain or even simply by being bullied by field companions, can also increase and perhaps even change an elderly horse's nutritional requirements. Take all this into consideration when deciding upon a diet for an old horse and you begin to realise just how important it is to consider his individual needs in accordance with not only his age, height, type and work being done, but also his state of health, daily management routine and his relationships with others. The key to maintaining an old horse's condition, therefore, largely relies upon your powers of observation and familiarity with your horse's physical and mental wellbeing. Whether wishing to extend the usefulness of your horse's life, or simply wanting to ensure he has a long and happy retirement, it is essential to feed an easily chewed, highly digestible and nutritious diet. Unsurprisingly it is the elderly horse who is lavished with that little bit of extra TLC who is likely to thrive throughout his pensionable years.

The Rules of Feeding

Whilst the basic rules of feeding apply to horses of all ages, they become increasingly important for the elderly horse, whose delicate digestive system can no longer compensate for any inconsistences or sudden changes in the diet. In the previous chapter, we discussed the importance of correct dental care and an efficient, thorough worming programme, both of which can have an enormous effect on your old horse's ability to chew, digest and utilize his food. We have also noted that the feed required by an elderly horse will be determined by his individual requirements. However, there are a number of other general, yet equally important, guidelines that must be taken into consideration.

Allow access to a clean and fresh supply of water at all times

Water is essential to maintain the efficient functioning of the digestive system, from the production of saliva, to the transportation of nutrients around the body and subsequent excretion of waste products. It is required by all bodily cells, tissues, fluids and joints and helps to regulate temperature. Your old horse will drink between five and ten gallons a day to support all life processes. Thirst may increase as a result of hot weather, hard work, transportation, disease or diets which are high in fibre or protein. Conversely, a decrease in thirst may be an indication of illness or simply the result of high levels of moisture in the diet, as a result of feeding soaked hay, for example. It should be noted that as elderly horses are increasingly prone to painful mouth problems, this may make them reluctant to drink very cold water during the winter months. This has potentially serious consequences since insufficient water intake will thicken and slow the flow of blood throughout the body, causing reduced functioning of the gut. Combine this with the high percentage of dry food (i.e. hay) being fed during the winter months and you have one of the primary causes of impacted colic. During particularly cold periods it is therefore advisable to take the chill off your old horse's drinking water whenever possible. Removing ice from troughs at least twice a day and insulating water pipes will also ensure your horse has a constant supply of fresh water. Similarly, remembering to keep water receptacles clean, both in the field and stable, will prevent stale and tainted water from deterring your horse from drinking.

Feed plenty of roughage

Microorganisms in your old horse's gut have evolved to digest fibre. Without adequate roughage, the digestive system simply cannot function properly as it loses the ability to move food through the gut, is unable to retain water as effectively within the intestinal tract and, as discussed, cannot manufacture adequate levels of essential B vitamins. A lack of fibre can, therefore, result in colic, laminitis, nervousness and even filled legs. Horses also have an inherent need to chew, which, if not satisfied, may lead to the development of compensatory stable vices such as crib-biting and wood chewing. Ideally, your elderly horse should be given ad lib access to forage in the form of either grass or hay.

Make all changes to the diet gradually

Though the majority of the billions of microorganisms within your horse's gut have evolved to digest fibre, some will have developed a preference for specific types of food depending upon the ingredients of your particular horse's diet. If these ingredients should suddenly change, the microbes will not have time to adapt to the new feedstuffs. Effectively this means that the new ingredients will not be digested and the microorganisms that developed to survive on your horse's original diet will begin to die off, releasing toxins into his digestive system. This can lead to anything from poor food utilisation to colic. In order to give the microbes time to adjust, it is essential to introduce new feed-stuffs very slowly over a period of at least two to three weeks (at no more than 100–200 g [$3\frac{1}{2}$–7 oz] a day depending upon the size of horse or pony) whilst at the same time gradually reducing the ingredients which are to be replaced. Even changing from one batch of hay to another or from winter to summer grazing should be done slowly, either by gradually mixing the two types of hay together or slowly building up the period of time during which the horse is allowed access to new pasture.

Any increase or decrease in the quantity of food given must also be made gradually if your old horse's delicate digestive system is not to be adversely affected. For instance, the practice of feeding elderly horses only on the days when they are worked can upset the balance of microflora in the gut. Similarly, sudden high intakes of concentrate feed can result in undigested food being passed through to the large intestine causing acid conditions in the gut which could trigger conditions such as laminitis or colic. Conversely, suddenly starving a fat horse or pony, can cause mobilisation of the body's fat reserves, causing a condition called hyperlipaemia, which can prove fatal.

Whenever changes are being made to your elderly horse's diet, giving a five- to ten-day course of probiotics which contain beneficial species of bacteria to support gut function, may prove beneficial in helping the older horse's slower, less efficient digestive system to cope.

Feed little and often

Your horse's digestive system is designed to function best when two-thirds full. Research has shown that if left for more than a few hours without food, the motility (movement) within his gut will decrease, making your elderly horse prone to digestive disorders. In the wild, a horse would consume small amounts of food at frequent intervals to maintain the effective functioning of his gut and so in order to mimic nature, if your old horse does not have free access to adequate grazing, hay should be given on an ad lib basis. Alternatively, if your elderly horse is on a diet, small amounts of hay or chaff should be offered at regular intervals to ensure the survival of the microorganisms in the gut and thereby the efficiency of the digestive process.

Despite his large frame your horse has a relatively small stomach, which is only the size of a rugby ball when empty. As his digestive system is strictly a one-way tract, he is unable to vomit and consequently there is a real risk of the stomach rupturing if it is overloaded. The intestinal tract is also poorly designed with a U-shaped bend in the colon which can become blocked if your horse is given large feeds or denied adequate amounts of water or fibre. As a general guide, therefore, you should split your horse's concentrate ration into at least two or three meals a day, none of which should weigh more than 0.4%

Unfortunately, many people believe that it is inevitable for old horses to appear thin and develop long, scurfy coats. However, the condition of semi-retired Rixilla, a 25-year-old veteran class winner, belonging to Sue Besnard, just goes to prove that, given a high standard of care, this does not have to be the case.

of his body-weight (i.e. 2 kg [4 lb] to an average 500 kg [1,000 lb] horse). Feeding more than this at any one time will result in food being pushed through the gut without being digested, which at the very least is wasteful and at worst could cause a fatal bout of colic.

Feed by weight, not volume

In order to avoid accidentally over or underfeeding, which could cause unexplained excitability, loss of condition etc., it is vital to ensure that you know how much you are actually feeding in either pounds or kilogrammes, rather than simply relying on the size of a particular scoop since the volume of a feed bears little relation to its weight. There are a vast range of scoop sizes and it is therefore essential that you take a set of kitchen scales into the feed room to enable you to ascertain the weight that your particular scoop will hold of each type of feed you use. You will find, for instance, that a scoop full of cubes will weigh heavier than the same size scoop full of coarse mix or chaff. With this knowledge you can then ensure you are feeding your horse the correct amount of each type of feed.

Only offer good quality feed

Inferior quality hay and feed will not provide adequate nutrients and will frequently contain high levels of dust and mould which could predispose your elderly horse to the development of chronic obstructive pulmonary disease (COPD). Purchasing good quality, highly digestible feeds, may cost more initially but actually makes economic sense when you consider that cheap, poor quality hay and concentrates may have to be fed in larger quantities in order for your elderly horse to derive comparable benefits. Such judicious spending could also save on veterinary bills and prevent unnecessary stress being placed on an ageing digestive system.

Do not work immediately after feeding

When work starts, blood is diverted from the gut to the muscles, thereby slowing down the digestive process which can lead to the poor utilisation of nutrients or colic. The positioning of the stomach also means that, when full, it will prevent the lungs from functioning efficiently, which in turn will place extra stress on your elderly horse's heart. As a rule of thumb, you should allow between one and one and a half hours after feeding before hacking or schooling. Similarly, if your old horse is kept out at grass, he should be brought in from the field at least an hour or two before being asked to work to allow for the majority of the contents of his stomach to pass into the intestines.

Do not feed a hot, tired horse

Water and electrolytes lost in sweat need to be replaced and normal circulation to the gut restored before a hot, sweating or tired horse is offered any concentrate feeds, otherwise digestion may be impaired, increasing the risk of the development of colic. Sweating horses should not however be allowed to take long drinks of very cold water, the shock may cause the ring of muscle between the stomach and the small intestine, known as the pyloric sphincter, to go into a spasm. This will cause a delay in the transfer of the stomach contents to the gut, resulting in the stomach becoming overdistended which may cause colic or even rupture of the stomach. Initially, a horse should be allowed to drink small amounts of water at frequent intervals (i.e. four or five sips of water every five minutes or about a quarter of a bucket every ten to fifteen minutes) until body temperature returns to normal.

Ensure feeds are given at the same time each day

Elderly horses thrive on routine and may become easily stressed if their feed does not appear when expected. This can have a detrimental effect on the population of microorganisms in the gut and may result in colic, a loss of appetite, aggressiveness or the manifestation of stable vices.

Keep work levels ahead of feed and reduce the level of concentrates fed before a rest day or if your horse is suddenly confined to his stable

Enforced idleness can cause a build up of excessive amounts of glycogen (fuel) within the muscles, which, when exercise is resumed, cannot be burnt off quickly enough and may result in severe, painful muscle cramps and subsequent damage to muscle fibres. If your elderly horse is working hard or needs high levels of concentrates in order to help him maintain weight, he should,

At eighteen years old, Greenan Grenadier became the UK National In-hand Part Bred and Anglo-Arab Gelding Champion, and at the age of twenty-one, became the Northern Part Bred and Anglo Supreme Champion. Now twenty-four years old, Gren is still ridden daily by owner Heather Campbell and continues to qualify for numerous championship competitions.

therefore, have his concentrate feeds reduced by a least half if his workload is suddenly reduced or if he is confined to his stable through injury, poor weather conditions etc. However, if digestive upsets are to be avoided, it is still important to keep to his usual feeding routine (i.e. giving the same number of feeds at the same time each day) and to retain the same ingredients in the diet, albeit in smaller quantities, whilst increasing the level of fibre. If continual box rest is required, your horse's rations will need to be reduced still further, and a supplement will be required to help maintain adequate vitamin and mineral levels. If necessary, a laxative diet can be provided by mixing 3 oz of Epsom salts with a little soaked sugar beet and alfalfa, which provides a much more nutritious and easily digested mash than bran.

Nutrient Requirements

In addition to water, your elderly horse's diet will need to provide adequate levels of carbohydrates, fats and oils as well as protein, vitamins and minerals.

Carbohydrates

Carbohydrates, in the form of fibre, sugar and starch, provide energy (calories). Slow-releasing energy provided by good quality fibrous foodstuffs, such as grass, hay, sugar beet or alfalfa, will prove particularly beneficial for your elderly horse. However, depending upon his type, health, condition and workload, he may also require a more instant source of energy in the form of concentrate feeds (which are high in sugar and starch) to help him maintain body-weight or perform the work expected of him.

Fats and Oils

Slow-releasing energy can also be supplied by feeding fats and oils, which provide approximately two and a quarter times more energy than carbohydrates. While most diets include between 2% and 3% fat, feeding additional quantities of oil as an extra energy source can prove particularly beneficial if your old horse has a poor appetite or worn teeth. It is also a very useful addition to the diet of laminitics where carbohydrate intake has to be restricted. Provided your old horse does not have any liver problems, anything from two tablespoons to up to half a pint of a vegetable oil such as soya, corn or sunflower oil can be fed on a daily basis, though if you are feeding a lot of oil, additional vitamin E may be required and advice should therefore be sought from a qualified equine nutritionist.

Fish oils, and to a lesser extent some pure unprocessed plant-based oils such as linseed (flaxseed), are also good sources of essential fatty acids, including the Omega 3 family, which can help regulate the inflammatory response to conditions such as arthritis and improve dry, dull coats and hoof condition. Fish oils, such as cod liver oil, should however be fed strictly in accordance with the manufacturer's instructions (especially if you are already feeding a vitamin and mineral supplement or compound feed), as they are also a good source of vitamins A and D, which if fed to excess could have an adverse effect on your horse's health.

Assessing the Energy Level a Feed Supplies

When trying to work out the energy level a feed supplies, look for the digestible energy (DE) content (i.e. the gross energy the feed contains, less the amount of energy it is estimated will be lost in the faeces). This is measured in megajoules per kilogram (MJ/kg) which is the equine equivalent to the number of calories contained within one kilogramme of any foodstuff. The lower the level of DE a feed contains, the less energy (calories) it supplies to the horse. As a guide, a low energy feed for those who maintain their weight easily may therefore contain between 7–9 MJ/kg. A feed suitable for horses in medium work or who need just a little extra help in maintaining condition may contain between 9–10 MJ/kg, whilst feeds that will help increase body-weight or provide energy for hard work will contain 11 MJ/kg or above. Feed too much DE, and your old horse will become fat or perhaps excitable. Conversely, if you feed too little, your elderly horse will lose weight and may become lethargic, irritable and prone to infection. When trying to determine the amount of energy a feed supplies, check that the levels you are quoted for each feed have been calculated on an 'as fed' basis and not a 'dry matter' basis in order to ensure that you can make a fair comparison between one type of feed and another. If energy and nutrient levels are calculated on a dry matter basis, which

Owned by riding school proprietor Hazel Walsh, 12.2 hh Maggie spent twenty-four years teaching children how to ride before being semi-retired and given to the Thompson family as a mount for their young children. These days, 38-year-old Maggi still brings home numerous rosettes and in the winter months goes out most Saturdays with the Hursley Hambledon Hunt.

will be indicated by the letters 'DM' after the quantity quoted, this means that the feed has been artificially dried out before being analysed. This results in apparently higher levels of energy and nutrients being quoted than if the same feed was calculated on an 'as fed' basis which takes into account the natural level of moisture normally contained within a feed at the time it is actually eaten by your horse. For instance, whilst a feed containing a digestible energy level of 12.2 MJ/kg DM may appear to provide more energy than a similar type of feed shown to contain 11.5 MJ/kg on an 'as fed' basis, the former feed actually only contains the equivalent to 10.7 MJ/kg on an 'as fed' basis when moisture levels within the feed are taken into account and therefore actually provides less energy (calories) for your horse to utilize, which could be important if you are desperately trying to put weight onto old bones.

Protein

If your old horse is healthy and easily able to maintain body-weight, protein levels will be adequately met by hay and feeds which contain approximately 8.5–10%. However where your elderly horse is having difficulty in keeping condition, research suggests that offering concentrate feeds which contain between 12% and 14% protein will prove beneficial in aiding the repair and replacement of body tissue, increasing resistance to disease, and improving both coat condition and hoof horn quality. However, there is no benefit to be gained by feeding higher levels of protein as it cannot be stored in the body to any great extent and is excreted in the urine. In fact, whilst a protein deficiency can result in the delayed healing of wounds, increased vulnerability to infection and poor coat and hoof condition, too much can also prove harmful because the removal of excess protein from the body puts unnecessary strain on the kidneys, heart and lungs and increases water requirements. Indeed, where liver or kidney problems are suspected, protein levels must be kept to a minimum.

Proteins are made up of twenty-two amino acids, twelve of which are synthesised adequately by the horse's gut. Of the remaining ten which must be provided by the diet, only lysine and methionine are likely to be deficient, the most obvious signs of which are poor hoof and coat condition. Elderly horses in particular require increased levels of lysine and diets should contain in the region of 0.6%. A lack of the amino acid tryptophan may cause increased nervousness.

Vitamins and Minerals

Amongst their many functions, vitamins and minerals help preserve a strong bone structure and healthy teeth, they aid energy metabolism and feed utilization, assist in the maintenance of fluid balance as well as nerve and muscle function and boost the efficiency of the immune system. Some will help to maintain skin, coat and hoof, whilst others may act as antioxidants which help to deal with problems such as infections and inflammation, and prevent the decay of body tissue, resulting in claims that antioxidants can help delay the signs of ageing. As a result, if your horse's diet does not provide adequate levels of vitamins and minerals, he may have difficulty in maintaining weight, become prone to infection, develop brittle bones or loose teeth, have poor hoof and coat condition or suffer from anaemia, delayed wound healing, nervousness or muscle damage.

Your old horse can, however, have too much of a good thing, and an overabundance of certain vitamins and minerals can adversely affect the absorption and action of others. A detailed discussion of the complicated relationship between various vitamins and minerals is beyond the scope of this book, but a basic knowledge of when and why elderly horses may require additional supplementation will prove useful. The following guidelines may be of assistance, but if you have any doubt as to whether or not it is necessary to supplement your old horse's diet, seek advice from a qualified equine nutritionist.

The majority of equine diets are deficient in **salt** but this is easily rectified by allowing free access to a salt block, or by adding a couple of tablespoons of loose salt to your old horse's feed (though this could be contraindicated if your horse suffers from heart disease). Salt blocks containing trace minerals can be useful in helping to make up for any shortfall of minerals in such a diet but if these are already being supplied by either a broad spectrum supplement or compound feed, trace-mineralised blocks are unnecessary and may even be contraindicated as excess consumption of certain minerals can prove detrimental.

Heidi, thirty-two years old, has been owned by Vanessa Staight for twenty years, taking her through Pony Club and winning many show jumping, cross-country and showing events, before being taught to drive at the age of twenty-five. Though having lost two front teeth, Heidi is still in good condition and winning both veteran and gymkhana championships.

Research has also indicated that elderly horses who have difficulty in maintaining condition, have a reduced ability to absorb **phosphorus**, and that a deficiency of this nutrient could be connected with weight loss, poor coat condition, bone abnormalities and lameness. At the same time, it is important to realise that excess phosphorous can actually prevent the absorption of calcium which is also essential for bone and tooth strength. The two minerals should therefore be present in an elderly horse's diet in the ratio of 1.5 calcium : 1 phosphorous. Adding a yeast supplement to the diet will also reportedly aid phosphorous absorption.

As previously mentioned, a declining population of microorganisms within your elderly horse's gut can lead to insufficient synthesis of **B vitamins**, a lack of which can adversely affect his health and condition. The production of B vitamins will be still further reduced if antibiotics have to be administered at anytime because these drugs are unable to discriminate between good and bad bacteria, and therefore kill both. On a therapeutic level, giving a course of probiotics (a source of live microbes) on completion of antibiotic therapy or during periods of stress, will help repopulate the gut with beneficial bacteria and help 'kick start' the digestive system. Thereafter the addition of a yeast culture to the diet of most elderly horses will enhance the ability of existing microbes to utilize fibre more efficiently, whilst at the same time providing a good source of B vitamins. Except in cases of veterinary emergencies, avoid the use of B vitamin injections as tonics for elderly horses as fatalities have been known to occur as a result of allergic reactions to the preservatives they contain. Wherever possible, use an oral alternative and seek advice from an equine nutritionist as to how best to provide a balanced diet, that will meet all of your elderly horse's nutrient requirements and prevent deficiencies arising in the future.

It has also been suggested that elderly horses may require increased levels of **vitamin C**, which acts as an antioxidant (reducing the signs of inflammation and infection), helps boost the efficiency of the immune system, aids the utilization of B vitamins and the absorption of iron. Though adequate vitamin C is normally synthesised by the liver, researchers have found that elderly horses, particularly those with Cushing's syndrome, frequently have low levels of the vitamin in their bloodstream. Whilst studies have yet to prove that additional supplementation is beneficial, this has lead some to suggest that a deficiency could be connected with delayed wound healing, joint pain, bleeding from the nose and an increased susceptibility to disease. Though nutritionists accept that it is poorly absorbed by a horse's body, some research has suggested that adding an extra 10–20 g of vitamin C (available from your local health food store) to the daily diet may prove useful. Fresh carrots, apples and green forage are also good sources of vitamin C.

Supplementation of **vitamin E** may also prove beneficial, particularly if your old horse is on a high fat diet or does not have access to good grazing. Like vitamin C, vitamin E acts as an antioxidant and is essential for the proper functioning of the immune system, though for optimum benefit, adequate levels of selenium are also required. However, whilst even quite high levels of dietary vitamin E have failed to show any adverse effects, there is a very fine line between adequate and toxic levels of selenium, which can prove fatal. Selenium, which also acts as an antioxidant, should therefore only be supplemented on the advice of your veterinary surgeon or equine nutritionist.

When to use supplements

If your elderly horse is on a restricted diet perhaps as a result of illness or obesity, is being offered straights (i.e. cooked cereal meal, oats etc.) or is being fed on old hay and kept on poor quality pasture (both of which will have low levels of vitamins and minerals), a broad spectrum vitamin, mineral and amino acid supplement will prove beneficial. Supplements specifically designed for veterans or feed/ration balancers which include adequate levels of calcium and phosphorous, lysine, B vitamins, vitamin C and E, as well as additional probiotics and yeast cultures to help support gut function, may prove particularly useful if your horse is showing signs of old age.

If, however, in addition to hay, you are also feeding a compound feed specifically formulated for elderly horses, this will contain elevated levels of all the vitamins and minerals your old horse is likely to require. Additional supplementation should then be unnecessary, unless you are feeding less of the compound feed than is suggested by the manufacturer (i.e. generally 3.5–4 kg [$7\frac{1}{2}$–9 lb] a day for a 500 kg [1,000 lb] horse). Similarly, if you are unbalancing the diet by mixing the compound feed with other 'straight' ingredients such as oats or barley, then your old horse may not be consuming adequate amounts of the vitamin and mineral premix contained within the compound feed to meet his needs. In such circumstances, you should contact the feed company's equine nutritionist for advice on how much extra of a broad spectrum supplement or feed balancer your old horse will need to compensate for the reduced amount of feed being given.

When adding extra vitamins and minerals to your horse's diet, remember that feeding more than one type of supplement, which may contain the same ingredients, is a dangerous practice. Contrary to popular belief 'more' does not necessarily mean 'better' and a supplement will only be of benefit if your elderly horse actually has a deficiency of the particular vitamins and minerals it contains. In fact some vitamins and minerals may actually prove harmful if fed to excess (e.g. selenium and vitamin A).

It is also worth noting that vitamins and minerals are easily destroyed by heat, light and air, so store both supplements and compound feeds in a cool, dark environment and remember to reseal containers. Hot water added to winter feeds will destroy their vitamin and mineral content and should be avoided, unless supplements can be mixed into feeds after they have had a chance to cool down. Remember also that the majority of supplements are only designed to supply your elderly horses *daily* nutrient requirements and they should be thoroughly mixed with and divided equally among your horse's feeds on a daily basis to ensure they are utilized effectively. Feeding such supplements once or twice a week is simply a waste of money.

Practical Feeding

Forage

The nutrient content and amount of forage consumed by your elderly horse is the most influential factor in determining the amount and quantity of other feedstuffs required. Allowing your horse access to well-managed pasture and feeding the best quality hay available not only makes economic sense but is the most natural diet that can be provided.

Grass

The value of grass must never be underestimated as it is easy for elderly horses to chew and its high moisture content aids the process of digestion. During the growing season, grass is also a good source of protein and carbohydrate, which explains why the condition of many elderly horses' skin and hooves will often improve in the spring, and why the body-weight of good doers can become difficult to control. Unfortunately, the nutrients that your old horse derives from grass varies, depending upon the weather and environmental temperatures, soil type and condition, varieties of grass grown and herbal content (if any), as well as stocking rates per acre and the length of time your horse is turned out. It is, therefore, very difficult to quantify the exact contribution grass makes to your elderly horse's diet. Indeed a certain amount of guesswork will always be involved in working out a horse's rations, hence the old saying 'it is the eye of the master that maketh the horse'. Consequently, you must frequently assess your old horse's body-weight and energy levels, in order to determine if, when and how much additional feed is required, remembering to be particularly vigilant in late autumn as winter approaches and the feed value of the grass declines.

Hay

If grass alone is insufficient to maintain condition, your horse's diet should be supplemented with good quality hay. A soft, leafy meadow hay, cut from permanent pasture is particularly useful for elderly horses as the variety of grasses it contains generally makes it more nutritious and easier to chew than coarse seed hay, which is specifically sown as a crop and contains only two to three different species of grasses. The only real way of determining the nutrient content of hay is to have it analysed, a service which is provided free of charge by some of the larger feed companies. When you consider that during the winter months hay is generally the largest component of your horse's diet and can vary in content from 5–10% protein and 6–11 MJ/kg of digestible energy, it makes sense to look at the nutritional contribution hay is making to your horse's rations, especially if he appears to have weight problems or suffers from conditions such as liver or kidney disease.

Even apparently good quality hay can contain high levels of dust and mould spores which, whilst not visible to the naked eye, will nevertheless compromise the efficiency of your horse's lungs. All hay should therefore be immersed in fresh, clean water for approximately 10–20 minutes. This will cause any spores present in the hay to swell to such a size that they are likely to be swallowed rather than inhaled, thereby reducing the risk of

Soaking hay for any longer than 10–20 minutes will result in the loss of valuable nutrients.

your old horse developing an allergic reaction which could damage the respiratory system. Excess water can be drained off before feeding, but the hay should not be allowed to dry out again otherwise the effects of the soaking will be lost, and the spores will once again become airborne. Soaked hay is also softer for your old horse to chew and may reduce wear on his teeth.

During the winter months, however, offering hay that has been soaked in freezing cold water could deter an elderly horse with neuralgia-type symptoms from eating. Where possible, therefore, take the chill off the water before soaking. Steaming hay cannot be recommended, as pouring boiling water over hay will reduce its nutrient content and have little effect on dust and mould spores. It is also important to note that mould will quickly develop on damp hay left over from the night before, therefore any uneaten soaked hay should be regularly cleared up and thrown out before a fresh supply is offered.

Haylage

Alternatively, feeding a dust free haylage can negate the need for soaking hay and prove particularly beneficial for elderly horses with severe respiratory problems. Made by baling the hay before it has completely dried, haylage is compressed and then wrapped in layers of plastic in order to exclude air. Provided that the wrapping remains airtight, the natural fermentation process that takes place inside the packaging will prevent dust and mould formation. However, if the haylage has been improperly made, contains soil particles or has been exposed to air during storage (as a result of the wrapping being punctured in some way), moulds and toxic bacteria can quickly develop, increasing the likelihood of respiratory problems, colic and even the development of botulism. Haylage which is slimy to touch or has an unpleasant sickly or ammonia type smell should therefore be discarded. In fact, once opened, haylage should generally be consumed within four to five days to prevent spoilage.

Though digestible energy and protein levels will generally be similar to early cut meadow hay (depending upon the variety of grasses from which the haylage has been made), it is always advisable to buy haylage which is accompanied by a nutritional analysis. It should also be noted that as haylage contains around

Seed hay, haylage and meadow hay.

50–60% moisture (compared with approximately 10–15% moisture in traditionally cured hay), an elderly horse may need to be fed around one and a half times more haylage in order to obtain sufficient fibre to keep the digestive system functioning properly. If, as a result, weight gain becomes a problem, additional fibre may need to be provided in the form of chopped straw or similar, and the level of concentrates being fed (if any) should be reduced.

Silage

In my opinion silage is not suitable for elderly horses. The nutrient content and increased acidity of silage is unsuitable for their fragile digestive systems, and the high moisture content (approximately 80%) means that it must be fed with other sources of forage such as straw or chaff to ensure an adequate fibre intake. A combination of low dry matter, high pH and an anaerobic environment, also has the potential to cause the *Clostridium botulinum* organism to produce toxins within the silage that can cause botulism, a disease which has already been proven to be responsible for a number of equine deaths. Although silage has been successfully fed to horses under professional guidance, the risks involved for the average owner are, I believe, unacceptably high, when there are plenty of other safer hay alternatives on the market.

Straw

Normally fed on a fifty-fifty basis with hay, oat or barley straw, which is low in digestible energy, can help to reduce the calorie content of your elderly horse's diet but it is worth noting that baled straw also has a low protein level and consists of particularly dry, coarse stems which means it is hard to chew. Whilst soaking the straw before feeding will help soften the stems and reduce the risk of the low moisture content causing impacted colic, a low-energy chaff may be a better alternative if your old horse has dental problems. If a compound feed is not being fed, then a good quality protein, vitamin and mineral supplement will also be required to help boost nutrient levels. As with all forage, straw should be clean with no visible signs of dust or mould. Wheat straw is particularly indigestible and often unpalatable and should not be given to your horse to eat.

Intermediate Feeds

Considered as a compromise between a forage and a concentrate, alfalfa (which is also called lucerne) and sugar beet both provide good quality protein and calcium, and are an extremely useful source of highly digestible fibre and slow-releasing energy. Though frequently used just to bulk out other feeds, a combination of alfalfa and sugar beet can in fact prove to be a very useful and easily digested feed for old horses. However, where relatively large quantities of such feed is offered (e.g. as a hay substitute for elderly horses with poor dentition), adding a little bran (which is high in phosphorous) to the mix may prove beneficial in helping to balance the calcium : phosphorous ratio of your elderly horse's rations.

Alfalfa

Available as a chaff or cube, alfalfa provides around 15% good quality protein (including the essential amino acid, lysine), between 9–10 MJ/kg of DE and is also an excellent source of naturally occurring vitamins and minerals. In fact research has shown that alfalfa is particularly useful for improving hoof growth and horn quality. Mixing alfalfa with oat straw reduces the level of energy and protein it provides to that of hay, and thus makes such mixes useful for good doers and laminitic ponies especially if combined with a supplement specifically formulated for elderly horses.

Sugar beet

Sugar beet, which is available as a cube or pulp, has a protein level of between 8% and 10%, provides approximately 10 MJ/kg of DE (though the DE in unmolassed sugar beet may be lower) and is rich in salt. It expands to two or three times its original volume and *must* be thoroughly soaked before feeding to avoid the risk of choke or impacted colic: the cubed variety must be soaked in three times its volume of cold water for twenty-four hours, whilst the pulp must be immersed in twice its volume of cold water for twelve hours. If left to soak for much longer than this, however, the sugar beet will quickly ferment. A fresh supply must therefore be soaked on a daily basis, and containers throughly cleaned after use. Do not be tempted to soak sugar beet in hot water in an effort to speed up the process, as this could also cause dangerous fermentation and would undoubtedly destroy the feed's nutrient content. In winter, care must also be taken to prevent the sugar beet freezing, which would stop the sugar beet from absorbing sufficient water. If time is short, consider paying extra for the type of sugar beet which has been presoaked before being processed and only needs to be soaked for a few minutes before feeding. Note also that whilst it appears to be common practice to drain off any spare liquid from sugar beet before feeding, this is in fact inadvisable as it contains water soluble nutrients and is therefore very nutritious.

Concentrate Feeds

If impaired digestion or the level of work your elderly horse is asked to perform means that he is unable to maintain condition on hay and grass alone, it is worth remembering that his digestive system is poorly designed to cope with high carbohydrate, low-fibre feeds and that the incidence of colic rises among cereal-fed horses compared to those fed forage alone. When choosing a concentrate feed you should therefore base you decision on the digestible energy, fibre and oil content of a feed and not just the protein level as is often thought (though this is still important).

Compound feeds

Feeding a good quality compound feed (e.g. cubes [pellets] or coarse mixes [sweet feeds]) produced by a reputable company, is undoubtedly one of the easiest and most convenient ways of ensuring your old horse is receiving a balanced diet as each feed will have a guaranteed analysis of nutrient levels which will be shown on the back of the bag. Remember to take your horse's type, health and level of work into consideration when choosing a feed, and not just his age. Feeds marketed for older horses are generally specifically formulated for those who have difficulty in maintaining weight and contain higher levels of digestible energy than the average horse and pony cube (pellet) which means they will not be suitable if your elderly horse is overweight or laminitic. Similarly, the higher oil and protein content of 'senior' feeds could hasten the demise of an elderly horse suffering from liver or kidney problems, hence a blood test to identify any pre-existing, sub-clinical illness is often recommended before changing to such feeds.

Coarse mixes (sweet feeds) containing micronised and extruded cereals which are easier for elderly horses to chew and digest, are the most popular type of feed, partly because even fussy feeders will generally find them appetising, but mainly because their ingredients are clearly visible, making them pleasing to the owner's eye. Cubed (pelleted) feeds however can be equally as palatable and are often even easier for elderly horses to chew, particularly if they have either a high oil content which makes the pellet softer, or if they are lightly soaked before feeding. The ingredients within good quality cubes (pellets) are often the same as those contained within a coarse mix, but they will have simply been ground down so that the shape of the pellet can be easily formed. Effectively this means that each ingredient has been 'prechewed' which can actually make them easier for old horses to digest. Whatever feed you choose, however, remember that just because a certain brand or type of feed proved ideal for your friend's or a celebrity's horse, it does not necessarily mean that the same feed will be as beneficial for yours.

Although mixing straights (cereals) with a compound feed will have the effect of unbalancing the vitamin and mineral level of your horse's ration, adding chaff, alfalfa or sugar beet can prove beneficial, not only in slowing down the rate at which the feed is eaten, but also in increasing the fibre content of each meal, both of which will help reduce the risk of choke and the development of colic.

Straights

For those who prefer to use straights (cereals) such as oats, barley and maize, you may be surprised to learn that, of the three, oats contain the highest level of fibre and the lowest level of energy (approximately 12 MJ/kg of DE). In fact, in the USA where maize is the most commonly fed cereal (with a DE of 14–15 MJ/kg), oats are considered a safe, low energy feed for temperamental horses, and barley is classified somewhere between the two (with a DE of approx. 13 MJ/kg). Hence the confusion when on arrival in England an American friend saw a feed which was guaranteed to be free from oats, but listed both barley and maize in the ingredients, described as a 'low energy' mix! However, as many owners in the UK are convinced that oats cause their horses to become excitable, feed companies simply respond to customer beliefs on a supply and demand basis, by excluding oats and replacing them with smaller quantities of barley and maize, the energy levels of which are then diluted by other high fibre ingredients. Even equine nutritionists cannot seem to agree as to whether or not oats cause hyperactive behaviour. Some claim that such effects are simply a result of overfeeding causing the natural characteristics of some horses to become exaggerated, whilst others say that any change in behaviour may be a result of an allergic reaction to a unique protein contained within the oats themselves.

Depending upon quality, the protein level of all three cereals can vary between 6% and 10%, and all contain poor levels of calcium, lysine and many vitamins, so are best fed mixed with alfalfa or sugar beet (to improve protein and calcium levels), and either a feed/ration balancer or good quality amino acid, vitamin and mineral supplement. Though there are many ways of processing cereals, elderly horses in particular will benefit from being offered flaked, micronised or extruded cereals as the cooking process makes them easier to chew, more palatable and increases the amount of starch that is digested in the small intestine, thereby reducing the risk of diarrhoea, colic or laminitis being caused by a carbohydrate overload. It is also worth noting that, contrary to popular belief, boiling barley is not worthwhile as it does little to improve its digestibility and will in fact destroy the cereal's nutrients levels. Oats which have had their outer fibrous husks removed (often referred to as 'naked' oats) will be low in fibre (generally no more than 3% compared with the 17% fibre contained in traditional oats), but are highly nutritious with a DE of 15 MJ/kg and a protein level of approximately 12.5% and may therefore be fed in smaller quantities.

A feed that may be found to be particularly useful for elderly horses who have difficulty chewing or maintaining condition, is cooked cereal meal. The low volume of the meal also means that it must be classed as one of the best feeds for elderly horses with limited appetites. It has a DE level of approximately 14 MJ/kg and contains more protein (approximately 15%) and lysine than any of the other commonly fed cereals. However, like most other cereals it is low in fibre, is a poor source of vitamins and minerals and has an incorrect calcium to phosphorus ratio. However, mixing the meal with alfalfa and/or sugar beet and adding a vitamin and mineral supplement to the diet will solve this problem. Alternatively a fully supplemented and sweetened cubed variety of the meal is also available.

Nutraceuticals

Feedstuffs which claim to have a beneficial effect on health are collectively referred to as nutraceuticals. Some may consist of large doses of particular vitamins and minerals, whilst others may be plant based (e.g. herbal remedies) or derived from animals (e.g. chondroitin sulphate). Many which claim to keep joints supple, improve immune response or aid the process of digestion are often recommended for old horses and, whilst few have been substantiated by independent trials, there has been a deluge of anecdotal reports from owners who swear that certain such additives have given their old horse a new lease of life, improved soundness etc. Do not believe everything you hear, however, for whilst some studies have supported the effectiveness of the various nutraceuticals, others have shown that, when compared with feeding a placebo, nutraceuticals show no advantage. Similarly, just because a substance has been proved to help human patients or other species of animals does not automatically mean it will be as beneficial for horses as some may be absorbed differently by the equine digestive system. Having said that, some nutraceuticals are now recommended by vets, and are definitely worth a try if your elderly horse has a specific problem. Inevitably, results vary depending upon on the individual horse and the cause and severity of the condition that you are trying to treat.

It should be noted that complicated interactions between some nutraceuticals and certain drugs can and do occur. It is therefore unsafe to assume that adding such supplements to the diet will do no harm. Even herbal remedies can have adverse effects if given inappropriately. If your elderly horse has a particular health problem or is being given any form of drug treatment, you should consult your veterinary surgeon before adding any form of nutraceutical supplement to his diet. Similarly if your horse is already being fed this type of product, you should advise your vet before any medication is prescribed.

Whilst a full list of nutraceuticals is beyond the scope of this book, some of those recommended for the treatment of specific conditions are mentioned under the appropriate headings elsewhere. However, those in most common use which deserve special mention are listed below.

Chondroitin sulphate and glucosamine

Chondroitin sulphate is one of two main glycosaminoglycans (GAGs) that are essential to the structure, strength and elasticity of cartilage and other connective tissues. It is claimed that supplements containing chondroitin sulphate can help to maintain and stimulate the repair of cartilage, increase joint lubrication, act as an anti-inflammatory and reduce damaging enzyme activity that can lead to cartilage degradation. However, there is great debate over whether or not oral supplements of chondroitin sulphate (commonly derived from bovine trachea or sharks' cartilage) can actually be utilized by the horse as some research has suggested that little, if any, of that fed by mouth is absorbed by the equine intestinal tract.

Glucosamine is a component of chondroitin sulphate and is required for the synthesis of GAGs. Manufactured in the body from a combination of glucose and amino acids, glucosamine production declines with age. Consequently, GAG production is also reduced and, as a result, elderly joints become increasingly prone to injury and arthritis. It has therefore been suggested that supplementation of glucosamine can help prevent or at least delay the onset of arthritis. Current evidence indicates that dietary glucosamine is well absorbed by a horse's body and can prove helpful in stimulating cartilage repair and improving joint lubrication. Trials carried out on human patients have also suggested that oral GAG supplements can effectively help to relieve the pain, soreness and inflammation associated with the early stages of arthritis to such an extent that the need for non-steroidal anti-inflammatory drugs (NSAIDs) may be reduced.

In addition to chondroitin sulphate and glucosamine, many 'joint supplements' also contain other substances said to be essential for joint health such as the following.

- Manganese – essential for the synthesis of GAGs.
- Copper – for the formation of cartilage.
- Vitamin C – for its antioxidant properties.
- Yucca – for its anti-inflammatory and pain relieving effects.
- Perna mussel – obtained from the sea, it is a source of chondroitin sulphate, glucosamine, trace minerals and beneficial fatty acids.
- Methyl sulphonyl methane (MSM) – to promote the health of joint tissues and aid the utilization of glucosamine.

Methyl sulphonyl methane (MSM)
MSM is a feed additive consisting of an easily absorbed form of sulphur which is an essential component of connective tissue throughout a horse's body. Although a deficiency in sulphur has been found in other animals, this has not been confirmed in the horse and it is generally thought to be provided in adequate amounts by several amino acids, the B vitamin thiamine and biotin, as well as certain enzymes and hormones. Blood levels in older horses have however been found to be low, which some claim could be connected to hoof, skin and joint problems as well as respiratory disorders and an increasing inability to combat infection. MSM is widely found in fresh plants and vegetables, though it has been discovered that it is destroyed when food is harvested, stored or exposed to heat, leading to suggestions that sulphur may be lacking in the conventional diet of the stabled horse. MSM is related to dimethyl sulphoxide (DMSO), and is said to have similar anti-inflammatory properties, without the associated risks. Anecdotal reports suggest that supplementary levels of MSM can prove beneficial when given to old horses suffering from, for example, infections, general stiffness, low-grade lameness, hoof and skin problems and laminitis.

Garlic

Garlic is a natural expectorant and antibiotic which makes it excellent for aiding the control of respiratory conditions. Blood tests have revealed that horses fed garlic show a slight increase in their white blood cell counts indicating its ability to boost the immune system and help guard against infections. Garlic is also said to aid the digestive system and act as a natural anthelmintic to help prevent worm infestation. It is also thought to help cleanse and thin the blood making it useful for horses with circulatory problems or navicular disease. Fed throughout the summer months, garlic will also act as a natural fly repellant as it seeps through the pores of the skin. Six to eight garlic cloves may be crushed and fed on a daily basis or, alternatively, garlic may be purchased in the form of a commercially produced powder, granule, pearl or oil.

Cider vinegar

Cider vinegar is an excellent general tonic that is said to cleanse the blood and reduce calcification of joints and arteries. It is thought to be particularly helpful in the prevention and control of arthritic conditions. Add approximately 50 ml (a scant US $\frac{1}{4}$ cup) to you old horse's feed or drinking water.

Echinacea root

Worldwide, echinacea is recognised for its ability to boost the efficiency of the immune system, thereby helping to improve resistance to, and the severity of, any infection. Recent studies have also shown that echinacea can help increase the size and number of red blood cells and increase the level of haemoglobin (the part of the blood which is responsible for transporting oxygen to body cells). Echinacea will therefore prove beneficial for preventing and treating infection, aiding wound healing and improving blood quality. It has been reported, however, that continual or overfeeding of echinacea may actually depress immune function; as a result it is suggested that for maximum benefit approximately 10–20 g ($\frac{1}{2}$–$\frac{3}{4}$ oz) of echinacea root or 10–20 ml (2–4 US tsp.) of the tincture should be fed daily for four weeks, and then eliminated from the diet for five to ten days before the cycle is repeated.

Devils claw

Trials have suggested that devils claw, which is well known for its anti-inflammatory pain relieving effects, can, in some cases, prove just as effective as a low dose of bute. Increasingly, numbers of owners are initially trying to help chronically lame horses by using devils claw and other supporting herbs (which, depending upon the cause of the lameness, may include willow, hawthorn, meadowsweet, celery seed and chamomile) before moving onto the use of NSAIDs if and when the herbs prove no longer effective. Most potently available in either root or liquid form, devils claw should not be given to those already suspected of having a gastric ulcer as it can aggravate the condition by stimulating bile production. Devils claw is also unsafe for use in pregnant mares as it can act as a uterine muscle stimulant.

Probiotics and yeast cultures

If at any time your elderly horse is stressed, perhaps through illness, fever, change in diet or environment, the beneficial bacteria in your horse's foregut (i.e. small intestine) that help him to digest largely non-fibrous feeds and prevent the proliferation of disease-causing bacteria within the gut, can begin to die off, adversely affecting nutrient absorption and making your old horse susceptible to digestive problems. As probiotics are a source of these beneficial bacteria, a ten- or twenty-day course (check product labelling) can help stabilize and repopulate your horse's gut with these microorganisms at a time when they are needed most, thus helping to improve condition and prevent digestive upsets. Available as a powder, paste or liquid, supplementation is particularly recommended following the administration of antibiotics which are unable to differentiate between good and bad bacteria and consequently kill both.

Whilst probiotics support the functioning of the foregut, yeast cultures (e.g. Yea–Sacc) enhance and stimulate the existing population of microbes in the hind gut (large intestine) thereby aiding the digestion of fibre which, as already mentioned, becomes more difficult with age. Yeast is also a good source of lysine and B vitamins and reportedly helps older horses to utilize phosphorus more efficiently.

As a result of these benefits some compound feed manufac-turers have included yeast and/or probiotics in the formulation of their 'senior' diets. However, additional supplementation of higher dosages may still prove beneficial in some cases, following antibiotic therapy or weight loss for example.

Antioxidants

Free radicals are a normal waste product of metabolism and the immune system's response to exposure to bacteria, viruses, air pollutants, drugs and chemicals. They are highly reactive, electrically imbalanced molecules containing oxygen that can cause damage to cells and tissues throughout the body, including cartilage. The body's natural defence against free radicals are antioxidants which normally mop up the free radicals and neutralize them before they can do too much harm. However, if free-radical production increases beyond normal levels, perhaps through illness, injury or any form of stress, the body may not be able to produce sufficient antioxidants to keep the free radicals under control. Left unchecked, free-radical damage may not only worsen a horse's condition, increase inflammation and delay healing, but may also be connected with the development of arthritis, immune deficiency, cancerous growths, the weakening of skin, tendons and ligaments, exercise intolerance and heart disease. These findings have lead to suggestions that the overproduction of free radicals may cause premature ageing.

Feeding a balanced diet containing a high proportion of green leafy forage, such as grass and alfalfa, which provides adequate levels of vitamins C, E and A, selenium, copper, manganese and zinc – all of which act as antioxidants – is thought to help support the body's defence mechanisms against free radicals and slow the process of ageing. Other substances such as bioflavonoids found in fruits (which enhance the effectiveness of vitamin C and strengthen capillaries) and beta-carotene which is the pigment that gives carrots and green forages their colour, also have antioxidant properties. However, additional supplementation of anitioxidants (often containing grape/grape seed extract which is a source of many antioxidant chemicals) may prove beneficial if your horse incurs a wound, suffers from an infection or allergy, develops a tumour, tendon strain or joint problem.

Electrolytes

These are mineral salts, present in a horse's body fluids, which conduct electricity throughout the body and are involved in nerve impulses and muscle contractions as well as oxygen and carbon dioxide transportation. Mineral salts can be lost through the evaporation of body fluids when a horse sweats due to exertion or as a result of illness or disease such as diarrhoea or pituitary tumours. If left unchecked this can eventually lead to an irregular heartbeat, dehydration, thickening of the blood, inadequate circulation, impaired kidney function, digestive malfunctions and fatigue. Electrolyte supplements are designed to help replenish body reserves. Most often available as a powder or liquid they should be mixed into a bucket of water, and then offered to the horse alongside another bucket full of clean, fresh water. A homemade electrolyte supplement may be prepared by mixing one and a half tablespoons of table salt with one and a half tablespoons of Lo Salt or Lite Salt in one gallon of water. Trials have indicated that a horse will only find electrolytes palatable when they are required by his body, hence an alternative supply of clean water must be available at all times if a horse is not to be deterred from drinking. Your vet may, however, need to give electrolytes intravenously or by stomach tube if your horse is seriously dehydrated.

Electrolytes cannot be stored in the body to any great degree making it pointless to add them to your horse's feed in an attempt to prevent the occurrence of dehydration. Electrolytes should only be offered if your horse has been sweating heavily or if a deficiency has been confirmed by your veterinary surgeon.

Determining the Amount of Food Required

In order to calculate the amount of food your elderly horse requires, it is essential to first determine his actual body-weight. Whilst this is most accurately obtained by taking him to a public weighbridge, this is not always possible. A weight tape will prove a useful alternative as, even though it may not be 100% accurate, it will, when used on a regular basis, at least give an indication of any increase or decrease in your old horse's weight which may otherwise initially be so subtle as to go unnoticed.

In general, elderly horses will need to be fed between 2% and

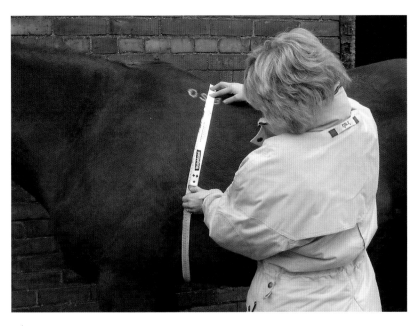

A weight tape will give a good indication of your old horse's body-weight.

$2\frac{1}{2}$% of their body-weight on a daily basis, though this will vary depending on your old horse's breed, type and condition. For instance, if he needs to lose weight then feeding $1\frac{1}{2}$% of his body-weight would be more appropriate, but if he needs to put on weight then the amount of feed he is offered may need to be gradually increased to between 3% and $3\frac{1}{2}$% (if he will eat that much). For example, a 500 kg (1,000 lb) horse who simply needs to maintain his condition will require between 10 kg and 12.5 kg (22 lb and 27 lb) of food a day, but if the same horse needed to lose weight this would need to be reduced to 7.5 kg ($16\frac{1}{2}$ lb) a day. However, if the horse was too thin for his frame, then he may need to be fed between 15 kg and 17.5 kg (33 lb and 38 lb) on a daily basis until his weight increased.

Working out the proportion of fibre to concentrates is not always easy. A diet of 100% fibre is ideal but if your elderly horse is unable to maintain his weight on fibre alone, slowly introduce up to 20% of concentrates whilst gradually reducing the fibre portion of the diet to around 80%. If he is still not obtaining sufficient energy (calories) to maintain condition, check that you are using a feed which contains a suitable level of digestible energy and then if necessary increase the concentrate portion of the ration again (up to 30–40%) until condition can be maintained. Note, however, that the fibre portion of the diet should never be less than 50% if the correct functioning of your elderly horse's gut is to be maintained.

Trying to calculate how much of your old horse's daily food allowance should be provided by fibre and how much should be offered as concentrates by using only his workload as a guide can be misleading. The amounts will also depend upon the quality of the fibre he is being given, as well as his individual type, breeding, temperament and lifestyle (i.e. kept at grass or stabled). For example, a retired old horse living out at grass who has difficulty in maintaining weight may need to be fed the same amount of concentrates as a horse in moderate work, whilst another old horse who is actually in moderate work, but who is prone to gaining weight or becoming overexcited, may perform happily on a ration normally suggested as suitable for those in light work.

As a guide, an elderly horse of average build weighing 500 kg (1,000 lb) who needs a little extra feed to maintain condition when in light work, may need approximately 12.5 kg (25 lb) of feed per day (2.5% of body-weight), offered as 80% forage (10 kg [22 lb]) and 20% concentrates (2.5 kg [4–5 lb]). Remember that if the concentrate portion of the diet consists of straights such as oats or barley, a vitamin, mineral and amino acid supplement will also need to be given at the manufacturer's recommended levels. Supplementation may also be required if you are feeding less than the recommended rate of a compound feed (check dose rates with the relevant feed company's nutritionist), since your old horse may not be obtaining enough of the vitamin and mineral premix contained within the feed to meet his daily requirements.

If you have any doubts about how to feed your individual horse, try calling one of the many feed companies who now run free telephone help lines manned by qualified nutritionists who are willing to provide advice. It is worth remembering, however, that a nutritionist who does not know your horse or see him on a regular basis can only provide guidelines as to the suitability of a particular diet, based upon the known requirements of certain types of horses. It is then up to you to observe how your old horse is doing on the suggested diet and make any necessary adjustments according to the time of year, varying work schedules and whether he is gaining or losing weight. It is important, however, to allow sufficient time for any change in a feed programme to take effect, particularly when trying to increase body-weight, but if after two or three months there is no appreciable difference in your old horse's condition, do not be afraid to go back to the nutritionist for further advice. Veterinary surgeons who have taken time to study equine nutrition in detail can also offer useful advice, however it is worth noting that most veterinary surgeons will have had only a few hours of tuition on the subject throughout their years at veterinary college and may not, therefore, always be able to offer the most up-to-date or practical advice.

Feeding Problems

Feeding horses who are thin, have poor dentition and/or limited appetite

Loss of condition is probably the most common feed-related problem of the older horse. Poor dentition as well as a decline in digestive efficiency are common causes but blood tests are worth considering to identify any other possible cause such as infection, worm damage, tumour or liver or kidney malfunction, that may be affecting food utilisation. Be aware that pain, whether sudden and severe as a result of an injury, or low grade due to conditions such as arthritis, may also reduce your old horse's appetite.

Having taken into consideration and dealt with any health issues, aim to boost your elderly horse's calorie intake by gradually increasing his overall feed consumption to approximately 3–3.5% of his bodyweight. Wherever possible, turn him out onto good grazing and offer the best quality hay you can find on an ad lib basis. If he is having difficulty in cropping grass or chewing long stemmed hay due to loose, worn or missing teeth, try soaking his hay or offering a softer source of fibre such as vacuum-packed hay, though in many cases short chopped fibre will provide the ideal solution. Research has shown that on a weight-for-weight basis, chaff will actually take your old horse longer to eat than ordinary hay and will therefore still satisfy his psychological need to chew.

Where even short chopped fibre cannot be eaten, your elderly horse's nutritional needs and fibre requirements may still be met by soaking various combinations of alfalfa pellets, high-fibre

Despite losing most of his teeth following a viral infection, Monty, owned by Julie Mancini, is still being regularly placed in veteran classes at the age of thirty-three.

cubes and conditioning cubes in either soaked sugar beet or warm water some twenty minutes before feeding. (Remember not to immerse them in hot water as this will result in the loss of vitamins and minerals.) As such mashes are eaten quickly, they will need to be given several times a day in order to ensure continued motility of the horse's gut. In these circumstances boredom is also likely to be a major problem since a horse would normally eat for some sixteen hours a day. Therefore, between feeds your elderly horse will still benefit from being turned out as much as possible in compatible company, even if he is unable to graze.

Concentrate feeds should be increased by no more than 200 g (7 oz) per day and should consist of 'senior' or conditioning feeds in combination with alfalfa and/or sugar beet as these are generally easily chewed and digested. No matter what is fed, the addition of oil to the diet will prove particularly beneficial in raising digestible energy levels (provided that your horse does not have liver or kidney disease) and a yeast supplement may prove useful in helping your old horse utilize the fibre in his diet more efficiently. Remember to monitor your horse's weight using a weight tape to ensure that weight gain is slow and steady, and thus avoid digestive disturbances that could lead to problems such as laminitis or colic.

It is quite common for a horse's appetite to diminish with age, and finding foodstuffs that will tempt his palate can become quite challenging. You may need to experiment a little with various types of feed, to which honey, apple juice, sliced carrots, or anything else he finds particularly appetising, may be added but be warned that your old horse's favourite foodstuffs may change with alarming regularity, in which case probiotics may prove beneficial in supporting microbal digestion. The addition of herbs such as mint and fenugreek have also proved beneficial in encouraging both appetite and weight gain, whilst other herbs such as meadowsweet, chamomile and valerian can help settle the gut if nervous tension is suspected.

Where the appetite is limited, it is particularly important to offer only small amounts of high calorie concentrate feeds (e.g. cooked cereal meal) at frequent intervals, in order to prevent overfacing your horse with large meals which may deter him from eating. It should also be noted that, as infuriating as it may be, hay left over from the night before is often considered by horses to be no more appetising than soiled bedding, and should therefore be discarded before a fresh supply of hay is offered.

Appetite may also be suppressed or energy unnecessarily wasted if your elderly horse is under any kind of stress, so it is worth considering if anything in his environment or management could be causing a problem. For instance, is he being bullied by field companions or does he feel threatened by being stabled next to another horse known to be aggressive? Does he get upset if his field companions are turned out before he is? Does he become distressed when left in the field or stable on his own? Did his loss of appetite coincide with a change in his workload? Does he eat better if he can see other horses eating at the same time, or does he prefer to eat his meals in privacy? Is he finding any new activity too difficult perhaps because he is conformationally unsuited to the job he is being asked to do resulting in painful muscles and joints? Does he weave, box walk, crib-bite or windsuck, perhaps through boredom or lack of fibre? Is he warm enough and is there adequate shelter from the elements in his field? All these factors and many more may need to be considered before the key to your horse's appetite may be found!

The trick in maintaining weight on elderly horses is to increase the feed before a difference in body condition becomes visible to the naked eye. Monitoring condition on a weekly basis by the use of a weight tape is therefore essential because, once lost, weight can prove very difficult to put back on to old bones. Remember that your horse's feed requirements will vary throughout the year in accordance with both his workload and the weather conditions. For instance, extra hay and feed may be required not just during the winter, but also during spells of drought in the summer when the grass stops growing.

Do not become too obsessed about your old horse's weight, however. Remember that some old horses simply have a faster metabolism than others and will always remain lean looking despite having the appetite of an elephant. If your old horse is happy, relaxed and otherwise in good health you probably have little to worry about.

Feeding the fat and/or laminitic horse

Many owners like their old horses to be in 'show' condition but if allowed to become seriously overweight, elderly horses can develop health problems, including heart, limb and joint disorders, muscular injuries, laminitis, lipomas and colic. In fact, excess fat can seriously shorten your old horse's life expectancy and every effort should therefore be made to maintain him in a moderate condition when the ribs, though not visible, can be easily felt.

Certain types and breeds, particularly native ponies, cobs and warmbloods will always be more prone to gaining weight more easily than their thoroughbred relatives. Similarly, whilst highly strung, nervy-type horses often find maintaining condition difficult, their relaxed, laid-back stablemates seem to get fat on fresh air. Ill health, such as heart disease, respiratory disorders and arthritis may also make your elderly horse unwilling to partake in much exercise and so contribute to weight gain.

As anyone who has been on a diet will know, success or failure is often determined by a combination of a reduction in food intake and an increase in exercise. Starvation diets are rarely, if ever, successful, especially for the horse in whom rapid weight loss can be extremely dangerous, resulting in the fatal mobilisation of body fat, a condition known as hyperlipaemia. Feed levels should, therefore, be reduced gradually and condition monitored regularly using a weight tape to ensure that weight loss is slow and steady.

Whilst aiming to restrict your elderly horse's diet to approximately $1\frac{1}{2}$-2% of his body-weight, remember that his digestive system has evolved to eat little and often and, left to his own devices, he would rarely fast for more than two to three hours. Leaving your old horse for more than seven or eight hours without food will in fact adversely affect gut motility and could predispose him to colic. Small amounts of fibre should, therefore, be offered at frequent intervals throughout the day. Whenever possible, choose a hay containing a relatively low level of digestible energy. Alternatively, try mixing your elderly horse's hay on a fifty-fifty basis with soaked oat or barley straw or chaff. A reduction in digestible energy levels does *not,* however, equate to a reduction in quality and should never be used as an excuse for feeding dusty or mouldy hay which would have a detrimental effect on the horse's respiratory health. Remember that when the diet is restricted, a broad spectrum vitamin, mineral and amino acid supplement will need to be fed to ensure your old horse's nutrient requirements are being met.

Invariably grazing will also have to be restricted. Recently much has been written about the dangers of allowing laminitics to graze when fructan levels in the grass are high. Unfortunately, the level of fructans (a form of carbohydrate which is stored in grass when not being used during periods of growth) can vary considerably from hour to hour depending on numerous factors, including light intensity and weather conditions, the type of grass grown and how it is normally managed. There is therefore no truly 'safe' period of the day during which laminitics may be allowed to graze freely, though current research suggests turning out late at night and bringing in at dawn may pose the least risk.

As a result of this confusion, some owners make the mistake of confining overweight horses to their stables but this can simply compound the problem as metabolic rates slow down when a horse is forced to stand still in his box all day. The situation can be made even worse if straw is used as bedding as, once hungry, a fat or greedy horse will start eating his bedding, thereby thwarting his owner's attempts to stay in full control of his diet. Whilst a gradual increase in ridden work, lungeing and loose schooling can all help towards obtaining a trimmer girth line, regular turn-out is still essential to ensure your elderly horse has sufficient exercise and does not become bored. Pottering around a paddock with field companions, interspersed with a few playful gallops will all help towards using up more calories and reducing fat reserves.

Where necessary, grass consumption should actually be restricted either by confining your elderly horse to a paddock with limited grazing or by the use of a muzzle. Alternatively, he may be turned out in the field for short but frequent periods throughout the day (provided he is easy to catch) or allowed to roam around an indoor or outdoor school (preferably with company). This type of approach will not only let you control your horse's diet, but the gentle movement will also help increase his metabolic rate and keep him mentally much happier.

Many owners are often horrified at the thought of using a muzzle, thinking that the practice is psychologically cruel.

The use of a muzzle can help prevent laminitis.

Correctly designed, however, it should still allow your old horse to drink and nibble at strands of grass which poke through the holes in the bottom of the muzzle, whilst still allowing him to exercise and socialize with his friends. This is surely a better option than confining an elderly horse to a life of virtual solitude locked up in his stable. To be safe, however, you must ensure that either the muzzle and headcollar straps will break easily should they become caught on anything in the field.

No matter how you choose to control your elderly horse's diet, particular care should be taken to restrict the grazing of those prone to laminitis during periods of rapid grass growth in the spring and autumn, or when rainfall follows a prolonged dry period in the summer. During the winter, turning out on bright, frosty mornings should also be avoided as, whilst sunlight will encourage the production of high levels of carbohydrates in the grass, the frost will reduce the rate of grass growth, resulting in an accumulation of fructans within the plant. Under such circumstances it is safer to wait until later in the day when the frost has gone before turning your horse out in the field.

Finally, it is worth considering that a fat horse is unlikely to feel the cold as much as his thinner stablemates, and that leaving him without a rug for as long as possible will encourage him to use up his energy in order to stay warm. Remember that horses can cope with even very cold conditions as long as there is no wind or rain to disturb the natural protection offered by their coat. Consequently, overweight horses rarely need to wear a rug when stabled, even when temperatures drop below freezing, and in all probability will only require a lightweight New Zealand rug to help them keep dry when turned out during the winter months.

Feeding the temperamental horse
Thankfully many owners are beginning to realise that horses who are considered to have a 'difficult' temperament are often just responding to pain from, for example, dental problems, incorrect bitting or an incorrectly fitting saddle, bilateral lameness, hoof imbalance, muscle soreness or trapped nerves, and that it is therefore essential to have a veterinary surgeon, equine dentist and a chiropractor or physiotherapist check the horse over in order to eliminate all of these potential problems before they start to blame the horse's diet. If any of the above are proven

to be the cause of, or are at the very least a contributory factor towards, your old horse's behavioural difficulties, you must understand that the memory of the pain will remain for sometime even after the cause has been removed. A miraculous change in your elderly horse's demeanour, although possible, should not be expected to happen overnight. It will take time for him to realise that the pain has indeed gone for good, and this may necessitate considerate and gradual reschooling to encourage the build up of muscles that may have atrophied as a result of pressure, imbalance or lack of use.

If it is a dietary problem, a lack of fibre in the diet can be one of the main contributory factors to temperamental problems. Insufficient fibre not only causes the horse to become bored as a result of being unable to satisfy his need to chew, but it also upsets the balance of microflora in the gut, causing acidity and an inability to produce adequate levels of B vitamins which can manifest itself as irritability and nervousness. A course of probiotics combined with increasing the level of fibre in the diet (preferably by offering ad lib hay) may be all that is required to remedy the situation. Supplementary B vitamins (particularly thiamine) may also prove useful.

When extra feed is required to increase weight or provide energy for work, choose alfalfa, sugar beet and cubed feeds in preference to cereal-based mixes and increase the level of oil in the diet. Some owners have also reported that calming herbal remedies have proved helpful.

Temperamental problems can also be caused by food intolerances and elderly horses who have a genuine allergy to certain foods (which can be confirmed by skin, blood and, in some cases, hair testing) will obviously benefit from the elimination of those ingredients from their diet. Cereals such as oats, barley, maize and peas are the usual culprits, though a few horses have reportedly had an allergic reaction to foodstuffs like sugar beet or garlic, so a process of elimination on a trial and error basis will be required.

Remember to feed by weight not volume to avoid unintentionally overfeeding your horse, and make sure that you are not overestimating his energy requirements. Keep your feeding programme flexible and take into account seasonal variations as well as changing workloads. Do not forget that during the summer months feed levels may have to be reduced in order to compensate for the extra energy which may be being obtained from good quality pasture.

Changes in a horse's day-to-day management can have the most dramatic effect on temperament. Regular turn-out with at least one other compatible equine is essential to help horses relax and burn off excess energy, and may help encourage weight gain in those who would otherwise simply fret when kept alone.

When all has been considered, it has to be said that some individuals are just naturally more highly strung and nervous than others. This type of elderly horse will need an experienced, knowledgeable and confident rider and attempts must not be made by more novice owners to starve such a horse into submission. A combination of regular routine, daily turn-out, training and work is essential to keep these horses 'sane'. If you are inexperienced and only able to ride occasionally owing to family or work commitments you may have to face up to the fact that a highly strung horse may not be your most suitable mount and that you may both be happier if you parted company.

Feeding the lazy horse

If your elderly horse appears thin, lacklustre or is constantly tired he should be examined by your veterinary surgeon and have blood tests performed to check for signs of anaemia or liver problems that could account for his condition and demeanour. Pain from a number of sources such as poor dentition, an incorrectly fitting saddle or arthritis may also make some old horses appear dull and unwilling.

Often, however, laziness may simply be the result of obesity and putting your elderly horse on a diet may be all that is needed to improve his enthusiasm for his work. If extra energy is required, try providing an instant source of energy, by feeding small quantities of high-energy cereal feeds, rather than giving large amounts of a low-energy mix.

Laziness may also be caused by boredom. Some old horses will simply 'switch off' if their life is filled with monotonous tasks. A combination of regular turn-out in the company of other horses, changes in activity including hacking, jumping, lessons or shows, for example, and improving your own riding and knowledge of how to keep schooling sessions interesting, can make a dramatic improvement in your elderly horse's willingness to work.

Hay bellies

Whilst the bellies of some elderly horses may appear to drop as their backs sag due to a loss of muscle tone, others may develop a hay belly as a result of inadequate nutrition. Although frequently thought to be fat, horses with an abnormally enlarged gut are actually often underweight, a fact that can be recognised by their protruding withers and spine, poor top line and quarters that appear sunken on either side. Gut distention can be the result of horses being forced to consume large quantities of poor quality forage in an attempt to meet their energy requirements. Unfortunately, such fibre will take a long time to pass through the gut as it will prove difficult to digest and is unlikely to provide the calories and nutrients your elderly horse requires. In these circumstances, condition may be improved by feeding better quality hay and other sources of fibre such as alfalfa and/or sugar beet. Additional concentrates may also prove useful in helping to increase the levels of digestible energy without also increasing bulk. A course of probiotics may prove beneficial, followed by the addition of a yeast culture to the diet on a daily basis to assist in the efficient utilization of fibre. Optimum vitamin, mineral and amino acid levels must also be maintained.

Gut distention may also be caused by a heavy worm burden or gut damage and, if suspected, veterinary advice should be sought, even if a regular worming programme has been followed.

Eating faeces (coprophagy), wood chewing, licking walls

All these problems can be indicative of stress and boredom, or a lack of fibre and/or nutrients. Changes in the environment (increasing turn-out and adjusting workload for example), combined with ad lib forage, and feeding either a broad spectrum supplement or suitable compound feed, can go some way towards helping to resolve these problems. A course of probiotics may also be required, particularly in the case of coprophagy which is often a horse's way of trying to re-establish or rebalance the level of microorganisms in his gut. It will also be worthwhile checking that your old horse is not suffering from a worm infestation, which could explain why he is not fully utilizing a diet which otherwise appears adequate.

Chapter Four

EXERCISE AND WORK

Whilst the amount and type of work that may be expected from an elderly horse will, to a certain extent, depend upon his individual breeding and constitution, as well as his attitude and enthusiasm for life, various other factors including years of inappropriate nutrition and worming, improper foot care, poor conformation, injury and overwork at a young age, can all affect long-term usefulness and may cause premature age-related changes such as arthritis, colic and nutrient malabsorption. Therefore, while some horses may be fortunate enough to continue to compete, even in quite high-level competitions, into their early twenties, others may need to have their workload reduced or participate in less demanding activities by the time they reach their mid-teens.

Whatever you do with your old horse, whether it be horse trials, endurance, dressage or simply hacking, the most important thing to remember is that if you want him to remain active, he must be given regular, steady and consistent work. In the same way that an elderly person living a fairly sedentary life would find it stressful, and indeed painful, to suddenly do an hour's worth of concentrated exercise, an old horse whose daily activity involves little more than pottering around the field, is unlikely to be fit and supple enough to cope with increased demands placed upon his body by work. Unaccustomed stress placed on ageing bones, muscles, tendons and ligaments by irregular exercise can cause painful muscular spasms, injury and

Over the years, three generations of Paula Killengray's family have had great fun with Rieben, a 16.2 hh Dutch Warmblood who at twenty-six years old still enjoys regular hacks.

Snowman, a 26-year-old grey, owned by Di Brown, is now enjoying his semi-retirement with Judi Gibbon and loves going for fun rides with his 21-year-old friend Mr T, who still competes in show jumping and one-day events with owner Zoë Northfield.

the breakdown of joint surfaces. A daily combination of formal exercise and turn-out in the field, is therefore essential to help increase lung capacity and cardiac efficiency, as well as to maintain optimum joint flexibility, preserve and develop muscle strength and tone and retain the elasticity of the tendons and ligaments, all of which may otherwise be compromised by age.

Even if your old horse can no longer be ridden, twenty minutes of formal daily exercise will help keep him healthy and may give him an additional interest in life, particularly if his work is varied between walking out in-hand, working over poles, long reining, (long lining) and driving. A combination of massage and passive stretching will also prove beneficial in helping to promote circulation, maintain joint flexibility and retain stretch tolerance of the muscles, tendons and ligaments.

Without some sort of formal exercise, the normal range of motion in an elderly horse's joints may soon be lost and muscle mass will quickly be replaced by fat. Sustained periods of inactivity are best avoided if you wish to maintain your horse's health and prolong his usefulness.

Passive Stretching

With the minimum amount of stress, passive stretching of the neck, back and limbs can help retain joint flexibility and elasticity in the muscles, tendons and ligaments, thereby reducing the rate of degenerative change and the occurrence of strains.

Application

Passive stretching should only be performed once the muscles have been warmed up (e.g. following a 10–15 minute period of walking) and must be done very slowly and carefully (particularly if your horse is known to suffer from arthritis) using gentle traction to stretch the muscles to the full extent of the range with which the horse is comfortable. Never attempt to stretch cold muscles, force your horse to stretch beyond his current capabilities or use quick jerking or twisting motions, all of which could result in tiny muscle tears and increased soreness. To be effective, muscles should be stretched to their current limit, held for up to thirty seconds and then returned gently to their original position. If at any time your horse shows resentment, indicating that you have gone beyond his comfort zone, he should be allowed to relax, before you try again.

Note If passive stretching is used to help prevent tissue shortening or loss of muscle tone during prolonged box rest, the muscles should first be warmed up using massage, magnetic therapy or hot packs. Following injury, passive stretching may also be used to aid healing or prevent the development of fibrous adhesions (i.e. a band of tissue, that bonds two structures together, causing restriction of movement) which may form following

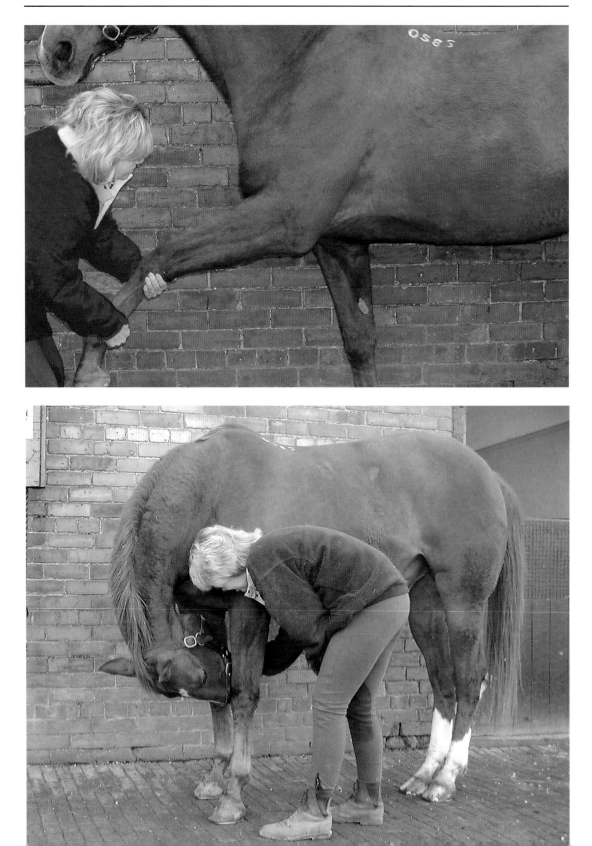

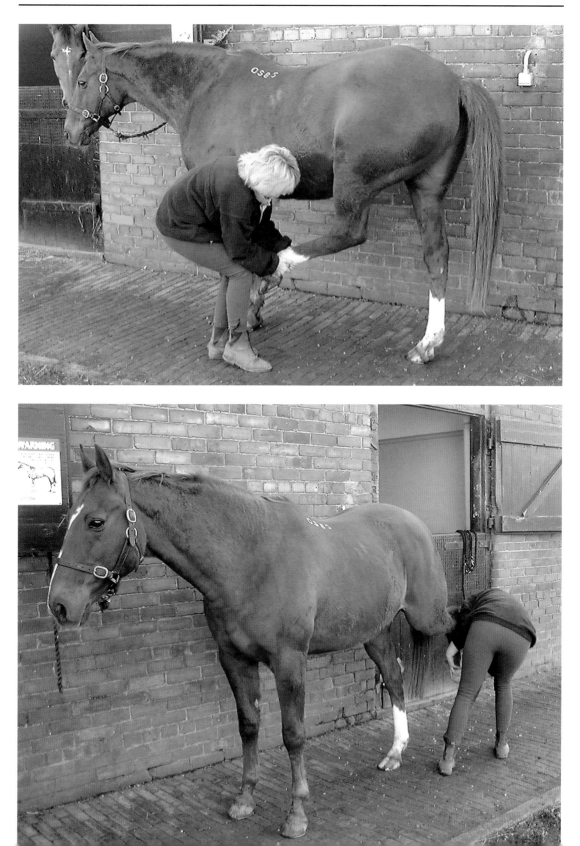

chronic inflammation. In such cases, stretching exercises should only be carried out on your vet's recommendation because, if performed too early before any tissue damage has had sufficient time to heal, stretching could prove detrimental.

Massage

Massage can prove useful in helping to stimulate blood flow, increase warmth, disperse fluid accumulation and promote relaxation. It is particularly beneficial for elderly horses who, as a result of stiffness in the joints or chronic lameness, frequently develop tension in the shoulders, back and hindquarters as a result of compensatory muscle use. This can lead to a reduction in blood supply to the affected muscles and the subsequent development of fibrotic tissue, causing less efficient use of the muscles which eventually begin to waste away. A general slowing down of the circulatory and lymphatic system can also lead to problems such as poor lubrication of the joints and filled legs.

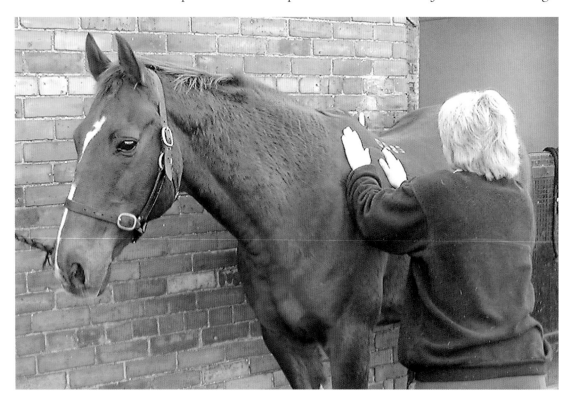

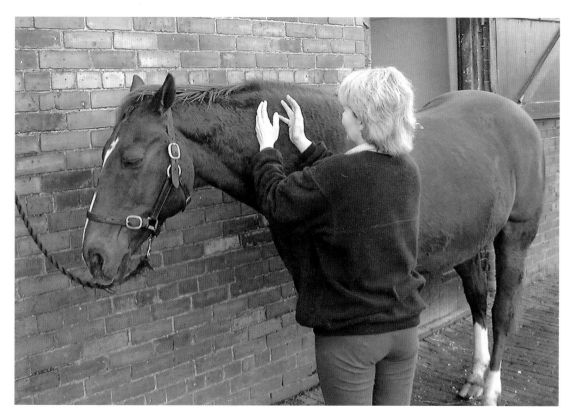

Application

In its most basic form, massage involves making either slow, firm strokes or small circular movements over the muscular areas of the body and can be easily incorporated as part of your horse's daily grooming routine. Using either your bare hands, a grooming mit or rubber groomer, start at the top of the neck and work down, move along the back and over the hindquarters in the direction of the muscle fibres. Avoid the abdomen and any bony prominences. Your horse's reaction and body language will tell you how much pressure he finds acceptable. Massage of the legs (using only the hands) should always be in an upwards direction towards the heart. Small circular motions over the coronary band (an area with a profuse supply of blood vessels) can help encourage hoof growth. Deep massage, required for more specific purposes, to promote healing for example, requires in-depth study and should only be peformed by, or under the direction of, a trained therapist.

Contraindications

Do not massage a horse who is suffering from azoturia, a skin infection or any form of undiagnosed illness or lameness.

The Benefits of Schooling

Regardless of whether or not you are interested in competitive dressage, regular schooling, following the principles of classical equitation and including plenty of changes of rein, circles, transitions, lateral work (e.g. shoulder-in, travers and half-pass) and pole work, will prove particularly therapeutic. If correctly ridden, this type of work will help develop equal strength and flexibility on both sides of your horse's body, and teach him how to support more of both his own and his rider's weight on his hindquarters, by helping to develop the abdominal muscles which will enable him to bring his hind legs further under him, thereby allowing him to arch and strengthen his back as he stretches forward towards the bit. This will lighten the load placed on the forelegs and, as a result, your horse will not only become a safer, more manoeuvrable and pleasurable ride, but also concussion and jarring of the joints, tendons and ligaments will be reduced as your horse learns how to lift himself across the ground rather than hammer into it with each stride.

Schooling should, therefore, be seen as a means of helping to maintain long-term soundness, but will only prove beneficial if, throughout, you work towards keeping your horse calm and relaxed and quietly accepting the bit whilst remaining responsive to your seat and legs. From this stage it is then possible to strive towards the ultimate goal of developing collection and self-carriage by establishing forward and rhythmical gaits, suppleness, straightness, balance, impulsion and engagement, all of which are inter-related and dependent upon each other.

Obviously physical limitations, caused by poor conformation, arthritis or injury, must be taken into account and will determine the type and standard of work that may ultimately be expected from your old horse. However, the success of any schooling work will be greatly influenced by your ability as a rider. In his book, *The Ethics and Passions of Dressage* (published by Half Halt Press Inc.), Charles De Kunffy writes 'There is no

neutrality in riding: you are either actively improving your horse, or actively breaking him down'. This is a quotation that many riders would do well to remember. If, for instance, you allow your horse to trundle along on his forehand and try to force him to drop his head and neck, by drawing back the hand and hauling on the bit or by the misuse of gadgets such as draw reins, you will only succeed in breaking down his muscular structure and joints more quickly. Similarly, if you sit heavily or vigorously drive your seat forward with each stride in a mistaken attempt to push your horse onto the bit and increase impulsion, you will only succeed in creating great discomfort, in response to which your old horse will almost certainly hollow (and thereby weaken) his back and concertina his neck muscles in order to try and escape from the pain.

In order to be a help, rather than a hindrance, to your horse you must, therefore, be able to sit lightly in a balanced position in the centre of the saddle, to ensure that your weight is

Elderly muscles can soon become tired. Your old horse will therefore appreciate plenty of short breaks during each schooling session to allow him to stretch and relax his muscles. Take care, however, not to just drop the contact and allow him to flop suddenly onto his forehand for this may easily cause him to stumble or lead to tendon strain. Rather you should keep him in a rounded outline, whilst allowing him to stretch over his top line into a gradually lengthening rein.

distributed over the strongest part of his back, and must aim to ride with a quiet, sensitive seat that allows the whole body to be used to give an aid, instead of relying on just the hands and heels. A detailed discussion of the rider's position and the most appropriate form of schooling exercises for horses with various individual problems is beyond the scope of this particular book. However, there are many other excellent books, including *The Classical Seat* (published by D. J. Murphy [Publishers] Ltd.) and *Dressage in Lightness* (published by J. A. Allen), both by Sylvia Loch, which cover such topics in great depth and are well worth reading as an adjunct to regular lessons with a classically trained instructor, which should be considered an essential contribution towards helping to prolong your elderly horse's useful working life.

Improving Your Horse's Fitness

If your elderly horse has been out of work for sometime, exercise should be introduced very slowly as an ageing body which may well have lost muscle tone and elasticity in the tendons and ligaments, will take longer to adapt to the stress of work. Note that throughout training protective exercise boots should be worn, as stiffness in the joints may make an elderly horse more prone to stumble or knock into himself. Prior to embarking on any fitness programme, you should ensure that all your old horse's nutritional needs are being met and have him examined by your vet in order to identify any health problems such as arthritis, COPD or heart murmurs that may limit his performance or need monitoring throughout training. With your veterinary surgeon's approval, your elderly horse should subsequently be given just twenty minutes walking every other day during the first week, allowing him alternate days to recover from any aches and pains that may develop. If all seems well at the beginning of week two, increase your walking exercise to five or six days of the week, allowing him one or two rest days turned out in the field. Thereafter, exercise should be increased by an additional ten minutes each week, until at the end of the fifth week, your horse is being walked out for up to an hour a day.

During this time, long reining in walk with frequent wide sweeping turns and changes of direction, may also prove beneficial in providing adequate exercise without the additional stress of the added weight of a rider. Lungeing, however, is probably best avoided in the early stages of training if you find it difficult to govern the pace or prevent your horse from cavorting around at the end of the lunge line. This could result in muscular spasms, strains and tissue damage, especially if your horse is also forced onto too small a circle as you try to regain control. In these circumstances, the introduction of up to twenty minutes lungeing a day is therefore best left until your horse is ready to start some trot work in week five or six. Even then, lungeing should be kept to a minimum or even avoided altogether if your old horse suffers from arthritis or navicular as the constant turning can aggravate such conditions by increasing torque on the joints, tendons and ligaments.

Though both you and your horse may find the initial slow work somewhat boring, never skip, nor underestimate the value of, walking, for it is the least stressful way to gradually build up muscular development, increase suppleness, improve cardiac function and maximise respiratory efficiency. Controlling overexuberant behaviour and insisting that your horse walks as much as possible during this phase of training will help reduce the risk of injury, and is least likely to exacerbate any health problems that may only become evident once work is introduced. If your horse does misbehave, however, some light schooling in walk may help concentrate his mind.

Before and after each workout your elderly horse should be checked for any heat, swelling or soreness. If at any time he should begin to trip more frequently, appear increasingly stiff or lame, become tired, breathless or even just uncharacteristically unwilling to go forward, his workload should be reduced and he should be checked by your veterinary surgeon before proceeding further. From the start, particular attention should also be paid to ground conditions and, wherever possible, very hard, unlevel or deep going should be avoided in order to reduce the risk of concussion, tendon strain etc. If possible, ride on level ground during the initial stages of training and only gradually introduce hill work from week five, once your old horse's stamina has started to improve.

During the sixth week of your fitness programme, walking work may be interspersed with short periods of a minute or so's trotting, which should initially amount to no more than five minutes per hour. Over the next three weeks, trot work may be slowly increased and exercise alternated between hacking and schooling. By week nine, short canters may be introduced, followed by periods of walk to allow heart and respiratory rates to return to normal. During the following three or four weeks, canter times may be slowly increased and, depending upon your horse's soundness, jumping may also be introduced.

Barring any injuries or set backs, at the end of thirteen weeks your old horse will be fit enough for general riding club work, including the participation in low-level dressage, jumping, week-end shows and lessons. Any extra fitness work required will depend upon on your ultimate aim and the type and level of work expected. If you are in doubt about how to proceed, seek advice from someone experienced in the relevant field. As a rule of thumb, however, note that you should never suddenly increase your old horse's workload beyond his normal range. Introduce everything gradually and increase either the length or the speed of the work-out, but never both at the same time.

If at any time your elderly horse's fitness programme is interrupted owing to illness or injury, allow at least one extra week of work for each week your horse has been rested. Of course, some elderly horses who are coming back into work after only a short lay-off may not need three months to regain their fitness. On the other hand, if your old horse is recuperating from an injury such as a tendon or ligament strain, you may need to take up to six months to return him to full work. This fittening programme should, therefore, only be used as a general guide but you will not go far wrong if you always err on the side of caution and monitor both your elderly horse's psychological as well as physical response to training on a day-to-day basis.

Warming Up and Cooling Down

No matter how fit your elderly horse becomes, never forget to spend at least the first ten to fifteen minutes of any exercise period in walk, before going onto more strenuous work. This will help to promote circulation, thus increasing the delivery of fuel (nutrients) and oxygen to his muscles in order to allow them to cope with the increased demands of work. The gradual stretching and flexing of your elderly horse's muscles and joints will also help relieve stiffness and prevent any sudden strain from causing further damage to his ageing tissues.

Similarly, spending ten to fifteen minutes in walk at the end of each session is equally important, not only to allow your old horse's heart rate and breathing to return to normal, but also to encourage the dissipation of body heat, allow blood flow to be rerouted back to the internal organs and permit the gradual removal of any toxins which have built up in the muscles, thus helping to prevent soreness.

It should also be remembered that, as age-related changes can make it increasingly difficult for your elderly horse to regulate body temperature, working in hot and humid weather conditions may become particularly problematic, especially if your old horse also suffers from respiratory or cardiac disfunction, is overweight (fat is a very effective insulator) or has a long, thick coat as a result of Cushing's syndrome. During the summer months, care should be taken to exercise during the coolest part of the day, that is the early morning or late evening, and if necessary your horse's coat should be partially or fully clipped so as to allow sweat to evaporate freely.

If he should become particularly hot and sweaty, you may help your old horse cool down by keeping him in the shade as much as possible, and repeatedly sponging cold water over his body and then scraping it off with a sweat scraper, whilst continuing to walk him around quietly until his temperature, pulse and respiration return to normal. In order to avert the development of dehydration or colic, he may also be allowed to drink a quarter of a bucket of water every fifteen minutes or so until his thirst is quenched. Do not forget that if your elderly horse has been sweating profusely, significant amounts of essential body salts may have also been lost, in which case he should be given a choice between drinking from a bucket of plain water and one containing an electrolyte supplement (*see* page 94). Feed should not be offered until at least an hour after work stops, in order to provide sufficient time for circulation to the digestive system to be restored.

Conversely, during the winter months, your elderly horse may tend to feel the cold more easily than his younger stable companions especially if he has been clipped or is underweight. Prior to being exercised he may therefore benefit from wearing a rug to help warm up his muscles in preparation for the work ahead. Subsequently, the warmth provided by a quarter sheet during exercise may also be appreciated. If your horse's work-load causes him to become overheated, care must be taken to ensure he does not cool down too quickly after work as the rapid loss of heat from the muscles due to cold environmental temperatures can cause painful muscular cramps. If sweating, your old horse should therefore be rubbed down with a towel before being covered with a cooler-type rug and then walked around until his temperature, pulse and respiration return to their normal resting rate.

Care of the Back

If your elderly horse is to remain comfortable when being ridden, care of his back and the provision of a correctly fitting saddle are essential prerequisites. As the condition and strength of the bones, joints, muscles, tendons and ligaments which hold the spine in a slightly arched position begin to decline with age, his back may eventually start to sag as it is pulled down by the forces of gravity and the weight of the abdominal cavity which is suspended below. Over time, a loss of muscle mass may also become evident just in front of and below the withers, as well as along the length of the spine, making the spinal process-es appear more prominent and the quarters more angular. As abdominal support is slowly lost, your elderly horse may take on a pot-bellied appearance and, as the back hollows further, saddle fitting will become increasingly difficult. In fact, some horses may eventually find ridden work painful if the back sags to such an extent that the dorsal spinal processes begin to collapse towards each other, causing discomfort as the bones rub together.

The rate at which such changes occur will vary from one old horse to another but even those with apparently strong backs may experience neck and back pain as a result of spinal

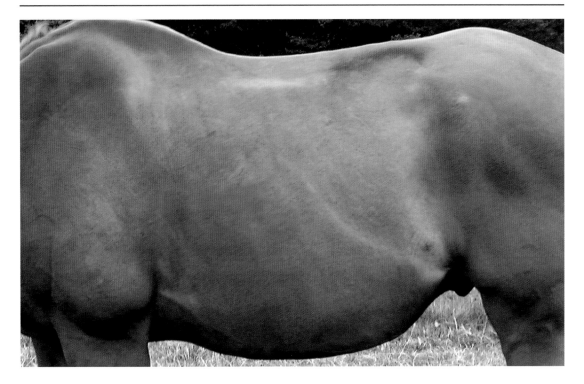

arthritis, lameness, muscle strain, dental problems or poor hoof balance, all of which can lead to compensatory muscle use, thus exacerbating the original problem. On the other hand, back pain caused by badly fitting saddles, poor riding or incorrect schooling can restrict an old horse's movement to such an extent that it actually causes lameness through placing abnormal stress upon the joints and causing muscular soreness. To prevent minor problems become major disabilities, all elderly horses, but especially those who are still in work, will benefit from having their backs checked once or twice a year (or whenever back pain is evident) by a vet or reputable animal therapist who is experienced in the detection and treatment of equine back pain.

Though correct schooling and passive stretching can help maintain the strength and flexibility of the spine, it is essential whenever your horse is ridden to relieve the weakening structure of his back by learning how to sit lightly in the saddle and rising to the trot as much as possible. Care should also be taken to prevent your elderly horse from becoming overweight as excess fat will place unnecessary stress on the

A loss of muscle mass can make the spinal processes appear more prominent.

121

back and its supporting structures. Similarly, forcing your old horse to stand for long periods in an abnormal position with his head raised and back hollow while feeding from a hay net will do nothing to stretch or relax his musculature and may cause spasms in the neck; feeding from the floor is recommended.

SIGNS OF BACK PAIN

- Uncharacteristic bad temper.
- Objecting to being saddled.
- Biting, kicking, tail swishing, pinning back of the ears.
- Difficulty in bending, rounding the back or stepping backwards.
- Shortened strides.
- Uneven muscle development.
- Being difficult when shod or groomed.
- Poor performance.
- Bucking, rearing, bolting, dipping the back, refusing to jump, grinding the teeth etc.

Saddle Fitting

Saddle fitting will need constant reassessment because the horse's back may change shape not only as a result of age, but also owing to seasonal variances in body-weight, standard of fitness etc. Though the basic principles of saddle fitting apply to all horses, compromises do sometimes have to be made, that is, it may occasionally be necessary to use a pad or numnah beneath a saddle that would otherwise prove to be too wide for your old horse at his current stage of development. If, for instance, there is insufficient muscle behind the withers or along the top line to support the bearing surface of the saddle, desperate attempts to maintain clearance of the withers and spinous processes commonly results in a saddle being used which is actually too narrow across the shoulders and which, as a result, tilts back towards the cantle. This causes restriction of the horse's movement and pushes the rider's seat to the back of the saddle, concentrating his weight over the weakest and most vulnerable part of the horse's back, causing soreness and eventually even lameness.

In these circumstances one temporary solution would be to compensate for the lack of muscle by using strategically placed padding beneath a wider-fitting saddle, which has been chosen to fit the horse's intended shape once the muscles have been built up by correct schooling, feeding etc. It is however important to ensure that the depth of the padding is such that it only replaces the degree of muscle loss in the poorly developed area, and that it does not cause the seat to become unlevel, thereby preventing the rider from sitting centrally in the saddle.

Alternatively you could choose to have four air bags inserted into the panels of such a saddle, with one air bag sitting each side of the front and rear of the saddle. Known commercially as the Flair system, the advantage of having air-filled panels resting on your horse's back is that they provide a soft and flexible bearing surface that will follow the contours of his back as he moves, thus making him feel more comfortable and helping to distribute the rider's weight over the largest possible area. If necessary, each air bag may also be inflated individually, giving your saddler a little more scope to compensate for any uneven

---

THE BASIC PRINCIPLES OF FITTING A SADDLE

The fit of the saddle must be checked with the girth tightened, when the rider is both mounted and unmounted.

- The gullet should be at least three inches wide along its entire length to avoid pinching.
- The panels should be broad and flat to distribute weight over the widest possible area.
- The saddle should give adequate clearance over the withers and along the length of the spine.
- To ensure the rider can sit centrally over the strongest part of the back, the saddle must not appear to tip forward or back.
- The saddle must allow sufficient room for rotation of the shoulder blades if freedom of movement is to be guaranteed.
- The entire bearing surface of the panels must rest evenly across the back and not bridge across its centre, otherwise weight will be concentrated only at the front and back of the saddle rather than throughout its length.
- When the girth is tightened the saddle should not move from side to side, or rock forwards and back.
- To avoid the rider's legs being pulled forward, thus forcing the seat onto the weaker part of the back, the stirrup bars should be positioned so that when the rider sits with the correct shoulder-hip-heel alignment, the stirrup leathers appear to drop vertically down the saddle flap from the bars, instead of being pulled back at an angle by the foot.
- Ideally, the saddle should fit the horse without the need for saddle pads or numnahs.

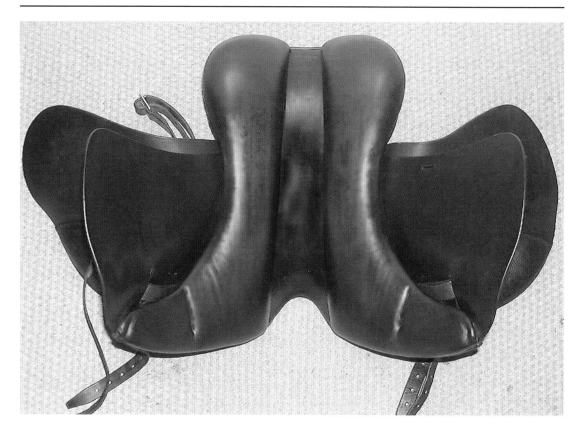

A saddle with a wide gullet and broad panels that will help prevent pinching of the spinous processes and aid weight distribution.

or poor muscle development, thus enabling him to balance the saddle more easily from both front to back and side to side. In some cases, the air bags may even be adjusted to help centralize the weight of a rider who may normally have a tendency to sit more heavily on one seat bone than the other. If the shape of your horse's back should subsequently change as a result of increased muscle development, it is then a simple process for a registered fitter to rebalance the saddle by adjusting the amount of air in the panels, provided of course that the original tree width of the saddle still remains adequate. Note that this system is not a cure for an ill-fitting saddle and that, in order to achieve the correct fit, the bags should never need overinflating to such a degree that they become hard like the tyre of a car.

For those who prefer the panels of a saddle to be flocked with more traditional materials, such as wool or foam, a made-to-measure saddle will prove particularly beneficial, and may not necessarily cost much more than a top-of-the-range premanufactured saddle. Correctly made, a custom-made saddle will not only conform to the contours of your individual horse's back, but will also be designed taking into account your own height, weight, body shape and ability. This ensures that it is constructed to help you sit in the best possible riding position with the minimum of effort, which will consequently make you an easier load for your horse to carry and thereby contribute to your horse's long-term soundness. Be aware that it takes an

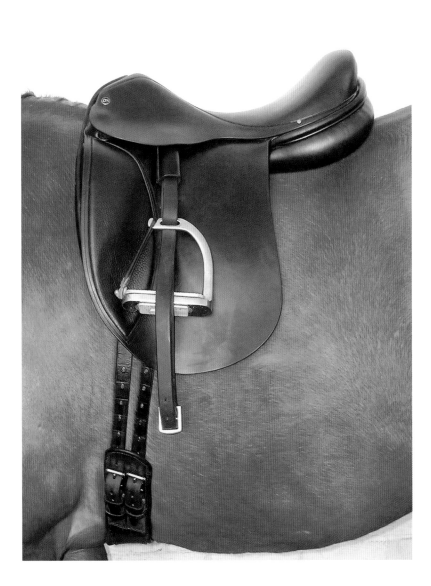

An excellent example of a well-fitting saddle that was made-to-measure for this particular horse by A. J. Foster Saddlemakers. The saddle conforms perfectly to the shape of the horse and allows the rider to sit centrally over the strongest part of the back.

experienced and knowledgable craftsman to design an individual saddle to such a high standard and you should, therefore, choose your saddlemaker with great care.

It is worth remembering that whilst there are some excellent professional saddle fitters, not everyone who sells saddles knows enough about the muscular development and movement of horses to be able to fit them correctly, let alone worry about whether or not the construction of the seat will actually suit the rider. Ideally, therefore, whenever a saddle is being fitted to your horse, you should try to have someone with you, such as an experienced riding instructor, who will be able to give you a knowledgable and unbiased opinion on the effect the saddle is having on both your horse's way of going and your own riding position.

Chapter Five

RETIREMENT

For many elderly horses, retirement may mean little more than a gradual winding down of their workload or participating in less demanding activities. An eventer, for instance, may be 'retired' to the hunting field, whilst a dressage horse who no longer has the athleticism required for advanced competition movements may act as schoolmaster or reliable hack for many years to come. If necessary, such horses can, therefore, often be rehomed with private individuals, riding schools and colleges, whilst those of a particularly quiet disposition may be eagerly accepted by riding associations for the disabled.

Unfortunately, once a horse can no longer be ridden, retirement options become severely limited. Though some elderly horses may be lucky enough to live out their days in familiar surroundings, being loved and fussed over by an owner whom they have faithfully served for many years, the reality is that the financial burden of maintaining a horse who has outlived his usefulness may be beyond the means of many owners, particularly if they do not have their own land. As a result, elderly horses with health or behavioural problems that prevent them from working may face an uncertain future.

In both the UK and USA, retirement homes for aged equines are few and far between, and those that do exist are run mainly by charitable organisations that almost exclusively take in abused or ill-treated equines referred to them by the police or animal welfare organisations. Though there are some homes that will

Helios, a traditional-type Hanoverian, competed in Advanced-level dressage in his younger days. Now at the age of twenty-five, Helios, owned by Vivien Carroll, still enjoys competing in hunter and veteran classes, and has raised thousands of pounds for charitable causes by participating in sponsored rides.

127

accept horses simply on the grounds that they are old and unwanted, waiting lists often span a number of years rather than weeks or months, and will hence be of little help if your horse is suddenly struck down by illness or injury. If you are hoping to place your old horse in a home, it is, therefore, essential to check out entry requirements well in advance of his retirement, including any age limit constraints, admittance fees or other financial contributions that may be expected whilst your horse remains in the home's care.

Since places at retirement homes are in such short supply, many owners will consider putting their horse out on loan as a companion animal but, again, these homes are extremely difficult to find and are usually only offered to 'low maintenance', easily handled individuals who are able to live out at grass all year round and require little in the way of special care.

Other options do exist. Some horses who are retired in their early teens may be accepted as donors by an equine blood bank, which supplies blood to hospitals and laboratories for use as an ingredient for culturing microbacteria for all human pathogens. Others may even be donated for non-invasive scientific studies, such as research into equine nutrition. However, such alternatives are rarely suitable for the very old horse and cannot be considered a long-term solution.

Regardless of the retirement option you are considering for your elderly horse, remember that it will remain your responsibility to ensure that your old friend remains healthy, comfortable and emotionally content for the remainder of his years, no matter who you entrust with his day-to-day care. Any prospective new homes must be carefully inspected, to provide answers to the following list of questions which will help you to choose the most suitable home for your horse.

1. **Are the facilities adequate and safe?**
   Is there sufficient grazing and shelter for the number of resident horses? Are the fences safe and secure? If stabling is required, are the boxes big enough for your horse and will his environment be as dust free as possible?
2. **Is there a sufficient number of knowledgable staff, to provide the sympathetic and individual care that an old horse may require?**

It is not unknown, for instance, to find retirement homes with three or four staff looking after sixty or so horses, which will obviously not only severely limit the amount of individual attention bestowed on each animal, but which may also put a horse's wellbeing at risk should the initial signs of health problems go unnoticed. An old horse or pony who is simply thrown out into a field, where the extent of any welfare checks involves nothing more than a head count, could easily become the subject of neglect.

3. **Will the level of care offered match your horse's needs?**
Ideally your horse's lifestyle during his retirement should not be too far removed from that which he has been used to throughout his life. Whilst some old horses may adjust well to living out all year round as part of a large herd in one big field, others who have been partially stabled and cosseted all their lives, have health problems or are easily bullied, may not cope well, either physically or mentally, if suddenly thrown out into a field and largely left to fend for themselves. A change of home is stressful enough for an elderly horse, without also having to contend with a completely new way of life.

Eventually the physical appearance of a very old horse may start to change as the back begins to sag, and the withers and hip bones become more prominent. Your horse's legs may take on an over-at-the-knee appearance and the fetlocks may drop towards the ground as support for the internal structures of the limbs slowly weaken. Facial hairs may begin to turn grey, and the head may take on a more chiselled look as deeper hollows appear above the eyes and the lower lip starts to droop. Setley Rose, owned by Anne McGrath, is thirty-eight years old.

Remember also to find out about the regularity of preventative health care measures, such as worming, hoof care and dental examinations, and to check whether or not the carer is willing to comply with any specialist feeding, care or drug therapy requirements your horse may have.

4. **Do other horses on the premises appear happy and in good condition?**

Whilst age may certainly change the physical appearance of a very old horse, they should not look like a 'bag of bones', have skin problems or look miserable and withdrawn. If you see any horse in this condition, try to tactfully enquire about any specific problems they may have and what, if any, treatment is being given to help improve their health. At the very least this will give you some indication of whether or not the carers are truly interested in providing the best of geriatric care, or whether they misguidedly believe such changes are simply the uncontrollable and inevitable effect of old age.

Trooper, bought by Les Gallop MFH as a 10-year-old, was hunted once a week throughout the season until he was twenty-three years old. Now twenty-six, Trooper is enjoying a well-earned retirement, acting as a companion for Ann Skinner's young horse.

Keep it in mind that it is not unknown for unscrupulous people to offer retirement homes for elderly horses, only to sell them on at auction as a riding horse before disappearing without trace. Therefore, even if you think you have found the perfect retirement situation for your old horse, always ask for references and never put him in the hands of others without first drawing up a contractual agreement, defining who is responsible for which aspects of your horse's care, in both routine and emergency situations. If you also reserve the right to periodically visit your horse to check on his wellbeing and comfort, it will not only put your mind at rest but will also ensure that his carers are

Seen here representing Ashford Valley Pony Club with young rider Lucinda Giles, it's obvious that no one has told 21-year-old Quizzy, a Super Solvitax Veteran Champion, that elderly ponies are supposed to slow down as they get older.

131

Admirals Cup, who won twelve races during his career was John Francombe's last winning ride before he retired. At the end of his racing career, Admirals Cup spent eight years at The Racing School in Newmarket before being given to Sue Cawthorn, who says the 23-year-old horse is 'the best hack on the heath'.

motivated to maintain high standards. In fact, if you apply the same care to finding a retirement home for your elderly horse as you would to finding a nursing home for an elderly relative, you will not go far wrong.

Chapter Six

THE OPTION OF BREEDING

Mares

It is when a mare can no longer be ridden that an owner's thoughts will often turn to the possibility of breeding. For some, the idea of having something to remind them of their beloved horse or pony is irresistible. For others it may be a way of justifying the animal's keep or perhaps be mistakenly seen as a cheaper way to get a replacement mount. Before any decision is made however, your elderly mare's health and suitability for breeding must be considered.

If, for instance, your old mare cannot even be taken for a quiet hack owing to back problems or chronic lameness such as severe laminitis or arthritis, do you really think she will be comfortable supporting the weight of an excited stallion during covering? Though this problem can be overcome by using artificial insemination, how can you subsequently rationalize forcing her to carry the increasing weight of a developing foal? This is bound to cause more stress and pain than any hour-long hack around the countryside would have done, particularly during the last trimester. Pain-relieving drugs can help, and some mares have given birth to normal foals whilst being maintained on low doses of NSAIDs (e.g. bute), however, no NSAID can be considered as safe for pregnant mares, particularly if dosages need to be

Despit having broken his pedal bone at the age of eighteen, Sam, owned by Nicola Gent, went on to compete in a Newcomers Regional Final at the age of twenty-one. Now twenty-nine, this 13.2 hh Welsh cross Arab still competes in show jumping, gymkhana and in-hand showing classes with his new 12-year-old rider Stacey.

Far from being a cheap way to provide a replacement mount, the cost of keeping a foal until he is old enough to be ridden will amount to thousands of pounds or dollars.

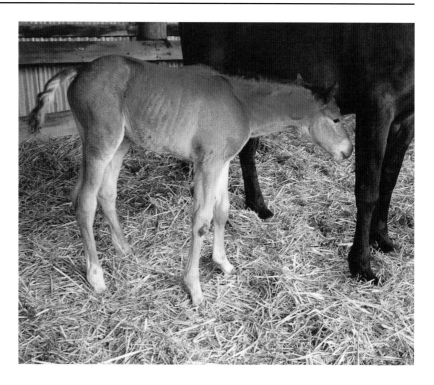

A mare's reproductive system

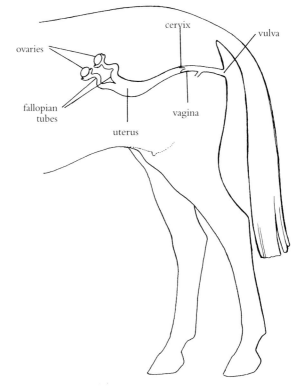

increased to keep the mare comfortable as the pregnancy progresses. Even common herbal remedies such as devils claw and rosemary cannot be fed safely to pregnant mares. Indeed, if your elderly mare is on any sort of drug treatment or herbal remedy for any reason you must talk over the risks of administration with your vet before considering putting her in foal.

Even though a good sire can help offset some of a mare's shortfalls, the truth is that if your mare is unsound, has poor conformation, a questionable temperament or 'isn't much use for anything else', then she is not a good breeding prospect. After all, a foal will be greatly influenced by his mother and will inherit many of her traits, including any predisposition to lameness, illness and even perhaps allergies. Similarly, it should be no surprise if a foal spending the first few months of his life with a mother who weaves, windsucks or crib-bites should subsequently display such habits himself during times of stress or boredom. Inherited temperament and learned behaviour are contributory causes to the development of so-called 'vices'.

If, on the other hand, your old mare appears healthy, has good conformation, an equable temperament and a proven track record as a good riding or driving horse, she may well produce a good quality foal that you can be proud of. Unfortunately however, the chances of a mare conceiving or carrying a foal full term begin to decline by the time she reaches her mid teens, especially if she has never been bred from before or has only had one or two foals in her distant past. In part, this may be due to a reduction in nutrient absorption, falling hormone levels, irregular cycling and aged eggs which are either unable to undergo fertilization or may develop abnormally. However, physical changes caused by weakening or excessive stretching of the muscles and ligaments supporting the reproductive tract also play a role. If, for instance, the vagina tilts forward so that the lips of the vulva no longer form a tight seal, this may allow urine, faecal material and air (a carrier of dirt and bacteria) to enter the reproductive tract creating ideal conditions for the development of infection.

Other common problems include scarring of the lining of the uterus due to increasing age, repeated infections or multiple foalings, and the formation of uterine cysts or tumours which can prevent normal development of the placenta. Similarly, a weakening of the muscular walls of the uterus and an age-related decline in the efficiency of both the lymphatic and immune systems, may contribute to delayed clearance of contaminants and fluids from the uterus following mating, causing inflammation and infection, and thereby thwarting pregnancy.

To evaluate your mare's chances of becoming pregnant, a veterinary examination is therefore recommended. This may include manual palpation and visual inspection of the reproductive tract (via ultrasound or endoscope), as well as taking a clitoral and uterine swab for culture and cytology to ensure your mare is free from disease and infection. A biopsy may also be performed to assess the extent of any damage to the lining of the uterus and a blood test may be taken to check for any viral infections that may cause abortion such as equine viral arteritis, and equine herpes. Other more specialised tests may also be recommended depending upon your mare's breeding history.

Even if problems are discovered, all is not lost, for some conditions may well respond to treatment. A course of antibiotics may, for instance, be sufficient to clear up minor uterine infections, whilst surgical procedures, such as the Caslick's operation, when the vulva is partially sutured, may help increase the chances of conception by reducing contamination of the reproductive tract. In some cases hormone replacement therapy may also prove helpful. Similarly, lavage (washing out) of the uterus anywhere from four hours to three days after mating, combined with the use of drugs to stimulate uterine contractions, can help promote the clearance of contaminants and fluids

The Caslick's operation involves partially stitching together the lips of the vulva to help prevent infection entering the vagina and uterus.

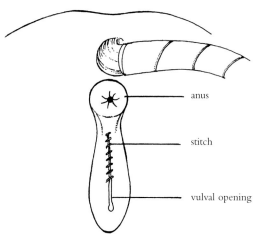

anus

stitch

vulval opening

from the uterus, without significantly affecting conception rates, as, within a few hours of mating, sperm actually move into the fallopian tubes (oviducts) to wait for ovulation, where the resulting embryo will also stay for a few days before entering the uterus.

It is important to realise that every time your mare is covered, it is inevitable that inflammation and contamination of her reproductive tract will occur, even if rigorous hygiene standards are imposed. In elderly mares with delayed uterine clearance this can increase the risk of the development of infection, which may subsequently prevent conception or lead to early abortion. In order to reduce the number of coverings required, you should therefore choose a stallion with a proven high count of active, viable spermatozoa, and have your mare scanned to ensure that mating need only occur once or twice as close to ovulation as possible, which is the time when fertilisation will take place. Alternatively, artificial insemination may prove a useful, if expensive, option.

Both before and during pregnancy your mare's normal worming, dental and foot care programmes should be maintained to ensure her continuing health. Vaccination programmes should be worked out with your vet to make sure that when the foal is born, he or she has some immunity against the most prevalent diseases. Your mare should be kept in good condition, being allowed neither to get too fat nor too thin. Ideally, at the time of covering she should be on a rising plane of nutrition, which means that she should be slowly increasing in weight as a result of being fed a high quality diet, as this has been shown to help increase conception rates. During the first eight months of her pregnancy, your mare should simply be fed to maintain optimum body-weight. It is not until the last three months of gestation that her nutrient requirements will increase beyond normal and her capacity for bulk feeds (hay) will be reduced as the growing foal takes up more abdominal space. At this time her additional feed requirements will probably be most easily met by gradually introducing a commercial stud mix or cube in combination with alfalfa/sugar beet and small quantities of good quality hay. However, if your mare is already overweight and you are unable to feed the recommended quantities of a stud diet due to the risk of laminitis, her increased vitamin, mineral and protein requirements may still be provided by feeding a good quality supplement or feed/ration balancer formulated for broodmares and growing youngstock. Such supplementation is vital, otherwise your elderly mare will be forced to use her own body resources to support foetal development, the consequences of which could be disastrous. It is not uncommon for instance for an elderly mare to loose all her teeth or develop brittle bones as a result of being robbed of her calcium and phosphorous reserves by the developing foetus.

During the last three or four months of her pregnancy, your old mare will become less agile particularly if chronic foot, back or joint pain becomes more intense as her weight increases. As a result she will become increasingly vulnerable to bullying by field companions and, if necessary, should be moved into a paddock either on her own or with a friend whose company she finds acceptable. A reduction in her activity levels can also cause poor circulation and fluid may tend to accumulate in the legs and along the underside of the belly. Quiet walks out in-hand, massage and passive stretching will all help to reduce oedema and improve blood flow, as well as helping to preserve muscle strength and tone which is so important in supporting the weight of the foal and making the birthing process easier.

Be aware that elderly mares are also more likely to suffer foaling complications. In particular it would appear that haemorrhaging from the artery supplying the uterus becomes more common, due to weakening of the artery walls. This is signified by colic-like symptoms and must be treated as an emergency because, whilst bleeding from a small tear may be contained by surrounding tissues, complete rupture of the artery can prove fatal. It should be noted that an elderly mare who recovers from even a minor tear of the uterine artery should not be bred from again, for any future increase in blood-flow demands to the uterus is more likely to result in severe haemorrhaging.

If foaling goes well and you want to continue breeding from your mare, many vets believe that your best chance of getting an elderly mare in foal again is to have her covered whilst she still has a foal at foot. But, mares in their late teens or early twenties are less likely to conceive during their foal heat (some 9–10 days after the birth) as their bodies need longer to recover from the

stress of foaling than younger mares. It is, therefore, probably best to wait until your mare starts cycling normally before having her covered again. This will also give you a little longer to assess your old mare's chances of maintaining her own body condition whilst supporting a foal at foot. If, despite good feeding, she begins to lose condition at this time then she is unlikely to be able to cope with providing sufficient nutrients for a developing foetus as well.

Though not all are so lucky, this mare in her early twenties had no trouble in maintaining body-weight whilst supplying sufficient milk for her ravenous and very cheeky foal.

Stallions

In comparison to elderly mares, there are few age-related problems that will affect a stallion's reproductive ability. Eventually, however, falling hormone levels, a declining libido (sex drive) and a reduction in the number of viable sperm may necessitate reducing the number of mares a stallion is expected to cover in any one season. Often, the simple act of breeding less frequently will prove sufficient to restore a stallion's interest and improve his sperm count, though in some cases hormone therapy may also prove helpful.

Provided they are well cared for, given a nutritious diet and kept relatively fit, many stallions will, in fact, continue to successfully cover mares well into their early twenties. In some cases, however, the development of abnormalities or tumours, such as squamous cell carcinomas and melanomas, on the penis or in the area of the sheath may eventually put an end to a breeding career, if surgical intervention is unsuccessful. Similarly, any pain in the back or hindquarters due to chronic lameness, arthritis or muscle soreness will undoubtedly affect a stallion's willingness to perform and may even adversely affect sperm quality. In these circumstances, however, the administration of pain-relieving drugs and nutraceuticals may be all that is required to see a stallion's enthusiasm for his job return.

Chapter Seven

EUTHANASIA

T hough it may not feel like it at the time, being able to put your horse to sleep to relieve the misery of severe pain or the torment of a quality of life that has become intolerable, is in fact the last act of kindness you can bestow. Knowing this does not make the decision any easier, however, and it is natural to feel overwhelmed by the enormity and finality of the instruction you are about to give. Even when you are sure there is really no alternative, being the one to order the death of a close friend will undoubtedly weigh heavily on your heart and you are bound to be filled with inner turmoil, wondering if there was anything else you could have done or, if given just a little more time, your old horse would have made a miraculous recovery. Rest assured however, that you will never forget your old friend, and that the guilt and grief you experience will eventually subside. You will then be able to look back upon your time together with great joy and affection, knowing that you gave your horse a good life and had the courage to ensure that in the end his passing was as quick and pain free as possible.

Unfortunately, horses rarely pass away quietly in their sleep, and most will eventually be euthanased as a result of colic, long-term lameness, catastrophic injury or some other illness. If you keep a horse long enough, it is almost inevitable that you will one day be responsible for ending his life. In such circumstances, your final decision will be largely influenced by your

Julianne Aston with Minty aged forty, the horse who inspired her to set up the Veteran Horse Society.

141

A valued and trusted member of Ruth Pimlett's family, Perky Pimlett was the National Reserve Veteran Champion at forty years old. Perky continued to be ridden until the age of forty-three but was sadly put to sleep at the age of forty-four when it became obvious that his quality of life was beginning to deteriorate. Though obviously sadly missed, Perky was a lucky pony indeed to have a caring owner who was willing to see him through to the end of his days.

veterinary surgeon's prognosis. That is why it is so important to employ the services of a specialist equine vet, who will be aware of all the up-to-date treatment options available for a wide range of conditions, and who will be able to give an objective opinion on your horse's chances of survival based on his past experience of similar cases.

Naturally you know your horse better than anyone else and are the best person to judge when your horse is still fighting for his life and when he has had enough, but you must be careful to ensure that in an effort to do everything possible to save him, you do not allow oversentimentality to cloud your judgement to such a degree that it actually prolongs suffering. Though there will always be someone who knows of a horse who became pasture-sound or was able to be used for light hacking after only being given a 5–10% chance of survival, it must be remembered that such horses are the extremely lucky ones and are, by far, in the minority. In reality, many horses in the same situation will

simply end up suffering unnecessarily because their owners cannot make that final decision or, worse still, are worried about being thought less of by their friends for giving up too soon. In an emotionally charged situation, it is also not uncommon for owners to commit themselves to long-term nursing only to regret it in the cold light of day when work and family obligations do not allow them to provide the level of care their horse truly needs.

We owe it to our horses to be pragmatic and, whether we like it or not, this often means that financial considerations and other commitments have to be taken into account. It will therefore prove helpful to give some prior consideration to what you would do if a crisis arose. If your old horse required investigative or life-saving surgery, for instance, would you be able to afford to go ahead with an operation that may cost thousands of pounds or dollars, bearing in mind that many insurance policies for older horses will not cover such treatment? Do you realistically have the time, dedication and facilities to cope with the intensive after-care that may be required? Does your horse have any pre-existing conditions, such as heart problems or severe arthritis, that may affect your decision? Would you want to proceed with the operation even if you knew your horse's chances of survival were slim or that he could never be ridden again?

Remember too that in an emergency, time is of the essence. Letting others know your answers to such questions will help ensure that your old horse receives prompt and appropriate treatment should he ever be taken ill in your absence. Indeed, if you ever intend leaving your horse in the care of someone else, while you go away on holiday, for example, you should complete and sign a veterinary care authorisation form (similar to that shown in Appendix 1). In our seemingly litigation happy society, this will give the carer and the attending veterinary surgeon confidence to act on your behalf in your absence, and will help prevent delays that could overwise cause needless suffering.

Other Considerations

Though it can be upsetting to think about, you should also give some thought as to whether you would prefer your horse to be put to sleep by lethal injection or gun shot. The administration of a lethal injection involves giving an overdose of anaesthetic into the jugular vein following which your horse will quickly lose consciousness and fall to the ground. (**Note** Since a lethal injection can take a little time to administer, some horses who are needle shy or showing signs of stress may first be given a sedative to ensure that they stand calmly for the vet). If planning to stay with your horse for the few minutes until he is pronounced dead, you should be aware that there will be some involuntary limb and muscle movement and a reflex 'gasping' as your horse slips into a coma and breathing stops. Though the fall and reflex actions can be distressing to watch, remember that from the time your horse is unconscious, he knows nothing of what is happening. The process is in fact much like putting your horse under an anaesthetic prior to an operation. However, subsequent disposal of the body can prove expensive since the use of drugs determines that the body must be incinerated or buried since it is no longer suitable for animal or human consumption.

The use of a hand gun is often considered the quickest method of euthanasia and is invariably cheaper as, provided no sedatives are given, the body may subsequently be used by the nearest hunt kennels or slaughter house. However, the efficacy of a bullet has recently become a matter of debate, since surprisingly little investigation has been carried out to ascertain just how 'humane' this method actually is. Nevertheless, it is thought that to ensure a horse dies quickly and cannot regain any degree of consciousness, the bullet must destroy part of the brain stem. Disturbingly, however, during a recent study, researchers found that six of fifteen brain stems taken from a group of horses shot routinely by an experienced slaughterer remained intact, and that there were varying degrees of damage to the other nine. In order to allow great attention to be paid to both the position of the gun on the head and the projected trajectory of the bullet, it has therefore been suggested that it is

Following a severe bout of laminitis, Tara, owned by Diane Hamlett, was retired from jumping and spent the remainder of her days hacking out and competing in show classes. Pictured here winning a ridden veteran class at thirty-one years of age it is clear that Tara enjoyed all the fuss and attention and was a credit to her owner. Sadly, however, Tara broke her leg in the field and had to be put to sleep just two weeks after this photo was taken.

preferable for horses to be given a sedative prior to being shot by a highly trained individual, as any sudden movement by a horse just as the trigger is being pulled could otherwise have dire consequences and result in immeasurable suffering. It is also thought that the attachment of a silencer in order to reduce distress in public places, may make the required accuracy more difficult to achieve owing to the increased length of the barrel.

Occasionally a horse may also be put to sleep using a captive bolt pistol. However, the bolt does not go far enough into the brain to actually kill the animal but simply stuns it. To ensure the animal dies, the veterinary surgeon then has to thrust an instrument into the resultant hole to destroy the brain and spinal cord (known as pithing). Since no drugs are used the body may sub-

Kenmuir, a 17 hh Irish Draught cross gelding, served in the Merseyside Police Force for twelve years before retiring at the age of sixteen owing to developing anaemia. He then went to live with Sue Green, under whose care he went from strength to strength, and successfully competed at both local and county level in side-saddle, ridden veteran and working hunter classes. At twenty-five Kenmuir still enjoyed regular hacks, and it was while showing his enthusiam with a buck that he lost his footing and damaged his superficial flexor tendon. Regrettably eight months after the intial injury, Sue felt that Kenmuir was no longer enjoying life and she and her sister made the brave decision to have their dearly loved horse put to sleep.

sequently be used by the local hunt kennels or slaughterman.

Taking each method into consideration my own preference, and that of many veterinary surgeons, is to put a horse to sleep by lethal injection as the method poses least risk and is less distressing for all concerned.

Your decision may however be influenced by the finances you have available and how you wish to dispose of your horse's body. In many cases burial of such a large animal will prove impractical and in some areas may even be prohibited by local government regulations. This means that if your horse has been given any sort of drug therapy or you do not wish his body to be used for human or animal consumption, then often your only choice will be to have him cremated. Whilst for a fee many slaughter houses may be willing to take the body away for incineration, some owners prefer to use pet crematoriums. Costs for cremation are, however, fairly expensive and vary considerably depending upon whether you wish your horse to be cremated on his own or with others.

Finally you will need to think about whether or not you would like some sort of keepsake. Some people may choose to keep a lock of their horse's mane or tail, or the last set of shoes he wore, whilst those who have their horse cremated, may ask for his ashes to be returned either in part or full. Alternatively, some owners may make a donation to an animal welfare charity, in return for their horse's name being placed on a plaque fixed to a tree or entered in a special Book of Remembrance, whilst other owners prefer just to look back at old photographs.

No matter what you decide, remember you will always have your memories of the special bond you shared.

Part Two

VETERINARY CARE

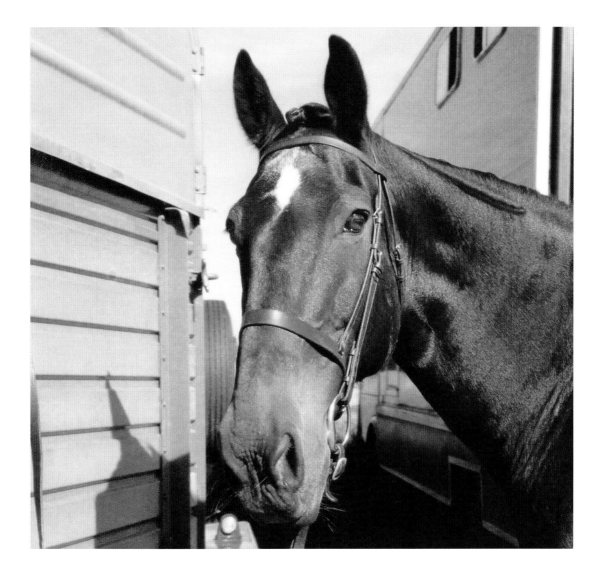

Previous page Harvey, a
16 hh Irish Draught cross
Thoroughbred gelding,
was given to Felicity-Jane
Nash by her father, who
had competed him in
open-level endurance
rides up until the age of
twenty-one. Now twenty-
six years old, Harvey is
shown in veteran horse
classes and helps Felicity-
Jane to relax after a
stressful day at work.

INTRODUCTION

This section covers some of the diseases and ailments to which horses become increasingly prone with age. The information provided is not in anyway meant to replace your veterinary surgeon's advice, but simply to help you understand how a particular condition affects your horse's body, what to do until the vet arrives and, hopefully, give you some understanding of why your vet is recommending particular treatments.

Guidelines are also given on related management techniques and nutrition, and in some cases complementary therapy such as herbal remedies and homeopathic treatments have been mentioned. For complementary therapy to prove effective, however, advice should be sought from qualified practitioners who will not only take into account your horse's particular ailment, but also his individual character, management and specific symptoms. In all cases, complementary therapy should never be undertaken without your veterinary surgeon's knowledge because, though invariably thought of as harmless, even herbal remedies can prove detrimental if given inappropriately, particularly if your horse is on concurrent drug treatment.

Where applicable, surgical options have also been discussed. Unfortunately, anaesthesia becomes an increasing risk with age, not only because of complications that may arise during surgery, but also because the excess stress placed on arthritic limbs during the recovery phase when your old horse is trying to clamber back onto his feet can increase the risk of further joint

Owned by Elizabeth Kay and now ridden by Kirstie Harrison, 25-year-old Connemara cross gelding Alfie continues to compete successfully despite suffering from arthritis.

damage and, possibly, fractures. In general, therefore, operations on elderly horses are only carried out in life-threatening situations. Regrettably, however, if your horse is of such an age that he can no longer be insured against illness or disease, such surgery may prove prohibitively expensive.

Chapter Eight

LAMENESS

Arthritis

What is it and how is it caused?

Arthritis refers only to inflammation within a joint but the term also tends to be generically used by horse owners to describe degenerative joint disease (DJD) and osteoarthritis (OA), which involve varying degrees of deterioration in the functioning of a joint. Specific names may also be used to describe degenerative changes in particular joints such as bone spavin in the hock, carpitis in the knee and articular ringbone of the pastern or coffin joint.

Arthritis, which is undoubtedly the number one ailment of elderly horses, is most frequently caused by an age-related thinning of articular cartilage combined with years of wear and tear. However, genetics, poor conformation, gait abnormalities such as toeing-in or toeing-out, infrequent or poor trimming and shoeing, overexertion and/or irregular exercise, can all compound the problem by unevenly loading, overextending or increasing the concussive forces placed upon the joints. Bone chips, fractures, ligament strains, and bacterial infections (most commonly caused by deep, penetrating wounds) can also initiate joint degeneration.

To understand both the causes and treatments of arthritis it is helpful to know that where the ends of bones meet they are

As well as being regularly placed in working hunter and veteran horse classes, 22-year-old Roxanne, belonging to Susan Loch, still enjoys participating in cross country, show jumping and dressage events.

There are four main types of ringbone based on the location of the bony changes. Articular ringbone is the only ringbone to involve a joint and is thus more likely to cause lameness than non-articular ringbone. Periarticular ringbone refers to bone proliferation around, but outside, the joint capsule.

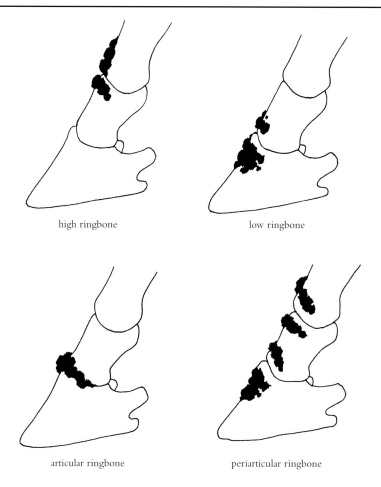

high ringbone

low ringbone

articular ringbone

periarticular ringbone

coated with a layer of cartilage which reduces friction and concussion and helps the joint move smoothly. The ends of the bones are then enveloped by a protective joint capsule which secretes thick synovial fluid to nourish the cartilage and provide lubrication. Structural support is given to the joint by ligaments on both sides preventing dislocation. When a joint is damaged, inflammatory substances leak into the synovial fluid, compromising its nutrient content and lubricating qualities. Without sufficient nourishment and protection, the cartilage starts to break down causing yet more pain and inflammation which sets off a vicious circle. Since cartilage does not have its own blood or nerve supply, healing, if it does occur, is extremely slow and even then the cartilage is likely to remain weakened. Eventually the cartilage may erode, and the bones will rub directly against

Bone spavin

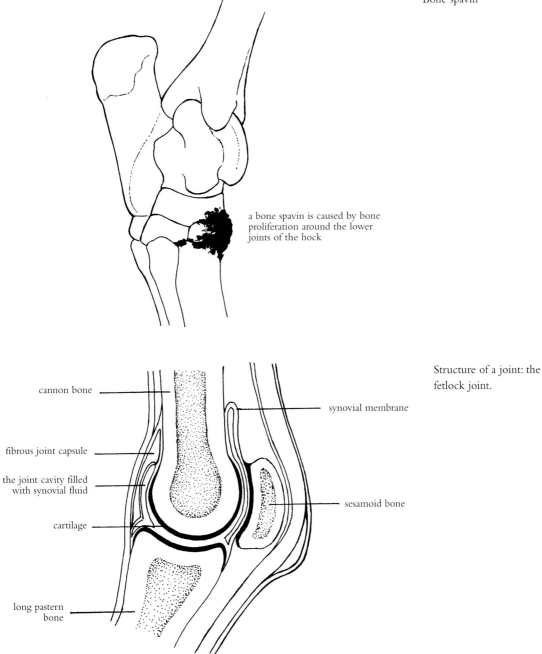

a bone spavin is caused by bone proliferation around the lower joints of the hock

Structure of a joint: the fetlock joint.

cannon bone

fibrous joint capsule

the joint cavity filled with synovial fluid

cartilage

long pastern bone

synovial membrane

sesamoid bone

each other. In an effort to try to strengthen the surface, bone growth will proliferate causing a narrowing of the joint space or bony spurs which will eventually fuse together to make the joint immobile.

155

What are the symptoms?

Symptoms may vary from a simple unwillingness to lengthen the stride to an obvious lameness which, depending upon the cause, may or may not be accompanied by heat, swelling and pain on palpation or flexion of the joint. Lameness may appear inconsistently depending upon which structures of the joint are involved, though symptoms are usually worse in cold, wet conditions and following periods of confinement.

How is it diagnosed?

Age, history and clinical signs are often sufficient for diagnosis of the condition, however your vet will test mobility of the joint involved and if a bacterial infection is suspected, will take a sample of synovial fluid for laboratory analysis. Your vet may also inject anaesthetic into the affected joint to check whether or not this relieves lameness, perform a bone scan (scintigraphy) to highlight areas of increased bone metabolism or turnover (areas of increased bone activity), and take X-rays to show up any bony changes or narrowing of the joint space. In some cases, an arthroscopic examination may also be performed. This involves the insertion of a tiny lens directly into the affected joint to view the extent of any soft tissue, cartilage or ligament damage, as well as to inspect for any bone abnormalities that may not have shown up on X-ray.

Coping with Arthritis

First aid

If lameness or joint inflammation develops, your horse should be rested until seen by your veterinary surgeon.

> JOINT INJURIES
>
> Since septic arthritis can occur as a result of a deep wound over a joint, such injuries should be treated as a veterinary emergency if rapid and irreversible degenerative changes are to be avoided. Whilst waiting for the vet to arrive, the injury may be cleaned with a saline solution and covered with a dry dressing and supportive bandage to prevent overdistention of the joint. Never apply a poultice without first consulting your vet, as this could result in precious synovial fluid being drawn out of the wound.

Medication

The aim of treatment must be to reduce inflammation of the joint capsule and its synovial membrane, normalise the production of synovial fluid and stimulate cartilage repair, so as to inhibit further degradation of the joint, reduce pain and improve mobility as much as possible. Your veterinary surgeon may therefore recommend a combination of the following.

- In the early stages chondroprotective agents may prove useful. These include:

  a. *Sodium hyaluronate* (i.e. Hylartil, Hyonate, [UK], Legend [US] etc.), is the key ingredient of synovial fluid which carries nourishment for articular cartilage, lubricates the joint and has shock absorption properties. Normally injected directly into an arthritic joint, it may also be given intravenously if more than one joint is affected.

  b. *Glycosaminoglycans (GAGs)* are a vitally important molecular component of synovial fluid and cartilage and as such are essential in maintaining joint lubrication and shock absorption. Injections of polysulphated glycosaminoglycan (PSGAG), i.e. Adequan, either directly into the affected joint or intramuscularly in an attempt to treat several joints at one time, has been shown to help stimulate the production of naturally occurring GAGs, promote the synthesis of sodium hyaluronate, reduce inflammation and aid cartilage repair. Although expensive, clinical trials have reported high success rates.

  c. *Nutraceuticals* including glucosamine, chondroiton sulphate, perna mussel, MSM, antioxidants etc. (*see* pages 88–94).

- Nonsteroidal anti-inflammatory drugs (NSAIDs), e.g. bute, to relieve pain and inflammation.

- Dimethyl sulphoxide (DMSO) is usually applied topically to help reduce inflammation, relieve pain and increase blood flow. DMSO must be used with care as it can blister the horse's skin.

- Corticosteroids, such as Vetalog, Azium and Depo-Medrol, are very powerful anti-inflammatories that relieve pain and prevent cell damage. Given orally or by injection, they can be very effective in the treatment of otherwise unresponsive joint problems. Although single injections of such drugs directly into a joint can help increase the production of sodium hyaluronate and can slow cartilage degeneration for anywhere between a few days to several weeks depending upon the product, repeated injections can have exactly the opposite effect and may actually hasten the breakdown of joint surfaces. However, this effect can sometimes prove useful in cases where joint fusion is actually required (*see* below). Where several joints are affected, elderly horses are sometimes given intramuscular injections in an attempt to treat all of them at the same time. However, once in the blood stream, corticosteroids can suppress the body's ability to fight infection and can disrupt hormone balance, as well as causing delayed wound healing, laminitis and gastric ulcers. If undergoing treatment, your old horse must therefore be monitored carefully for any adverse effects. (**Note** As these drugs can compromise the immune system, their use is normally contraindicated in cases of joint infection.)

Blisters The application of these substances to the overlying skin does not increase blood flow to the underlying structures of a joint and their use cannot therefore be recommended.

> JOINT INJURIES
> Where it is suspected that a wound has penetrated a joint, laboratory analysis of the synovial fluid may be recommended. If infection is found, the joint will be extensively flushed (known as lavage) with large volumes of sterile saline solution (ideally whilst the horse is under a general anaesthetic), and a course of antibiotics will be given.

As a last resort, where advanced degeneration of a low-motion joint (i.e. a joint which quite normally has only a limited range of movement) is causing lameness (e.g. bone spavin in the lower joints of the hock), your vet may aim to relieve the associated pain by encouraging joint fusion provided this will not significantly affect functional mobility. In some cases this may be achieved surgically or chemically via intra-articular injections of sodium monoiodoacetate (MIA) which will hasten the process of joint degeneration.

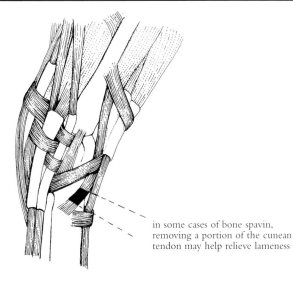

in some cases of bone spavin, removing a portion of the cunean tendon may help relieve lameness

Surgical options

Bone chips, damaged cartilage and other debris, which could result in persistent inflammation and deterioration of a joint, can sometimes be removed using arthroscopic (keyhole) surgery.

Where the aim of treatment is actually to speed up the process of joint fusion of a low-motion joint, surgical options include the use of screws or drills to destroy the space between the joint and thereby reduce joint instability and pain. In some cases of bone spavin, removing a portion of the cunean tendon (which may be irritated by new bone growth in the hock), may also help relieve lameness.

Trimming and shoeing

The proper trimming and shoeing of a horse with arthritis will depend upon any existing conformational faults or hoof imbalances but, in general, a wide-web shoe with a rolled or square toe will help reduce concussion and encourage breakover.

General management

In acute cases of joint inflammation, box rest followed by passive stretching and short periods of controlled in-hand exercise will be necessary. Once the initial inflammatory response has subsided, your old horse may be turned out and normal exercise may be gradually introduced. If at any point symptoms should reoccur however, he should be rested immediately and his

Described as a real character, 22-year-old Robins Ruin, 16.1 hh, owned by David Hunt was regularly hunted and successfully competed in working hunter classes, novice eventing and show jumping until diagnosed with low ringbone a year ago. Being very much a part of the family, Robin now spends his days taking David on some lively hacks and enjoys participating in the occasional veteran class.

treatment and exercise programme re-evaluated in consultation with your veterinary surgeon.

Where lameness is due to degenerative changes, daily turn-out and gentle exercise are essential to increase blood flow and promote the production and circulation of synovial fluid within the joint, thereby providing nourishment for the cartilage and helping to maintain mobility. The amount and type of work your old horse can be expected to perform will depend on the degree of lameness, though those who 'work sound' are generally capable of doing more than those who do not show an exercise-related improvement. Almost invariably, your horses workload will have to be reduced and if his long-term soundness, rather than short-term competitive success, is the ultimate goal, work on hard, deep or uneven ground and the participation in activities which involve jumping, galloping and sharp turns, should be kept to an absolute minimum. Your vet may, however, recommend a combination of relatively hard

work and NSAID therapy in cases where joint fusion is required.

To avoid placing extra stress on your old horse's joints, he should not be allowed to become overweight. Incorporating a little massage and passive stretching into his daily routine may also help relieve stiffness. Magnetic therapy may also prove useful in increasing circulation and reducing pain and inflammation. Remember that in the majority of cases, cold, damp conditions will make arthritic joints more painful. Therefore, in poor weather conditions your elderly horse will benefit from wearing a waterproof rug and may need to be brought into the warmth of his stable at night if shelter is not available in his field. In fact, keeping records of how your horse's lameness is affected by the weather, environmental temperature, ground conditions etc., will help ascertain optimum management and treatment strategies.

What does the future hold?

Though not generally life threatening, arthritis, DJD and OA may eventually affect your old horse's quality of life and limit his athletic usefulness to such a degree that long-term drug therapy (most frequently in the form of NSAID administration) may be required to keep him comfortable, though in some cases homeopathy, acupuncture and herbal remedies such as devils claw may prove useful alternatives.

Laminitis

What is it and how is it caused?

Laminitis is the term used to describe the breakdown of the bond between the sensitive and insensitive laminae which interlock to hold the pedal bone in position within the hoof capsule. Whilst research into the actual pathology of the disease is still on-going it is thought that a systemic response to, for example, illness, stress or overeating, results in laminitis 'trigger factors' being carried to the foot. The eventual effect of which is an interruption in the blood supply to the sensitive laminae (connected to the surface of the pedal bone) which weakens their finger-like grip to the insensitive laminae (attached to the hoof wall). If left unchecked, even for just a few hours, the stretching and tearing of the laminae (initially around the toe), combined with the pull of the deep digital flexor tendon at the back of the bone, may result in the tip of the pedal bone dropping down towards and eventually through the sole. Vets frequently refer to this stage as 'rotation' of the pedal bone or say a horse has 'foundered'. Without specialised treatment, the laminae attachment may be completely lost around the entire foot, whereupon the whole bony column drops straight down to rest on the base of the sole. A horse with this stage of the disease

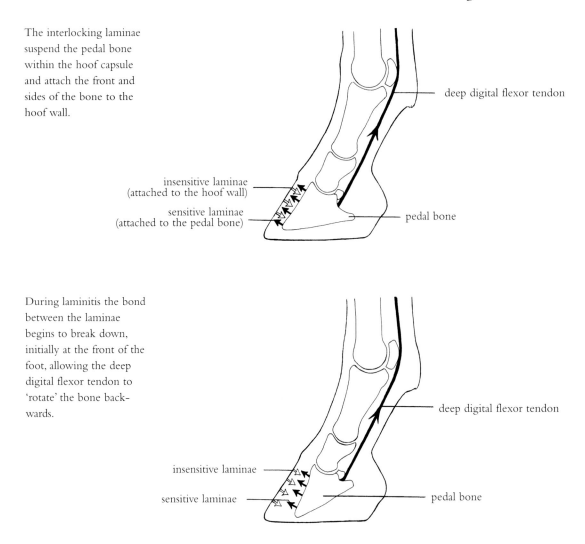

The interlocking laminae suspend the pedal bone within the hoof capsule and attach the front and sides of the bone to the hoof wall.

deep digital flexor tendon

insensitive laminae (attached to the hoof wall)

sensitive laminae (attached to the pedal bone)

pedal bone

During laminitis the bond between the laminae begins to break down, initially at the front of the foot, allowing the deep digital flexor tendon to 'rotate' the bone back-wards.

deep digital flexor tendon

insensitive laminae

sensitive laminae

pedal bone

is referred to as a 'sinker'. Laminitis, which can affect all four feet, but is most common in the forelimbs, must therefore be treated as a veterinary emergency.

As the efficiency of their bodily processes decline and risk of diseases such as Cushing's syndrome increases, elderly horses can become increasingly susceptible to laminitis which research has shown may be triggered by any one of the following predisposing factors.

- Obesity and mismanagement such as sudden changes in diet, feeding an excess of soluble carbohydrates or a lack of fibre.
- Various illnesses including colic, Cushing's syndrome, diarrhoea, dehydration, shock, severe viral/bacterial infection, organ failure, womb infections or poor cleansing following foaling.
- Mechanical overload or trauma, perhaps due to enforced weight bearing on one leg following injury to the opposite limb or constant pounding/jumping on hard ground.
- Drug therapy such as long-acting corticosteroids.
- Improper or irregular trimming and shoeing.
- Stress as a result of long journeys, overheating, exhaustion, surgery etc.

What are the symptoms?

During the developmental stage there may be no obvious signs of pain but, as the disease progresses, any combination of the following symptoms may be observed depending upon the severity of the condition.

- Lameness may vary from a stiff, pottery gait to complete inability to bear weight.
- Your old horse may be seen to shift his weight uncomfortably from one foot to the other, or rock his weight back onto his heels in an effort to relieve the pain associated with weight bearing on the front of the foot. If forced to turn in a small circle he may appear to sit back on his hocks and give little half rears in order to manoeuvre around.
- The affected feet will have an increased digital pulse, though occasionally this can be difficult for owners to feel.

163

An increased digital pulse (taken where the digital arteries pass over the sesamoid bones at the back of the fetlock) is indicative of an increase in blood pressure to the foot, one cause of which could be laminitis.

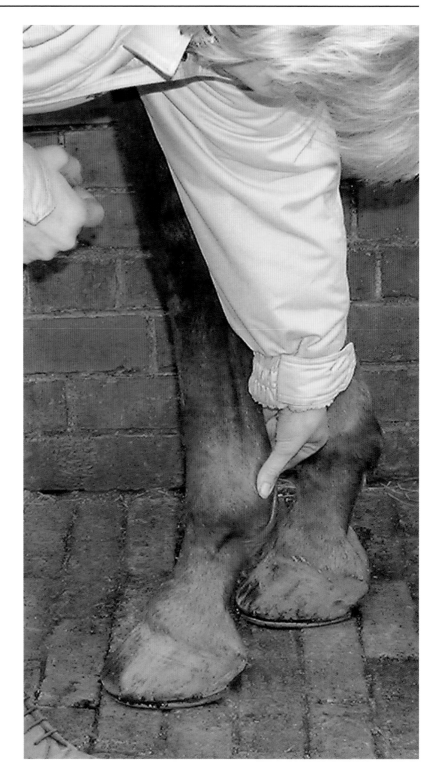

- Pressure applied to any part of the sole between the point of frog and toe will prove painful.
- As the severity of the laminitis increases, your old horse will become more and more reluctant to allow you to pick up his feet.
- Your horse may lie down, refuse to get up and sweat profusely. If in severe pain, his temperature, pulse and respiration rate will increase.
- If the pedal bone starts to rotate, a depression may be felt at the front of the coronary band, and a crescent-shaped bruise may appear on the sole. If the whole bony column starts to sink, the depression of the coronary band will extend all the way round towards the heels.

Note Heat in the feet is not a reliable sign of laminitis, as this will vary with the stage of development and environmental temperature.

How is it diagnosed?

Diagnosis is made on the presence of symptoms and a history of any predisposing factors. Initial X-rays will help determine the severity of the condition as well as providing a useful baseline from which progression of the disease may be monitored.

Coping with laminitis

First aid

Laminitis is a veterinary emergency. If it is suspected, call the vet immediately. The condition can deteriorate rapidly and without specialised treatment there may only be a twelve to twenty-four hour gap between the onset of symptoms and the development of severe, irreversible damage within the foot.

If your old horse is out in the field and refuses to move or allow you to pick up his feet, do not force him to walk back to his stable as this could hasten the tearing apart of the laminae and sinking of the pedal bone. Instead, wait for your vet to arrive, and if the field is some distance away from the stable yard make arrangements for your horse to be transported home in a trailer. Even if your horse is happy to walk a short distance to his stable,

A temporary frog support made from a thin roll of bandage, which should be taped securely into position.
Note the frog support must sit within the perimeters of the frog and must not be so thick as to become the only point of weight bearing. The shoe should still remain in contact with the ground.

the fitting of frog supports will help minimise the risk of pedal bone rotation in all cases. In an emergency these can be made from a thin roll of bandage taped into position within the margins of the frog. However, where pain is severe, forcing your old horse to support his weight on just three legs whilst you apply the frog support could cause him to collapse. Therefore, if he is unwilling to lift his feet, it may be more prudent to wait for veterinary assistance.

Once stabled, your horse should be given a two foot thick bed of shavings or sand to help support his soles and encourage him to lie down. Shoes must not be removed without veterinary approval because, if the soles of your horse's feet are flat or dropped, this could cause further damage and increase pain. Whether or not there is to be any benefit gained from soaking the feet is a matter of controversy. However, at the time of writing, recent research suggests that where it is suspected a horse may suffer an attack of laminitis as a result of grain overload or toxicity, the immediate and continual application of ice-cold wraps or boots to the limbs for the first twenty-four to forty-eight hours, before symptoms appear, may, by constricting the blood vessels, limit the laminitis trigger factors that reach the feet and thereby prevent, or at the very least reduce, the severity of any subsequent attack.

Medication

If your horse has overeaten, he may initially be stomach tubed with mineral oil and Epsom salts. Fluid and electrolyte therapy may also be required if he appears dehydrated. To help reduce pain and inflammation your vet will then administer NSAIDs (e.g. bute). Dosage must, however, be kept to a minimum as these drugs can upset intestinal function still further and may completely relieve pain, thus encouraging increased weight bearing and movement, which could hasten the breakdown of the laminae attachment. It is for this reason that desensitising injections of anaesthetic into the affected feet (nerve blocking) cannot be recommended, even though they may help increase blood flow. A certain degree of pain during laminitis is in fact beneficial as it encourages the horse to lie down, which relieves stress on the internal structures of the foot. Acepromazine (ACP) will also be administered to help reduce blood pressure and dilate the blood vessels thus increasing blood flow to the laminae. The tranquillising effects of ACP may also be useful in encouraging some horses to lie down.

The anti-inflammatory effects of DMSO and/or MSM may also prove useful in some cases, whilst the administration of high dosages of antioxidants may help limit the damage caused by free radicals.

Most recently, research has suggested that the use of nitro-glycerine patches placed at the back of the pastern can help in some cases by restoring normal blood flow and reducing the degree of lameness.

The choice of further medication will be determined by the underlying cause (e.g. organ failure or Cushing's syndrome).

Trimming and shoeing

As a first-aid measure in the acute stages of laminitis, your vet may continue to use frog supports or may choose to apply styrofoam pads taped in place which when compressed by the

When taped to the underside of the foot, styrofoam pads will compress to provide uniform support. (For illustrational purposes the tape has been removed from the horse's foot.)

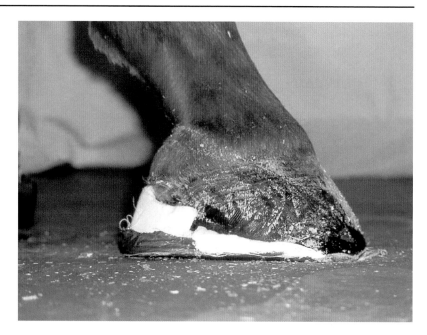

horse's weight will provide uniform support to the underside of the foot. (**Note** If styrofoam pads are used, it is essential that your horse stands on hard ground, so as to ensure even compression of the foam. In this instance, therefore, stable bedding should actually be kept to an absolute minimum. Without the uniform support that styrofoam pads provide, however, remember that it is essential to keep your horse on soft, deep footing as an alternative method of support.)

Subsequently, a Natural Balance shoe with additional frog support may be recommended. Alternatives include either a heart-bar or a heart-bar/egg-bar combination which may be nailed or glued onto the foot (depending upon pain levels) in order to provide support for the pedal bone. It is imperative, however, that such shoes are only fitted in conjunction with reference to X-rays because, if the frog support is incorrectly placed, it can damage blood vessels and cause abscesses. Most recently the use of the Equine Digit Support System (involving the use of a wide-web shoe, impression material, a pad, frog support and wedges that can be screwed into the branches of the shoe) has proved particularly beneficial in helping to transfer weight bearing to the back two thirds of the foot away from the most painful area around the toe.

In the early stages of severe laminitis, the application of wedges

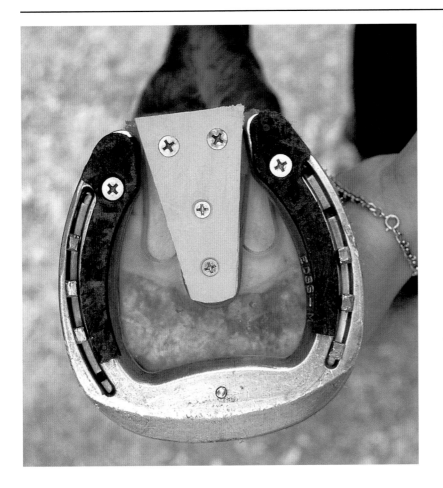

is considered by some as a life saver, in that they can help reduce the pull of the deep digital flexor tendon on the back of the pedal bone, and thus limit pedal bone rotation. They must, however, be used with caution and the horse's response must be monitored carefully, as in some instances they may make the condition more painful. The use of wedges without the concurrent use of supportive sole-packing materials is inadvisable.

As a result of the impaired blood flow, horn at the front of a laminitic foot will grow more slowly than that at the heel. However, as a laminitic horse will transfer the majority of his weight to the back of the foot in order to relieve pain, the toe will actually grow out longer. Reflecting such hoof growth, rings may appear around the hoof wall which are typically narrow at the toe, becoming progressively wider at the heel. The white line (which signifies the division between the hoof wall and the sensitive inner structures of the foot), may also become wider. Potentially this can allow infectious agents to invade the area and, as the white line becomes weaker, abscesses may develop. Your farrier will therefore need to trim your horse's feet on a four weekly basis to keep the toes short, restore/maintain the correct hoof/pastern angle and ensure the correct positioning of surgical shoes.

Surgical options

Though now a relatively uncommon form of treatment, the gas, blood, serum and dead tissue that can build up between the hoof wall and the pedal bone as the laminae bonds break down, may be removed by drilling a drainage hole into the hoof wall or, if particularly severe, by cutting away the separated wall of the hoof in a procedure known as a 'dorsal wall resection'. This will allow the bond between the hoof wall and the pedal bone to re-establish as new hoof grows down from the coronary band. Where horn growth is distorted because of pressure on the blood vessels at the coronary band, the removal of narrow strips of wall just below the coronary band can help restore normal blood flow and, therefore, growth.

In those cases of laminitis where, for some as yet unknown reason, the deep digital flexor tendon starts to contract, increasing its pull on the back of the pedal bone and thus hastening rotation, it may be recommended that the tendon be surgically cut. In some cases this has proved successful in halting pedal bone rotation and may allow some horses to eventually resume very light work, though it should be primarily considered as a salvage procedure.

General management

During laminitis, blood pressure within the hoof capsule rises (hence the bounding digital pulse) and blood is shunted away from the laminae. Exercise will not, therefore, help to restore circulation to the damaged tissues and is, in most cases, contraindicated as the mechanical forces placed upon weakening laminae will increase the risk of either pedal bone rotation or the sinking of the whole bony column. Box rest is, therefore, advisable until your old horse can be taken off pain killers and is able to move comfortably around his stable. Exercise should only be resumed on veterinary advice and in general will initially start with short periods of in-hand walking.

Whilst resting, your elderly horse should be given a high fibre diet of soaked hay or chaff. If recumbent, both hay and water should be placed within easy reach. Remember that, regardless of the cause of the laminitis, your old horse will still require adequate levels of protein, energy, vitamins and minerals in his diet to help support bodily functions and repair damaged tissues. Nutrient levels must, therefore, be maintained even if he is placed on a diet. In the long term, these are best supplied by a high fibre, low carbohydrate diet in conjunction with a good quality vitamin, mineral and amino acid supplement (*see* pages 100-103). In cases of laminitis caused by carbohydrate overload or toxicity, a probiotic may also prove helpful in repopulating the gut with beneficial bacteria. Never put your horse or pony on a starvation diet as this will force his body to mobilise fat reserves in order to obtain the energy it needs, causing the potentially fatal condition known as hyperlipaemia in which fat levels in the blood increase and the liver fails. If the laminitis was not caused by overeating and your horse actually needs help to maintain weight, try adding alfalfa, cooked cereal meal or high fibre cubes (pellets) to his diet, along with an oil supplement. Avoid the use of coarse mixes (sweet feeds) and highly molassed feeds.

What does the future hold?

With early diagnosis and prompt, appropriate therapy the majority of laminitis cases, will make a good recovery, even if initially they appear to be in great pain. However, where the pedal bone has rotated, the prognosis for returning to ridden work is guarded, and in cases where the bony column has started to sink, no more than a 20% chance of survival can be expected.

When considering the long term prognosis, it is important to be guided by your veterinary surgeon. However it is worth noting that success or failure in treating varying degrees of laminitis will depend largely on your commitment as an owner. You should be aware that, if severely affected, your old horse may require long, expensive and complicated treatment, as well as intensive nursing for many months, and even then there can be no guarantee of success. In severe cases, therefore, the harsh reality is that if you are either unwilling or unable to afford the time or money to see your old horse through the recuperation period, it may be more humane to put him to sleep rather than prolong his suffering.

Most recently, the daily feeding of a tiny amount of an antibiotic called virginiamycin (not available in the USA) has been shown to help prevent laminitis if it is present in the hind gut when it is overloaded by soluble carbohydrates, either as a result of overfeeding concentrates or the consumption of too much rich grass. Sold as Founderguard, the product works by reducing the build up of acidity in the hind gut, but should not be used instead of proper management. Though a useful preventative, virginiamycin is not a cure for laminitis and will not work if administered as a treatment for those who are already suffering from the condition. As the antibiotic is not absorbed by the gut it has no residual effects. Unfortunately the product is not currently licensed for general sale in the UK, though veterinary surgeons can apply for a special licence in most cases. It must be noted, however, that Founderguard is only useful in cases of dietary induced laminitis. Regrettably, where laminitis is caused by pituitary tumours or organ failure, for example, prevention may not always be possible unless the associated conditions can also be controlled. In most cases, however, if it is possible to treat and manage/alleviate the underlying cause of the disease, there is no reason why repeated attacks should occur provided daily care, feed regimes and weight etc., are also managed and monitored carefully.

Navicular Syndrome

What is it and how is it caused?

Navicular syndrome is the term given to describe lameness which develops as a result of pain in the heel area of the horse's foot, due to inflammatory or degenerative conditions in the navicular apparatus. It may also be referred to as navicular disease, palmer heel pain, caudal foot syndrome or simply sore heels. Navicular syndrome most commonly affects horses by the time they reach middle age, though it only rarely appears to affect ponies and Arabs.

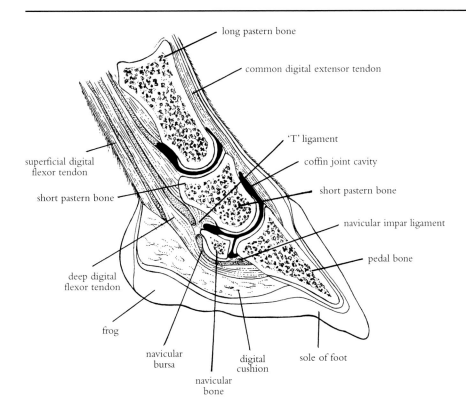

long pastern bone

common digital extensor tendon

'T' ligament

coffin joint cavity

superficial digital flexor tendon

short pastern bone

navicular impar ligament

short pastern bone

deep digital flexor tendon

pedal bone

frog

navicular bursa

digital cushion

sole of foot

navicular bone

The purpose of the navicular apparatus is to absorb concussion. It consists of the navicular bone, the navicular bursa and the deep digital flexor tendon (DDFT), and is supplied by nerves and blood vessels. The role of the navicular bone, which is held in place by surrounding ligaments, is to act as a pulley for the DDFT as it passes over the back of the coffin joint, to its attachment at the rear of the pedal bone. The navicular bursa provides a protective cushion between the DDFT and the navicular bone and prevents rubbing between the tendon and the bone. Excessive stress placed upon any of these structures can cause the following.

- Impaired blood supply.
- Inflammation or erosion of the navicular bursa.
- Degeneration of the navicular bone causing either roughening of its surface, a thinning or fracture of the bone, or the development of holes and cysts. Bone spurs may also form as a result of tension from the supporting ligaments.

- Adhesions (i.e. a fibrous band of tissue) developing between the DDFT and the navicular bone or bursa can limit movement and may result in a mechanical lameness without the presence of pain. However, pain may also be present if the forces placed upon the bone and tendon are such that it begins to tear the adhesions apart.
- Inflammation of the synovial membrane at the joint between the navicular bone, pedal bone and short pastern.
- Thinning of the tendon as it passes over the navicular bone.

Causes of navicular include:

- Genetic tendency.
- Poor hoof conformation as well as irregular or improper trimming and shoeing.
- Hard, fast and/or irregular work combined with a lack of fitness (e.g. those horses only ridden at weekends) which puts extra strain on the DDFT thereby delaying breakover and increasing pressure on the navicular bone.
- Poor riding and an incorrectly fitting saddle can cause back pain and restriction of the shoulder, both of which may result in a compensatory shortening of the stride and increased concussion on the forelimbs. It should also be noted that since some 60% or more of a horse's weight is naturally carried on his forehand, the extra weight of a rider on top of an improperly trained horse allowed to work on his forehand will also predispose him to the development of navicular.
- Frequent exercise on hard, uneven surfaces causes compression of the bones within the foot as well as an unnatural twisting of the limb that will put pressure on the DDFT and supporting ligaments.
- Excessive tension on the supporting ligaments surrounding the navicular bone. In particular strain, inflammation and eventual thickening of the impar ligament, through which blood vessels carry the majority of the blood supply both to and from the bone, can cause a reduction in blood flow.

What are the symptoms?

Navicular syndrome is almost always seen in both front feet, though one may be more painful than the other. In an effort to reduce pain in the heel region, your old horse will be seen to either constantly shift his weight from one foot to another or stand with the most painful foot pointed out in front of him, with the weight tipped onto the toe.

Navicular horses may appear particularly lame when first brought out of their stable, but will generally improve with slow, gentle exercise. Lameness is usually intermittent, with the degree of soreness varying depending upon the stress sustained by the navicular apparatus on a given day. Where there is a bilateral shortening of the stride due to pain in both front feet, your horse will appear to potter in front, land toe first and may frequently stumble. Compensatory muscle use may also lead to back pain. Lungeing, circle work, jumping, going down hill and hard ground will all generally increase soreness.

How is it diagnosed?

Since the clinical signs of navicular syndrome are often inconsistent and are similar to those caused by corns, pedal osteitis, low ringbone etc., a definitive diagnosis can be difficult and is generally achieved via a process of elimination. Indeed, some researchers have suggested that, because of the difficulties involved, navicular syndrome is often overdiagnosed. Knowledgable veterinary surgeons will therefore take great care not only to assess a horse's conformation, age, breed/type, workload and symptoms, but will also closely scrutinize your horse's pain response to hoof testers, hoof flexion tests and nerve blocks. X-rays will also prove useful, though it should be noted that even sound horses may show evidence of bony changes within the navicular bone, and such findings are not therefore conclusive proof of the disease. Other diagnostic techniques that may prove useful in certain cases include injecting anaesthetic into the navicular bursa, nuclear scintigraphy, thermography and diagnostic ultrasound.

Coping with navicular

Since the pain which causes lameness can originate from various parts of the navicular apparatus, no single treatment will prove

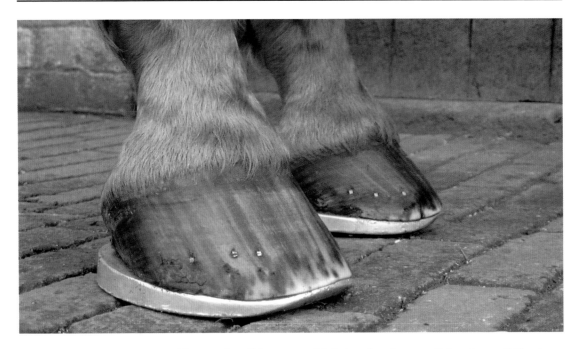

A graduated egg-bar shoe with rolled toes can help reduce tension on the deep digital flexor tendon and ease breakover.

effective for all horses, which is why the condition is so difficult to treat. Corrective trimming and supportive shoeing, combined with a change in lifestyle and, where necessary, the use of drug therapy, can in most cases prove successful in managing the condition, though it should be understood that 'cures' are not possible.

Medication

NSAIDs will prove helpful in reducing pain and inflammation, whilst vasodilators, such as isoxsuprine, may help improve circulation within the foot. Though now rarely used, warfarin (a blood thinner) has also proved successful in some cases, though great care must be taken to constantly monitor blood clotting times and adjust dosages accordingly if haemorrhages are to be prevented. (**Note** Bute must not be given at the same time as warfarin is being administered as the reaction between the two could prove fatal.)

Injections of cortisone and sodium hyaluronate (*see* page 157) directly into the foot may prove helpful in some cases.

Though further trials are required, recent test results have suggested that feeding a glucosamine/chondroitin sulfate supplement in the early stages of navicular may also prove beneficial.

Trimming and shoeing

It is essential that every four to five weeks, a qualified and experienced farrier ensures that the correct hoof/pastern axis is restored/maintained. The type of shoes required will depend upon your horse's individual foot conformation. However, in order to ease breakover, to support and encourage expansion and growth of the heels and to increase the area over which weight is distributed, wide-web shoes that have plenty of length and width at the heel and a rolled or square toe will generally prove beneficial. The exact choice of shoe will depend on your horse's foot conformation and the severity of the problem, but those most commonly recommended include Natural Balance shoes (with or without the additional support offered by a pad and sole-packing material), egg-bar shoes, a heart-bar/egg-bar combination, or the Equine Digit Support System.

In some cases, raising the heels may also help by reducing tension placed on the navicular apparatus by the DDFT. Pressure from heel wedges can however cause further contraction of the heels and create excess tension on ligaments and tendons at the front of the foot and fetlock. Over time their use may also lead to compensatory shortening of the DDFT which simply restores tension on the navicular apparatus. Graduated bar shoes and wedge heel shoes should therefore be used with caution.

Surgical options

Where none of the above treatment options prove successful, a navicular suspensory desmotomy, which involves cutting the ligaments which attach the navicular bone to the pastern bone, may reduce stress on the bone sufficiently to resolve some cases. This technique is, however, becoming increasingly uncommon as many veterinary surgeons have reported poor results.

As a last resort, cutting the palmar digital nerves (known as a neurectomy or denerving) will eliminate some feeling in the back of the foot. This may not always be successful, however, as occasionally complications may arise including the development of painful neuromas (i.e. swellings at the cut end of the nerves), or tendon rupture as a result of the restoration of normal foot flight (due to lack of pain) tearing apart adhesions between the navicular bone and the DDFT. Unfortunately, regeneration of the nerves over a period of one to two years, means that a

A neurectomy involves cutting the palmar digital nerves in order to eliminate feeling in the back of the foot.

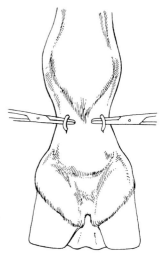

177

neurectomy can often only be considered as a temporary solution. The procedure may be repeated two or three times, but will often prove less effective on each occasion. A neurectomy is still worthy of consideration, however, as a last ditch attempt to save your old horse's life, as, if successful, it could prolong his usefulness and offer a pain free existence. If a neurectomy is performed, you must subsequently be particularly vigilant about injuries to the back of the foot which your horse may not feel, such as puncture wounds, but which if missed could lead to serious and equally debilitating infections.

General management

To reduce compression on the navicular bone and promote good quality hoof growth, overweight horses should be put on a diet and fed a good quality hoof supplement. Long periods of pasture turn-out are imperative as slow, gentle movement will increase circulation and help relieve the constant compression on the navicular apparatus that is caused by standing still. Box rest is therefore contraindicated as this will simply impair blood supply to the feet still further and may make the development of adhesions more likely. Once corrective trimming and supportive shoeing have been performed, your old horse should be given a minimum of thirty minutes in-hand or gentle ridden exercise each day, depending upon the level of lameness shown. Work which may aggravate the condition such as jumping, galloping or lungeing should be avoided or at the very least kept to a minimum.

What does the future hold?

At one time a diagnosis of navicular syndrome was almost a sentence of death. These days, a greater understanding of the condition means that many horses can still lead fairly active lives. In the early stages, lameness may be very subtle but if it is recognised and treated early, some 60-70% of horses will become sound enough to resume work as hacks, dressage horses etc., for many years. Whilst some horses have returned to full athletic function, it is important to remember that, at best, treatment generally only slows down the degenerative processes, therefore long-term soundness is unlikely in the majority of horses, especially if their workload is not reduced. Eventually, continued use of NSAIDs may be required to keep your old horse comfortable.

Sidebone

What is it and how is it caused?

Sidebone is the progressive ossification of the large pieces of flexible lateral cartilage that lie either side of the pedal bone, the purpose of which is to offer support and protection to the soft tissues at the back of the foot, whilst helping to absorb concussion. Often only discovered when an elderly horse's hoof is being X-rayed for some other reason, sidebone rarely causes lameness. In fact, research has shown that it is quite normal for one or both of these cartilages to begin to calcify as a horse ages. In many cases this is simply due to years of wear and tear but sidebone may also be caused by poor conformation (particularly toeing-in or toeing-out), a direct blow to the hoof, or improper shoeing and trimming resulting in uneven loading to your horse's foot.

What are the symptoms?

In those rare incidences where sidebone formation causes soreness, lameness is generally mild and your elderly horse will show

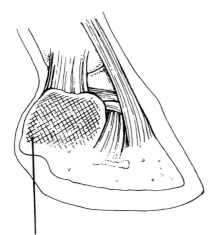

sidebone is the progressive ossification of the normally flexible lateral cartilage that lies either side of the pedal bone

179

evidence of pain in response to pressure on the lateral cartilages which may be felt just above the coronary band at the back of the foot. Lameness associated with sidebone is most commonly seen in the forefeet. Contracted heels may develop as a result of a reluctance to bear weight in the heel region.

How is it diagnosed?

Diagnosis is made on the presence of the above symptoms and thermographic pictures of the foot which will show up heat and inflammation of the lateral cartilages as brightly coloured 'hot spots'. X-rays and nerve blocks are of limited use since even sound elderly horses will show X-ray evidence of sidebone formation, and nerve blocks of the back of the foot will also eliminate pain originating from other structures.

Coping with sidebone

Where active calcification of the lateral cartilages is shown to be causing pain and inflammation, your vet may simply advise a few weeks of box rest in conjunction with the administration of NSAIDs until the bony changes settle down. Extended periods of confinement will only be necessary where fracture of the new bone is evident on X-ray or where bone chips have had to be removed surgically.

Trimming and shoeing

Corrective trimming to rebalance the hoof combined with supportive wide-web, rolled-toed shoes with plenty of length at the heels will help spread your horse's body-weight evenly across each foot and reduce concussion. The combination of a full pad and impression material across the sole may also aid shock absorption. Alternatively egg-bar shoes may prove beneficial.

What does the future hold?

Once ossification is complete, sidebone is unlikely to cause further problems provided the correct hoof balance is maintained.

Tendon and Ligament Injuries

What are they and how are they caused?

As the strength and elasticity of connective tissue reduces with age, elderly horses become increasingly vulnerable to tendon and ligament strains. Most commonly, such strains occur in the lower limbs where the tendons form a connection between the muscles above the knee or hock to the pastern and pedal bone, to facilitate either flexion or extension of the limb. Ligaments also consist of fibrous tissue, but their job is to support bones and joints and to prevent the tendons from overstretching.

Veterinary surgeons refer to inflammation of a tendon as tendonitis, whilst inflammation of the tendon sheath (which

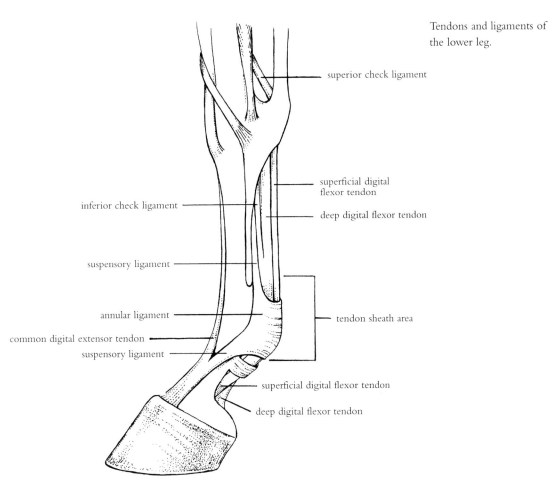

Tendons and ligaments of the lower leg.

superior check ligament

superficial digital flexor tendon

deep digital flexor tendon

inferior check ligament

suspensory ligament

annular ligament

tendon sheath area

common digital extensor tendon

suspensory ligament

superficial digital flexor tendon

deep digital flexor tendon

surrounds, protects and lubricates the tendon as it passes over a joint) is known as tenosynovitis and inflammation of a ligament is referred to as desmitis. All may occur either suddenly or as a sequel to repetitive low-grade stresses caused by poor conformation, incorrect or irregular shoeing and trimming, tightly applied bandages, a direct blow, overwork, muscle fatigue or overextension of a limb.

Although it is relatively rare, older horses may also suffer from an age-related degeneration of the suspensory ligament which will result in a gradual sinking of the fetlock. The condition is usually bilateral (i.e. both forelegs or both hind legs are affected) and though the actual cause is not yet known, it appears to most frequently affect horses with long pasterns and very straight hind legs.

What are the symptoms?

The signs of tendon or ligament inflammation can vary from a barely perceptible heat, pain and swelling to the classic appearance of the typical bowed tendon. Signs of lameness may or may not be present and it is, therefore, essential that you become familiar with and examine your elderly horse's legs on a daily basis to ensure that even minor abnormalities are quickly recognised. In

Bowed tendons

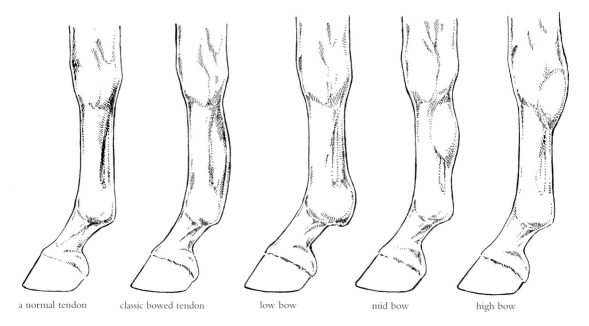

a normal tendon   classic bowed tendon   low bow   mid bow   high bow

very severe cases, your horse may, depending upon the structures involved, be unable to put his foot flat on the floor, may drop his fetlock to the ground or knuckle forward onto his pastern.

How are they diagnosed?

Initially your veterinary surgeon will palpate each tendon and ligament looking for any signs of pain or subtle swelling. If available, a thermographic camera may also be used to show up any 'hot spots' on the leg, which would indicate the presence of low-grade inflammation. Thereafter diagnostic ultrasound will be used to determine the extent of the injury.

If it is suspected that the suspensory ligament has torn away from either its origin at the back of the cannon bone (often referred to as high suspensory desmitis or suspensory origin desmitis), or its attachment onto the sesamoid bones (known as suspensory branch desmitis), radiographs will also be taken to ascertain whether there is any associated new bone growth or damage at either of these locations.

In cases of high suspensory desmitis, local anaesthetic may be injected into the area surrounding the origin of the suspensory ligament to see whether or not this relieves lameness. However, as this test also invariably blocks pain emanating from nearby structures, it does not represent a definitive diagnosis of high suspensory desmitis. Scintigraphy may therefore also be recommended as it can prove useful in highlighting areas of bone stress caused by the attachment of the strained suspensory ligament.

Coping with tendon and ligament injuries

First aid

No matter how insignificant the symptoms may first appear, if a tendon or ligament strain is suspected, your old horse should be confined to his stable until seen by your veterinary surgeon. Whilst waiting for your vet to arrive, the immediate application of cold therapy (i.e. cold boots, ice packs, hosing etc.) for ten to fifteen minutes will help reduce inflammation. Thereafter the skin should be thoroughly dried to prevent skin irritation, before a supportive bandage is applied in order to keep swelling to a minimum.

In cases where it is suspected that a tendon may have been severed, for example if there is a deep wound to the back of the leg, your veterinary surgeon must attend as a matter of urgency. If your vet is to have any hope of suturing the ends of the tendon back together, an operation should be performed within six to eight hours of the injury occurring in order to reduce the risk of complications as a result of bacterial infection. In such circumstances it is best to wait until your veterinary surgeon arrives before trying to move your elderly horse, otherwise the severed ends of the tendons could be pulled further apart. However, if the situation dictates that he must be moved to a safer area, then a wooden wedge or similar should be taped to the foot to raise the heel and so relieve the stretching forces placed upon the tendon by walking. Whilst waiting for your vet to arrive, make every effort to keep your horse still and if possible immobilize the lower leg by applying a splint. Similarly, if a tendon sheath infection is suspected (most commonly as a result of injury to the back of the pastern or fetlock), your veterinary surgeon must operate to flush the bacteria out of the sheath within twenty-four hours if your old horse is to have any realistic chance of returning to soundness. In either case use nothing more than a saline solution to clean the wound, before saturating a pad in the same solution and bandaging it firmly to the leg in order to keep the wound moist until your vet arrives.

APPLYING A SPLINT
To reduce pull on the flexor tendons following serious injury, cut a piece of board to the same width as the hoof and to a length that will reach from the ground to the top of the cannon bone. Tape one end of the board to the sole of the foot and then press the other padded end against the back of the cannon, before securely bandaging it in place.

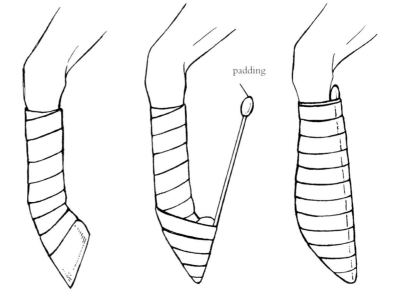

padding

Medication

To help control initial inflammation, a short course of NSAIDs such as bute will be given in preference to corticosteroids which have been shown to slow tendon healing. Cold therapy will continue to prove beneficial until the acute inflammatory reaction has subsided. If the tendon is severed or the tendon sheath has been infected, broad spectrum antibiotics will also be administered. Strained tendons and ligaments may benefit from the anti-inflammatory effects of the topical application of DMSO though this should be stopped immediately if the skin becomes irritated. In cases where the tendon sheath is inflamed, injections of sodium hyaluronate (*see* page 157) have also been shown to be of benefit in helping to lubricate and protect a tendon within its tendon sheath, reduce inflammation and limit the development of adhesions. Oral glucosamine and chondroitin sulphate supplements may also prove beneficial, whilst an antioxidant supplement may be useful in helping to limit the damage caused by free radicals.

Most recently, a new drug known as Bapten (beta-amino-propionitrile fumarate or BAPN-F) has been shown to aid tendon healing by inhibiting the cross-linking of replacement collagen fibres, thereby encouraging them to form in parallel alignment. Though such treatment can prove very expensive, research indicates that when combined with controlled daily exercise, the drug can help to strengthen the repair of damaged tissue, and reduce the likelihood of reinjury in some cases.

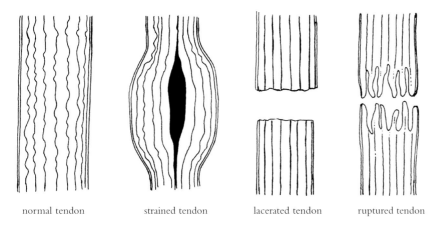

Types of tendon injury

normal tendon   strained tendon   lacerated tendon   ruptured tendon

Surgical options

On rare occasions when injury results in laceration of a flexor tendon, it may be stitched back together provided that the ends are not too far apart and no infection is present. Unfortunately where such a tendon has ruptured, stitching the 'frayed' ends together may be almost impossible.

Other surgical procedures include:

- Tendon splitting, which involves pricking a severely inflamed tendon with a scalpel to create tiny holes through which accumulated blood and fluid may drain, can promote healing by relieving stress caused by distention of the damaged tissues.
- The insertion of carbon fibre implants into the middle of a tendon can provide a framework along which collagen fibres are encouraged to develop in a parallel alignment. Results can be disappointing, however, and this technique is, therefore, now rarely used though it may help in some cases where a flexor tendon has been severed.
- Cutting of either the superior check ligament (in the case of a strain of the superficial flexor tendon) or the inferior check ligament (in the case of a strain to the deep digital flexor tendon) to give a tendon which has repaired with lots of inelastic scar tissue more freedom of movement, can help reduce the risk of overstretching the replacement fibres.
- In cases of tenosynovitis, arthroscopic (keyhole) surgery may be used to clean up the site of the injury and break down any adhesions which may have developed between the tendon and tendon sheath.

There is no one universally successful treatment but firing, which involves the application of red hot irons either poked directly into the leg or across the overlying tissue, cannot be recommended because research has been unable to substantiate claims that either of these very painful procedures will promote healing of damaged tendons or ligaments. Invariably, pin or line firing will simply increase a horse's distress. The only apparent 'benefit' of this procedure is that it creates a severe, visible injury which will encourage an owner to allow a horse sufficient rest, rather than being tempted to work the horse too early, just because they cannot actually see the damage within the structure of the leg.

Trimming and shoeing

In the majority of cases, maintaining the correct hoof/pastern axis, whilst keeping the toes short to ease breakover and applying shoes with plenty of length at the heel, e.g. egg-bars, will be all that is required to provide extra support beneath the damaged structures. However, where the deep digital flexor tendon has been badly injured, raising the heels by using either a wedged heel or patten shoe can help reduce tension and thereby encourage healing. It must be noted, however, that when heels are raised, the tendon will heal with shortened collagen fibres that could be overstretched when a normal shoe is reapplied. If used, therefore, the height of the wedge must be gradually reduced over a number of months, to allow for gentle stretching and strengthening of the replacement tissue, in order to help reduce the risk of reinjury. Note that in cases of damage to the superficial flexor tendon or the suspensory ligament, raising the heels will in fact increase strain on these tissues and is therefore contraindicated. If the flexor tendons have been severed, fitting a shoe with a long heel extension can help prevent the toe from tipping up and the fetlock from dropping further towards the ground. In very severe cases when support of

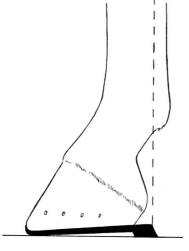

The patten or rest shoe

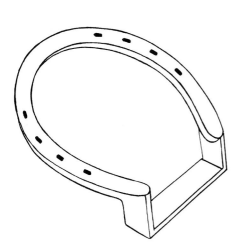

raising the heel, slightly reduces the tension on the deep digital flexor tendon

187

the fetlock has been lost, a shoe with heels that extend upwards to form a sling beneath the back of the fetlock may be required in order to give direct support.

If the extensor tendon has been lacerated and the horse is unable to bring his foot forward to place it flat on the ground, a shoe with a toe extension may be required to help prevent the horse from knuckling over.

General management

Depending upon the severity of the condition and the structures involved, rest may be recommended for anything from four weeks to eighteen months. Initially this will mean that your old horse must be confined to his stable, since it is obviously impossible to control the stresses placed on a tendon when a horse is turned loose in a field. During this period, support bandages should be applied and, in severe cases, a frog support should be placed on the opposite weight-bearing limb to help prevent the development of laminitis induced by mechanical overload.

In-hand walking starting with just ten to fifteen minutes, two or three times a day, will subsequently help to encourage the collagen fibres within the damaged tendon or ligament to heal in parallel alignment and reduce the development of adhesions. Without such exercise, which gently stretches the damaged tissues, replacement collagen fibres will be laid down in a random formation resulting in a weak repair that is liable to reinjury. Physiotherapy including passive stretching and the use of therapeutic ultrasound, lasers and magnetic therapy may also prove useful in promoting healing. (**Note** If your elderly horse has severed a tendon he must *not* be exercised until diagnostic ultrasound shows that the gap in the tendon has knitted together. This will mean strict box rest for at least three to four months [for part of which time your horse may wear a cast or splint] before short periods of exercise are introduced.)

Depending on the severity of the injury, when ultrasound examination indicates that the injured tendon or ligament has healed sufficiently, ridden work may be introduced starting with just five to ten minutes a day and thereafter building up work periods at five-minute intervals every five to six days. All being well, your horse should be capable of an hour's gentle work at the end of three months, but if at any time signs of reinjury (i.e.

A former riding school and RDA mount, 36-year-old Just Jaffa has been owned by Susan Young for the last ten years. Though in the past Jaffa has sustained numerous injuries including tendon and ligament strains, a shattered splint bone and a broken jaw, he now still succesfully competes in gymkhana games and veteran classes, despite also having been diagnosed with navicular, sidebone and ringbone! Proof indeed that with excellent care, even a horse or pony with a chequered health record can live a long and happy life.

heat, swelling or lameness) should appear, work should be stopped immediately and the tendon reassessed by ultrasound.

Your vet will only recommend turning your horse loose in the field once he feels that the damaged fibres have healed sufficiently to withstand the associated stresses and strains. However, after a long period of confinement, it is not unusual for horses to cavort around so much that they reinjure themselves. Initially your vet may therefore recommend administering a sedative such as ACP to help quell your horse's excitement.

What does the future hold?

Remember that your elderly horse will heal more slowly than his younger companions, and that during periods of enforced rest he is also likely to lose muscle tone much more quickly, consequently rehabilitation may take much longer. However, low-grade inflammation of a tendon, tendon sheath or ligament can heal very well and your old horse is likely to be able to return to work within a matter of months without experiencing any long-term effects, provided that no other structures are involved and that you allow your horse sufficient rest and reintroduce work very slowly. It is worth remembering that owner impatience is probably the single biggest cause of secondary breakdowns.

Where a severe strain has caused damage to the collagen fibres, however, the restructured tendon or ligament will be permanently weakened and prone to further strains. Although operations are not always the best policy for elderly horses, research has shown that in severe cases, surgical intervention may actually prove beneficial in promoting the development of stronger collagen fibres, making reinjury less likely. Nevertheless, it is probable that an elderly horse suffering a severe tendon or ligament strain may have to spend the rest of his days in the 'slow lane'.

Surprisingly, a laceration of the extensor tendon can heal very well with just rest and supportive shoeing. In fact, provided that there has been no associated damage to other structures, your elderly horse is likely to be able to return to normal levels of work. On the other hand, if the superficial or deep digital flexor tendon is severed, the best that can often be hoped for is a pasture-sound horse with a future as a companion animal, though it has to be said that depending upon the extent of the damage and the strength of the repair, a lucky few may be able to be very lightly ridden. Regrettably, however, if the initial injury is complicated by serious infection, euthanasia may be the most humane course of action.

Degeneration of the suspensory ligament also has a poor prognosis, though, once again, some elderly horses may recover sufficiently to live happily in retirement. Similarly, if a suspensory ligament tears away from its attachment causing either new bone growth or bone fragments to break away, chronic lameness may be the inevitable result.

Fractures

What are they and how are they caused?

Whilst bone may appear to be a solid, static structure, it is in fact living tissue that relies upon adequate levels of calcium and phosphorous in the diet for its strength and stability (though other minerals are also important) and on the protein collagen for a certain degree of flexibility. Indeed, throughout life, the bones of an adult horse are constantly being remodelled, as existing bone is eaten away (to release minerals for use elsewhere in the body) and is subsequently replaced by the formation of an equal amount of new bone which is laid down by the cells which deposit minerals in the bone for storage. With increasing age, however, a combination of the poor absorption of nutrients and a reduction in cell rejuvenation, can result in the demineralisation of bone, causing them to become weak and brittle, and making them prone to fracture. Unlike in people however, osteoporosis in horses is more likely to be a result of poor phosphorous absorption than a lack of calcium, though the correct ratio of both is essential to bone structure. Bone demineralisation may also occur as a result of inactivity or reduced weight bearing. Thus the bone structure of elderly horses who are lame or stabled for long periods will

Following surgery to remove a shattered splint bone at the age of twenty-two, Thoroughbred gelding Alfie (show name: Poppa Joe), owned by Jacqueline Baird, made an excellent recovery, and at the age of twenty-four years now regularly competes in working hunter, riding club horse and veteran classes.

not be as strong as those who are sound and regularly exercised.

Fractures most commonly occur as a result of a direct blow, compression (caused by the overloading of a limb) or torque (the twisting forces placed on a bone during a sudden turn or stop). However, tiny stress fractures may also develop as a result of years of wear and tear, poor conformation and unbalanced trimming and shoeing, which place abnormal stresses on bones and joints throughout the body.

There are many terms to describe the type of fracture a horse may sustain, the most common of which are as follows.

Articular   The fracture extends into a joint.

Complete   The bone is divided into two or more pieces.

Hairline, stress or micro fracture   The fracture does not penetrate the full thickness of the bone.

Simple   A single crack through the bone.

Comminuted   The shattering of the bone causes multiple fracture lines and bone fragments.

Displaced   A complete fracture results in the bone separating so that the two (or more) pieces are no longer in alignment with each other.

Chip   A small fragment of bone.

Closed   The skin over the fracture is still intact.

Open or compound   There is an open wound over the fracture site.

Avulsion   A weakened tendon or ligament has torn away from its attachment to a bone, pulling away a small piece of that bone.

What are the symptoms?

The symptoms of a fracture will vary depending upon the severity and type of fracture. A complete, displaced fracture may for instance cause sudden, nonweight-bearing lameness, extensive swelling and extreme pain. On the other hand, a hairline fracture or chip fracture at the end of a bone forming part of a joint, may initially only cause a mild, inconsistent lameness, and minimal swelling, symptoms which may be easily confused with arthritis. Similarly, the signs of fractured vertebrae in the neck or back may range from head shaking or napping, to complete paralysis if the fractured bone impinges on the spinal cord.

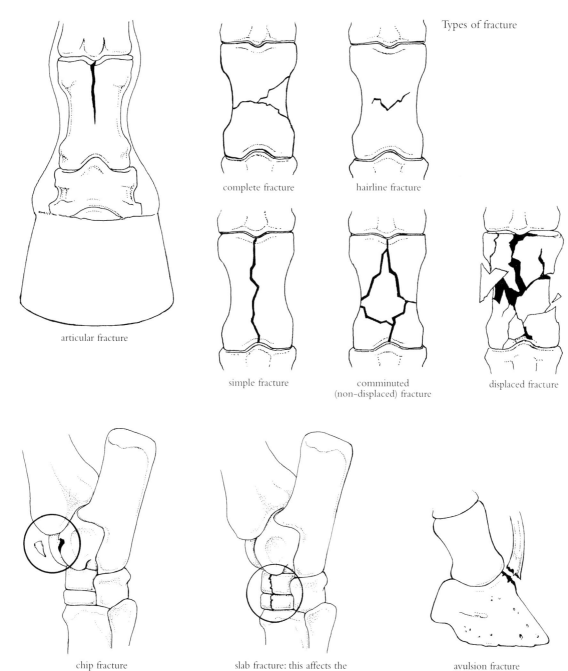

Types of fracture

articular fracture

complete fracture

hairline fracture

simple fracture

comminuted (non-displaced) fracture

displaced fracture

chip fracture

slab fracture: this affects the cuboidal bones of the hock or knee

avulsion fracture

How are they diagnosed?

Though the diagnosis and severity of a fracture can usually be confirmed by X-ray, some hairline fractures may initially be difficult to detect. In these cases repeat X-rays or a bone scan (scintigraphy) will prove valuable.

Coping with fractures

First aid

If sudden severe lameness leads you to suspect your old horse has sustained a fracture, he must not be moved until veterinary help arrives. Forcing him to take weight on the fractured bone could increase the severity of the injury and quite literally mean the difference between life and death. If there is an open wound over the site of a suspected fracture, it should be cleaned only with a saline solution, as antiseptics can irritate bone surfaces. Where a bone in the leg is affected, every effort should then be made to immobilise the limb to prevent further damage. This may be achieved by applying a home-made version of a 'Robert Jones' bandage, which involves first covering any open wound in a dressing soaked in a saline solution and then wrapping several layers of gamgee tissue (gauze) or cotton wool round the limb, from the hoof, up and over the joint above the injury, before securing them tightly with a cohesive bandage. This should be repeated two or three times in order to stabilize the injured bone and prevent the horse from flexing the injured leg. If there is insufficient padding or bandages available, pillows and strips of blanket may be used as an alternative. Splints made from sections of drainage pipe cut in half lengthways, planks of wood or even broom handles cut to the required length (i.e. so that they reach from the ground to the top of the bandage) can then be secured with tape or rope over the bandages. In most cases it is best to apply one splint to the side of the leg and one to the front or back of the leg in order to restrict movement still further. (**Note** When trying to stabilize a fracture of the upper leg, you will find it impossible to immobilize the elbow or stifle. However, applying a 'Robert Jones' type bandage as far up the limb as possible will still prove beneficial in helping to limit movement.) If, however, as a result of trying to apply a splint, your old horse becomes increasingly agitated, it may be best to just allow him to stand quietly until your veterinary surgeon can administer a sedative. In the meantime, arrangements should be made for a low-loading trailer to be made available to transport your horse home, or, if necessary, to a nearby veterinary hospital.

Medication

Subsequent treatment will depend upon the severity, type and extent of the fracture as well as the bone affected and the degree of lameness. Your old horse's temperament will also prove to be an important factor because not all horses will cope well with the necessary treatment. Unfortunately, despite recent advances in fracture repair, the sheer size and weight of a horse means that some fractures are untreatable and euthanasia will be the only option. With complete rest, however, some hairline fractures may heal by themselves, with or without the aid of a fibreglass cast or supportive bandage. Similarly, some fractures of the bones of the foot may be stabilised by applying bar shoes with clips or raised rims.

During recovery, NSAIDs will often be administered to help reduce pain and inflammation and where the fracture has extended into a joint, joint therapy will also be required in an effort to prevent the subsequent development of degenerative joint disease.

A fracture stabilized with screws

Surgical options

Other fractures may require surgical intervention to remove bone fragments or to stabilize the fracture by inserting screws, plates, pins or wire. Bone grafts may also be performed if it is thought necessary to speed up fracture repair.

General management

Regardless of whether or not surgery has been performed, the majority of horses will require box rest for at least six to eight weeks. During this time your old horse may initially have to be cross tied in order to prevent him from lying down, as the strain of repeatedly rising to his feet could cause further damage to the injured bone. Whilst the fracture heals, weight bearing will be transferred to the contralateral limb, putting its tendons and ligaments under increased strain. The weight-bearing limb should, therefore, also be supported by a bandage, and a frog support should be applied to the foot in an effort to prevent the development of laminitis as a result of mechanical overload. The provision of a deep bed of shavings or sand will also prove beneficial in offering yet more support for the sole of the weight-bearing limb. Such bedding will also make it easier for your old horse to move around his box, unlike long straw which can become entangled around the legs. In severe cases, however, your horse may need to be supported by a sling, to give the damaged bone a chance to heal. To aid recovery it is important to ensure that all your old horse's increased nutritional requirements are met, particularly in respect of protein and the correct calcium : phosphorous ratio.

Once X-rays and/or bone scans confirm that the fracture has healed, pasture turn-out will often be recommended for at least six months to allow bone density and strength to increase. However, rehabilitation may take much longer as elderly bones can take a long time to heal. If your horse recovers sufficiently to be ridden, start off with just five minutes walking per day, and increase by a further five minutes every five days or so. Only when your old horse is coping well with an hour's walking per day should any increase in pace be introduced. If at any time lameness reoccurs, ask your veterinary surgeon for a reassessment.

What does the future hold?

Whether or not your old horse will return to full athletic function will depend not only on the type, site and severity of the fracture, but also on the development of any complications such as implant failure, bone infection, joint problems and laminitis. Displaced, comminuted or open fractures generally have a very poor prognosis and, in many cases, elderly horses with these types of fracture may be euthanised. However, hairline or stress fractures may heal sufficiently well to allow the horse to resume normal work. Similarly, old horses with complete, non-displaced fractures which have been successfully stabilised with screws or plates may become sound enough to resume light hacking. On the other hand, if the repair of a fractured bone is relatively poor, an elderly horse may only ever become pasture-sound or suitable for breeding. Only the attending veterinary surgeon can give a prognosis for each individual case.

Notes on the Long-term Use of Non-steroidal Anti-inflammatory Drugs

Though some of the aforementioned conditions may result in varying degrees of chronic lameness, the subsequent long-term use of pain-relieving non-steroidal anti-inflammatory drugs (NSAIDs) such as bute, when combined with changes in lifestyle and workload, can extend the life of many old horses, allowing them to live comfortably for many years doing light work as hacks and schoolmasters. From the outset, however, it is essential to establish the minimum effective maintenance dose, and thereafter to only increase the dosage in consultation with your veterinary surgeon, as prolonged use (or high dosages) of these drugs can occasionally have serious side effects, which, even though fairly rare, include the formation of gastric ulcers and the development of kidney problems.

As a result of the risk of side effects, horses on NSAID therapy should be monitored for signs of drug toxicity throughout the duration of treatment. Periodic blood testing can prove useful in giving an early indication of drug intolerance, provided your old horse's normal blood parameters have previously been established. However, on a daily basis you should watch out for the development of such problems as mouth ulcers, diarrhoea, oedema of the limbs and abdomen, colic, lack of appetite, urticaria and depression. If any adverse reactions should occur, advice should immediately be sought from your veterinary surgeon.

Although by no means a guarantee, it has been suggested that adding up to a cupful (approx. 250 ml.) of a plant-based oil to a horse's daily diet (or half this amount for ponies) may help protect the lining of the stomach and reduce the risk of the development of gastric ulcers. A 10–20 g ($\frac{1}{4}$–$\frac{1}{2}$ oz, 2–4 US tsp) daily dose of MSM is also thought by some to help reduce the risk of gastrointestinal damage.

Despite the risk of side effects and the fact that the long-term use of bute and other NSAIDs only mask the symptoms of a condition and do nothing to treat the cause, the value of such therapy in both prolonging and improving the quality of life of a chronically lame horse must never be underestimated. It must be understood, however, that the long-term use of NSAIDs should be used only as a last resort when all other pain relieving alternatives have proved ineffective.

Chapter Nine

DIGESTIVE PROBLEMS

Colic

What is it and how is it caused?

Colic is the generic term used to describe the symptoms of pain originating from the abdominal cavity which houses the urinary, reproductive and digestive systems. From their teenage years onwards, horses become increasingly susceptible to episodes of colic which are most frequently caused by a problem within the digestive tract. This may be due to an age-related decrease in gut motility (movement), poor dentition, years of parasite damage, the effects of long-term drug therapy, a reduced ability to cope with dietary or management changes, or an increasing vulnerability to infection and disease. Whilst many cases of abdominal pain can be resolved quickly with prompt treatment, it is a sad fact that colic is still considered to be the number one killer of elderly horses.

Depending upon the cause of the condition, colic may be further classified as spasmodic (i.e. spasms of the muscular wall of the intestines), flatulent or tympanitic (i.e. gut distention as a result of gas or fluid build up), impacted (i.e. blockages) or surgical (i.e. serious displacement, twisting or interssusception of the gut, along with some impactions).

The causes of colic are many and varied, but may include any of the following.

Humphrey, a 26-year-old 15.3 hh cob cross gelding spent sixteen years of his life as a riding school horse. Now owned by Claire Thomas he is regulary hacked out and loves competing in shows during the summer months.

The digestive system

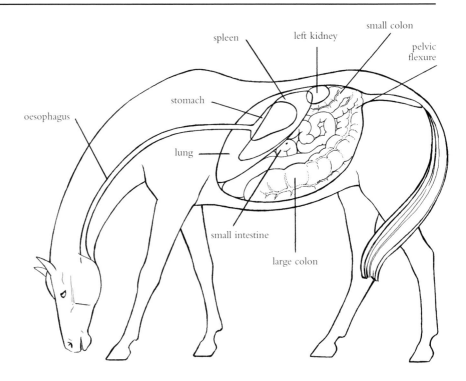

spleen

left kidney

small colon

pelvic flexure

stomach

oesophagus

lung

small intestine

large colon

- **Digestive upsets** A lack of fibre or water or a sudden change in diet. The consumption of poorly made/spoiled haylage, unsoaked sugar beet, improperly chewed food or indigestible materials (e.g. bedding). The digestive process may also be upset by unexpected stable confinement (perhaps as a result of injury), working too soon after feeding, and the stress of travelling, competition etc.

- **Illness and disease** Horses over the age of fifteen are five times more likely than younger horses to develop lipomas, which are benign tumours formed from an accumulation of fat cells, hanging from a fibrous stalk in the small intestine. These and other cancerous tumours have the potential to cause strangulation or impaction of the gut. Colic may also be caused by infections which cause inflammation and fever which can destroy the beneficial bacteria in the gut leading to digestive upsets. Intestinal stones (known as enteroliths) which comprise mineral deposits collecting around a foreign object such as a piece of cloth or baler twine, can cause recurrent colic, as can gastric ulcers, parasite damage, and the inadvertent consumption of sand or dirt (perhaps as a result of

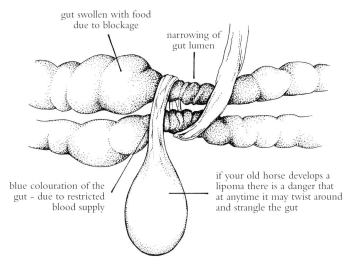

gut swollen with food
due to blockage

narrowing of
gut lumen

A lipoma

blue colouration of the
gut – due to restricted
blood supply

if your old horse develops a
lipoma there is a danger that
at anytime it may twist around
and strangle the gut

being grazed on bare paddocks or being fed from the ground on the synthetic surface of an outdoor arena).

- **Drug Therapy** Long-term use of NSAIDs which can lead to the formation of gastric ulcers, though this is relatively uncommon in comparison to the number of horses to whom such drugs are actually administered.

It should be noted that colic-type symptoms may also appear as the result of conditions such as azoturia, pregnancy and renal failure.

What are the symptoms?

In the early stages of colic, your elderly horse may simply appear depressed and dull and have little appetite. A change in the consistency of his droppings may be noted. He may also be seen to wrinkle his nostrils in pain or roll back the upper lip. (**Note** Not all horses rolling back the upper lip are in pain as this is also the means by which horses trap a strange smell for further investigation by their senses.) As the condition progresses he may appear uneasy and may be seen to paw at the ground, look at his flanks, stretch out or straddle his limbs as if trying to urinate, kick at his belly and lie down either repeatedly or for long periods. Patchy sweating, rolling and increased respiration and heart rate will all become apparent.

How is it diagnosed?

To determine the actual cause of the pain and the severity of the condition your vet will monitor your old horse's temperature, pulse and respiration, and will look for signs of circulatory problems indicated by a change in gum colour from pale pink to red, blueish purple or greyish white. He may also press the gums with his fingers firmly enough to make them blanch. If the normal colour of the gums does not return within three seconds, this is indicative of cardiovascular shock. Your vet will use a stethoscope to listen for any abnormal increase or decrease in gut activity, and may perform a rectal examination to feel for any blockages, distention or displacement of the gut. In order to check what is going on at the front end of the digestive system, a soft, flexible tube may be passed down your horse's oesophagus into the stomach to act as a drainage pipe for any trapped gas or fluid. Remember that horses cannot vomit or belch in the same way as we do and that on the rare occasions that ingesta is seen rushing out of the nostrils this may indicate that the stomach has ruptured.

If the reason for the colic still remains unclear, a worm egg count, blood tests, peritoneal tap (i.e. collection of a small amount of fluid from the abdominal cavity) or rectal biopsy may be performed. The insertion of an endoscope or arthroscope may also help determine the actual cause in some cases, though occasionally the only way of really finding out what is causing the problem may be to perform exploratory abdominal surgery.

Coping with Colic

First aid

In the early stages, it is impossible to know whether or not the cause of abdominal pain is of a mild, relatively trivial nature or a serious life-threatening, even fatal condition. **Colic must therefore always be considered an emergency, and immediate veterinary advice should be sought.** If the cause of the colic should turn out to be one of the 5–10% of cases which require surgery, any delay in treatment could mean the difference between life and death.

If your elderly horse is showing signs of colic he should be brought into the stable and all feed and hay should be removed, as eating could increase the severity of any impaction that may be present. Whilst waiting for your vet to arrive, do not leave your horse unattended. Record on paper his pulse, temperature and respiration rates every fifteen minutes, as well as the frequency and duration of any periods of particular distress. Any droppings your horse manages to pass should be kept to one side for veterinary inspection. If symptoms appear mild, walking in-hand for ten to twenty minutes may help to keep your old horse on his feet and improve gut motility (movement) which could help clear blockages or release gas build-up. There is nothing to be gained, however, by forcing him to walk for excessively long periods. If exhaustion sets in this will undoubtedly hinder his rate of recovery. Be guided by your horse's response and if he is more comfortable lying down then allow him to do so. Do not panic if he starts to roll. Contrary to popular belief this will not cause twisting of the gut. If displacement, strangulation or intussusception of the gut is going to occur, it will do so, regardless of whether or not your horse rolls. The main danger presented by rolling is, in fact, the risk of injury should your old horse go down on a hard surface or become cast in his box. If he is continually rolling and thrashing about violently in response to the pain, it may be safer for all concerned to lead or turn him out into a riding arena or small paddock (if necessary wearing a muzzle to prevent him from eating) where he is less likely to injure either himself or his handlers.

Do not administer any drugs or drenches without veterinary approval. However, the homeopathic remedy colocynthis given every fifteen minutes may help relieve intestinal spasm and will do no harm. Aconite and Dr Bach's Rescue Remedy may also help to keep your horse calm and reduce the effects of shock. Massaging the ears may also help relax your old horse and bring down his pulse and respiration rates. Start by pulling both ears gently yet firmly through your hands, then move onto the acupressure point located a quarter of an inch down from the centre of the ear tip. Press this point gently for one to two minutes between your thumb and index finger before pushing the skin gently around in small circular movements for at least another minute.

Medication

NSAIDs e.g. flunixin meglumine (Finadyne [UK], Banamine [USA]), muscle relaxants, antifermentatives, fluid and electrolyte therapy and/or sedatives may be given depending upon the suspected cause of the condition and the horse's specific symptoms. If necessary, liquid paraffin and saline solution may also be administered by stomach tube to help soften any impaction. Your vet may also recommend using an anthelmintic (wormer) if parasite infestation is suspected.

Surgical options

Whilst colic surgery success rates have increased over recent years to somewhere between 70% and 80%, your horse's chances of survival will be determined by the severity and extent of the damage found upon investigative surgery. The success of such operations has also been shown to be largely dependent upon the length of time between the first onset of symptoms and actual surgical intervention. Therefore, if your elderly horse does not appear to be responding to medication, or appears to recover only for symptoms to return with increased severity, arrangements should be made immediately to transport him to the nearest veterinary hospital. A premature, or even unnecessary, admission is always preferable to one that arrived just to late. Do not forget to check your insurance details, as the cost of colic surgery can run into thousands of pounds or dollars and, since insurance for elderly horses is unlikely to cover illness (most only offer cover against accidental injury), you will have to consider whether or not you can afford to proceed.

Major surgery will only be performed if your elderly horse is considered to have a fighting chance of survival and even then no guarantees can be given. In fact, it is not unusual for the attending veterinary surgeon to ask for your permission to euthanase your horse on the operating table should he find his condition inoperable. Even if your horse makes it to the recovery room, complications such as blood poisoning, muscle damage, intestinal scarring and wound infections may still be sufficient to claim his life and so, following surgery, intensive, twenty-four hour post-operative care will be required, after which your horse may need box rest for in excess of eight weeks.

A full recovery is possible however, and even horses who have had a section of their intestines removed have been known to return to normal levels of work.

General management

Following an episode of colic, your old horse should be monitored every few hours so that any signs of a relapse are quickly spotted. Hay and feed should be withheld until your horse has begun to pass normal faeces, otherwise additional food stacking up behind an impaction will only make the problem worse. With veterinary approval, the administration of a probiotic (*see* page 92) may aid recovery by helping to re-establish levels of beneficial bacteria in the gut. Once droppings have been passed, an easily digested and palatable mash can be provided by combining soaked sugar beet, bran and alfalfa or similar chaff (depending on the usual ingredients of your horse's diet). This type of mash is more nutritious and therefore more likely to aid recovery than the traditional type of mash made from bran alone. (**Note** The fibre content of bran is not very digestible, it has an incorrect calcium : phosphorous ratio and is likely to cause further digestive upset and diarrhoea if fed suddenly in large quantities when it is not normally a part of your horse's diet.)

No matter what is being fed, the addition of a broad spectrum supplement to a mash will help ensure your horse is receiving all the vitamins, minerals and amino acids he requires to recover quickly. Thereafter, slowly reintroduce small amounts of good quality, soaked hay to help maintain gut motility and assist water absorption. If your horse appears to make a good recovery, normal feed and exercise levels may be introduced over the next seven to fourteen days, though his condition must be monitored very carefully for any signs of the colic reoccurring.

If surgery has been performed, your horse will initially be starved in order to allow the gut to rest. Ideally, however, small, frequent feeds should be introduced within the first twenty-four to forty-eight hours, and certainly within seventy-two hours, otherwise there is a risk that starvation may lead to wasting of the lining of the intestines, compromised wound healing, or a susceptibility to infection. If your veterinary surgeon is worried about the possibility of disrupting suture lines he may initially suggest giving soup-like mashes consisting of soaked complete or hay cubes. Alternatively a liquid diet may be given by stomach tube in some cases. If your horse appears very weak, your veterinary surgeon may even resort to feeding intravenously until your horse appears well enough to eat on his own.

Subsequent feeding recommendations should then be worked out with the veterinary surgeon and a qualified equine nutritionist, as these will be determined by the actual surgery involved. Where the intestines remain intact your horse may be slowly reintroduced to his usual diet. If, however, a portion of the large colon has been removed, a good quality reduced-fibre diet may be required. Conversely if a portion of the small intestine has been removed a good quality high-fibre diet will be needed, since digestion of concentrate feeds will be adversely affected.

If, despite thorough veterinary investigation, your elderly horse continues to suffer from repeated bouts of unexplained colic, keeping a meticulous record of his daily care may prove to be the only way to link cause and effect, though in some cases it may take many months for the true picture to develop. In the meantime, feeding a live yeast culture may prove useful in helping to stabilise the gut and aid fibre digestion. Anecdotal reports have suggested that where elderly horses are prone to intestinal stones, adding a cupful (approx. 250 ml) of cider vinegar to each feed may help prevent/reduce their formation. (Half this amount is likely to be sufficient for ponies.)

What does the future hold?

It is sobering to know that some 90% or so of colic cases are related to dietary or management factors and are often entirely preventable. It is, therefore, essential to remember to follow the rules of feeding (*see* pages 66–71) and maintain a regular and appropriate worming and dental care programme. Whilst the majority of colic cases that do occur can be resolved quickly with prompt veterinary treatment, it is important to remember that any delay in treating your elderly horse could at best result in prolonged and unnecessary suffering and, at worst, could prove fatal. It is also worth noting that once your old horse has had one attack of colic, he is more likely to suffer from the condition again.

Choke

What is it and how is it caused?

Choke is the term used to describe a blockage of the muscular tube known as the oesophagus which carries food from the mouth to the stomach. In older horses incidences of choke appear more frequently as a result of the improper chewing of food due to dental problems. Other causes of obstructions include the consumption of unsoaked sugar beet, eating too quickly, and the swallowing of irregular-shaped lumps of food such as carrots and apples. Choke may also be caused by a tumour, abscess or scar tissue within the oesophagus itself, or any other illness or injury which effectively narrows the space through which food is forced to travel. Although in horses choke does not cause asphyxiation, a veterinary surgeon should be called as once food is trapped in the oesophagus, the soft pallet blocks its return to the mouth and occasionally pneumonia may result if fluid passes into the lungs as a result of the obstruction.

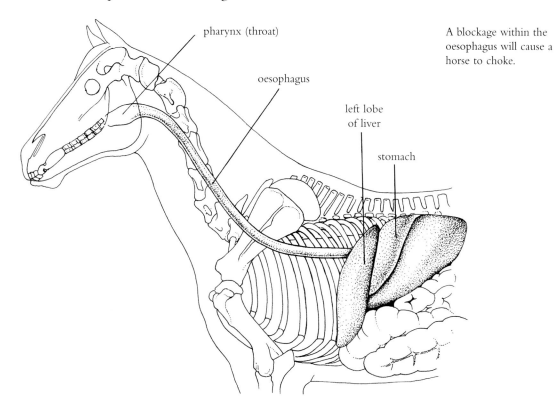

pharynx (throat)

oesophagus

left lobe
of liver

stomach

A blockage within the oesophagus will cause a horse to choke.

What are the symptoms?

If your elderly horse is choking he will repeatedly cough and stretch his neck in an attempt to dislodge the blockage which may or may not be visible on the left side of the neck. He will experience difficulty swallowing and will become increasingly distressed. Food and fluid may be seen draining from both nostrils and saliva may drool from his mouth. A prolonged episode of choke can cause dehydration and electrolyte imbalance.

How is it diagnosed?

Generally choke is confirmed as a result of the presented symptoms. If your old horse is afflicted by recurrent, unexplained episodes of choke, an endoscopic examination can prove useful in determining whether or not the oesophagus has narrowed and, if so, for what reason.

Coping with choke

First aid
If the blockage is small and can be felt on the left side of the neck, try gently massaging it down the oesophagus. If the obstruction is not visible or does not appear to be clearing, remove all food and water and keep your elderly horse under careful observation within his stable until your veterinary surgeon arrives.

Medication
Depending upon the severity of the condition, your vet may administer a light sedative to relax the horse in the hope that the blockage will then pass down the oesophagus on its own. In a few cases, it may be necessary to carefully pass a nasogastric tube down the oesophagus in an attempt to dislodge the blockage. Your vet may even decide to try to flush the obstruction out by pumping warm water down the oesophagus. However there is a risk that such procedures can occasionally do more harm than good (eg. causing rupture of the oesophagus) and they should only be performed when absolutely necessary and with the horse under heavy sedation.

Surgical options

In extreme cases, surgery may be the only answer, unfortunately postoperative scarring can cause a narrowing of the oesophagus, making subsequent episodes of choke more likely.

General management

Once the obstruction has been cleared, food should be withheld until the effects of any sedative that has been given have worn off as such drugs can hinder swallowing and reflex coughing, a factor that could lead to further choking. Subsequently your old horse should be given small amounts of soft, dampened feed and soaked hay, as he will undoubtedly have a sore throat. Fluid and electrolyte therapy may also be required if he has become dehydrated.

Thereafter every attempt should be made to prevent reoccurrences. For instance, if, despite regular dental checks, your old horse still has difficulty eating, the feeding of very moist, soft mashes and chaff will help prevent improperly chewed food from causing blockages. Conversely, if he tends to bolt his food, try placing large flat stones amongst his concentrate feed to slow down the rate of consumption. You should also ensure your horse has plenty of time to eat in a relaxed atmosphere where he does not have to compete with others for the food available.

What does the future hold?

Horses generally recover well from choke, provided they receive prompt veterinary attention and management practices are changed to prevent a reoccurrence.

Diarrhoea

What is it and how is it caused?

Many factors, including low-fibre diets, sudden changes in feeding, drug therapy, stress, illness, worm-associated gut damage and the improper chewing of food (caused by sharp or missing teeth) can cause loose, watery faeces, the effects of which can range from mild to life threatening. Neoplasia (i.e. tumours of the stomach or intestine) and malabsorption syndrome (i.e. the poor absorption of essential nutrients caused by inflammation and thickening of the wall of the small intestine) can also cause chronic diarrhoea in elderly horses. That said, diarrhoea is nowhere near as common in the horse as it is in other species, owing to the water absorption capacity of the horse's large colon.

What are the symptoms?

Droppings become increasingly watery and, depending upon the severity of the condition, colic, dehydration and sudden weight loss may also develop.

How is it diagnosed?

Diagnosis of the cause is not always easy, and needs to take into account your old horse's management and feeding routine as well as any history of illness. Investigative blood tests, dung samples etc. may also be required.

Coping with diarrhoea

General management
Veterinary advice should be sought immediately as diarrhoea can be a symptom of serious illness and can quickly cause dehydration. Until you have spoken to your vet, you should bring your elderly horse into his stable, offer him good quality soaked hay and give him free access to fresh water in order to encourage fluid intake. If his symptoms are not severe and his history does not give any cause for alarm, your vet may initially suggest just monitoring his condition for twenty-four hours as some cases may simply resolve themselves. In this instance, ask for your vet's approval to administer a probiotic supplement, to help restore gut microflora, and to offer an electrolyte supplement alongside your horse's usual water supply to help replace any body salts that may have already been lost. To avoid further digestive upset, keep to his normal feeding routine and offer small amounts of his usual feed. Do not offer bran mashes. To make him comfortable, tie up his tail to prevent soiling and regularly wash away faeces

from the dock, hindquarters and legs to prevent soreness. The application of Vaseline or similar soothing ointment will prove beneficial in helping to protect the sensitive skin around the anus.

Chronic (i.e. long term) or recurring diarrhoea in the elderly horse caused by an age-related impairment of digestive function can be particularly difficult to manage. Following an initial course of probiotics, a yeast supplement may prove helpful in aiding the digestion of fibre and providing essential B vitamins. Alternatively, clay-based additives such as the commercially available Thrive (in the USA, check with your veterinary surgeon for a similar product) may prove useful in slowing down the passage of food through the gut allowing more time for digestion. Feed small amounts of highly digestible and nutritious feeds at frequent intervals and offer the best quality hay you can find. Where the diarrhoea appears to be related to grass consumption, moving your elderly horse to a less rich pasture or limiting grazing time and offering other sources of fibre may prove beneficial. Whilst large quantities of oil can cause and indeed worsen diarrhoea in some horses, the addition of small quantities of fat to the diet can actually help boost energy levels, thereby aiding recovery and reducing weight loss in others. (**Note** Do not feed extra fat or oil if the diarrhoea is associated with liver disease.) Herbs such as slippery elm, which is known for its ability to soothe the digestive tract can be particularly useful in helping to resolve diarrhoea in elderly horses, especially when fed in combination with meadowsweet and comfrey.

Medication

If the condition does not resolve itself, any drug therapy given will be determined by identifying the cause. For instance, wormers may need to be given if parasite infection is thought to be involved, whilst gut sedatives, antispasmodic and analgesic drugs may be required to help relieve any colicky pain. In very severe cases your vet may wish to administer electrolytes intravenously or by stomach tube and may even consider tubing your old horse with fluid strained from another horse's normal faeces in an attempt to repopulate the gut with beneficial bacteria. This sounds disgusting, but coprophagy (dung eating) is in fact something that ill or malnourished horses will do instinctively in an attempt to rebalance the microorganisms within their gut. Indeed, where available, one of the most effective treatments for very severe diarrhoea involves stomach tubing the affected horse with the caecal contents drained from a deceased horse within 3–6 hours of its death.

In some cases however where the cause of chronic diarrhoea cannot be easily identified, steroids and codeine phosphate can prove a very effective treatment.

Surgical options

Where tumours in the stomach or intestines are found to be responsible, surgical removal will be required (if possible) in order for the diarrhoea to be resolved.

What does the future hold?

Diarrhoea is often alleviated by treating the underlying cause. However, any damage to or loss of intestinal function may prevent your elderly horse from making a complete recovery and diarrhoea may become a persistent problem that will require careful management based upon each individual horse's response to both orthodox and complementary medicine, as well as to changes in their diet and routine. Indeed, for some otherwise healthy old horses, long-term mild diarrhoea may become just a fact of life.

Chapter Ten

RESPIRATORY PROBLEMS

Chronic Obstructive Pulmonary Disease

What is it and how is it caused?

If affected by chronic obstructive pulmonary disease (COPD), your old horse will experience difficulty in exhaling, which means he cannot adequately clear his lungs of air before taking another breath. As the condition progresses he will be forced to use increasing muscular effort to push air out of his lungs causing the abdominal muscles to become thickened resulting in what is known as a 'heave line' along the belly, which is why COPD is sometimes referred to as 'heaves'. COPD is caused by a hypersensitivity to air pollutants such as dust, mould and fungi, and is aggravated by high levels of ammonia emanating from urine soaked bedding. If the condition is caused by an allergy to pollen from various plants, crops and trees it is commonly referred to as pasture associated pulmonary disease (PAPD). You may also, however, hear your vet refer to both COPD and PAPD as allergic airway disease (AAD), small airway disease (SAD), recurrent airway obstruction (RAO) and even 'broken wind'. Whilst it is thought that a previous viral or bacterial infection may be responsible for making a horse's airways hypersensitive,

Owned by Jill Alder since 1995, Whizz (show name: Let's Pretend), has proved an excellent all rounder for her daughters Caroline and Sharon. Now at the age of twenty-five, Whizz still enjoys the occasional day's cub-hunting with Jill and is regularly show jumped and shown in-hand during the summer months.

213

the exact reason why some horses develop an allergy and others do not still needs further research. The fact remains, however, that an increasing number of horses suffer the effects of COPD by the time they reach old age.

To understand the effect of irritants on your old horse's respiratory tract it is helpful to have an idea of how the system should normally work. It is important to realise that your horse cannot breath through his mouth, therefore air is inhaled via the nostrils into the nasal cavity where large dust or mould particles are filtered out. The air then enters the trachea (windpipe) which, just before reaching the lungs, splits into two branches, called bronchi, with one branch entering each lung. The bronchi then divide and subdivide into smaller and smaller branches, ending in grape-like clusters of tiny thin-walled alveoli air sacs. It is via the alveoli that oxygen is passed into the blood and waste carbon dioxide is taken into the lungs for exhalation. The entire airway is lined with a thin mucous membrane which traps any previously unfiltered dust particles, bacteria etc., and then transports them back up the trachea via the movement of tiny hair-like projections called cilia. The unwanted debris is then coughed up and swallowed for excretion by the digestive system.

When exposed to irritants or infection, the airways become inflamed and spasm of the muscular walls causes a narrowing of the space through which air may travel. In an effort to remove the allergens, mucus production increases. However, as the irritants and inflammatory substances build up, the mucus becomes thick and sticky and the cilia are unable to move it quickly enough back up the trachea, resulting in yet further narrowing of the airways as the mucus accumulates within the bronchial tree. As the condition progresses, permanent damage is caused as pressure within the lungs eventually causes the individual grape-like alveoli to collapse and join together to form one unit. Gaseous exchange is therefore limited as the surface area of the alveoli reduces and increased effort is required to clear the lungs.

What are the symptoms?

- In an effort to clear his lungs, your old horse may cough during the first few minutes of exercise. As the condition progresses intermittent coughing will become gradually

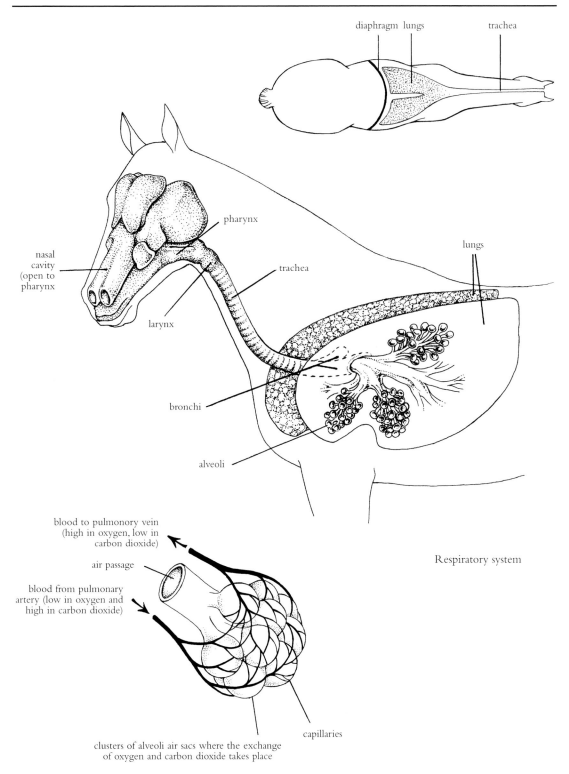

diaphragm lungs   trachea

pharynx

nasal
cavity
(open to
pharynx

trachea

lungs

larynx

bronchi

alveoli

blood to pulmonory vein
(high in oxygen, low in
carbon dioxide)

air passage

blood from pulmonary
artery (low in oxygen and
high in carbon dioxide)

Respiratory system

capillaries

clusters of alveoli air sacs where the exchange
of oxygen and carbon dioxide takes place

more persistent and may even be evident during rest periods.

- Initially a thin white discharge may be seen coming from the nostrils particularly after exercise or following exposure to specific irritants. However, if a secondary infection develops, thick yellow mucus may be seen on the floor and walls of your horse's stable.
- Your horse's respiratory rate (normally between eight and sixteen breaths a minute at rest) will increase and as his nostrils flare in an attempt to inhale more air, he may be heard to wheeze as air rushes through the constricted airways.
- A quick but firm pinch of the trachea, will cause coughing.
- Exercise intolerance will become apparent.
- Initially your horse's temperature and appetite may remain normal. However, if a secondary bacterial infection develops, his temperature may rise and he may go off his feed.
- In severe cases, a heave line may be visible along the abdomen and your old horse may have to concentrate on breathing so much that he is unable to eat comfortably, resulting in a loss of condition.

In time, constant coughing combined with the effort it takes to exhale will overdevelop the abdominal muscles causing a visible 'heave line'.

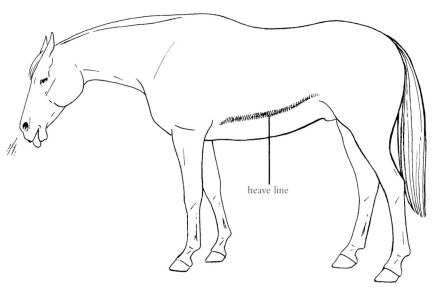

heave line

How is it diagnosed?

The symptoms of COPD and PAPD are generally specific enough to confirm diagnosis, though your vet will use a stethoscope to check for any abnormal sounds within your elderly horse's lungs, both when at rest and following exercise. Depending upon the severity of the condition, a fibre optic endoscope may be passed, via the nasal cavity, into the trachea, looking for a build-up of debris at the lowest point, samples of which may be removed for laboratory evaluation. A blood sample may also be taken to check for infection.

The use of skin testing or blood analysis to identify the exact allergens responsible for causing respiratory problems in an individual horse is controversial, as it is thought by many that the allergic response is localized to the lung tissue and is therefore unlikely to be reflected in skin or plasma tests. Though the results of such tests may appear to indicate that a horse with a respiratory problem is allergic to a number of substances, trials have demonstrated that even horses with functionally normal lungs may have very similar allergic responses. Nevertheless, such tests do little harm, and may be recommended by some veterinary surgeons or complementary health practitioners who have found them useful.

Coping with COPD

Chronic respiratory disease cannot be cured but early treatment of the condition can help reduce the extent of the damage caused within the respiratory tract, and therefore veterinary advice should be sought as soon as even very mild symptoms are noticed.

General management

It must be understood that once your elderly horse has become hypersensitive to certain allergens, he will remain allergic to them for the rest of his life. Therefore if damage to his respiratory system is to be kept to minimum, it is essential that his environment, management and feeding programmes are changed so as to reduce his exposure to the suspected allergens.

Your elderly horse should be maintained and stabled next to others who are kept on a clean air regime (see page 14). He should be fed soaked hay or haylage from the floor to reduce the risk of dust inhalation and to encourage mucus to drain from the trachea. Stables must be well ventilated and if possible wooden stables should be avoided as the walls, which can harbour various allergens in the form of dust, mould and mites, are virtually impossible to clean thoroughly. If your horse suffers from COPD turning him out in the field as much as possible will, in many cases, alleviate his symptoms. Conversely, if he has PAPD, he may need to be stabled during the day, especially when pollen counts are at their highest. Smearing a light coating of petroleum jelly onto his nostrils could help trap fine dust, mould or pollen particles before they enter his airways, though to be effective this would need to be removed and reapplied at least twice a day. Feeding a course of B vitamins along with 10–20 g of vitamin C or a general antioxidant supplement will help aid recovery. Note that since an allergic reaction is caused by the immune system recognising an often otherwise innocuous substance as harmful, the feeding of immune system stimulants, such as echinacea, may in fact worsen the condition and are best avoided.

If your old horse is wheezing badly he should not be worked as this will increase his oxygen requirement thereby putting his airways under extra pressure as he tries to forcibly clear his lungs, a factor which could lead to permanent respiratory damage. However, if your horse's symptoms are very mild, light exercise (gentle hacking) will actually prove beneficial in helping to remove mucus from his lungs, provided he does not have a temperature as a result of secondary infection. Only after his symptoms have been brought under control should his workload be gradually increased under the guidance of your veterinary surgeon.

Medication

In the acute stages, bronchodilators and mucolytics may be given to help open up the airways and liquefy mucus build-up, making it easier for the cilia to transport it out of the lungs. In most cases, a cough suppressant should not be given as this will inhibit mucus removal thereby increasing the likelihood of serious damage to his airways. The only instance where cough suppressants may prove useful is if your vet believes that the actual act of coughing has given your old horse a sore throat, and it is the subsequent irritation that is the cause of yet more frequent coughing rather than an inability to clear his lungs.

To help reduce inflammation, MSM may prove beneficial,

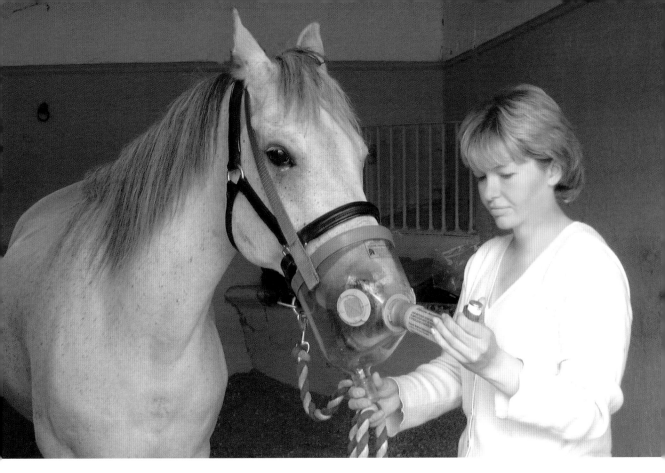

though in severe cases the anti-inflammatory effects of corticos-teroids will be required. Unfortunately the circulation of corticosteroids in the blood can have a number of serious side effects including a reduction in the functioning of the immune system, the development of laminitis and delayed wound healing. To keep corticosteroid levels in the blood to a minimum, they are, therefore, best administered directly into the lungs via a metered dose inhaler or nebuliser which necessitates the use of a special mask. Antibiotics will only be given if a secondary bacterial infection has been identified.

In some cases it may be possible to prevent an allergic reaction occurring in the first place by the administration of a drug called sodium cromoglycate via a nebulizer. The drug is only effective if given to a horse when it is not currently showing symptoms of COPD and works by suppressing those cells in the lining of the airways which respond to allergen invasion. As a result, it prevents the allergic reaction which triggers your horse's symptoms. Initially, treatment may continue for up to four days and is then repeated every 3–20 days depending upon the severity of your horse's condition.

The administrations of Corticosteriods directly into the lungs via a metered dose inhaler.

Alternatively, it may be worth asking your veterinary surgeon for a referral to the REACT equine allergy clinic which, at the time of writing, is the only centre in the UK that uses skin testing to identify the exact allergens which cause a reaction in each individual horse. In the USA, ask your vet for a referral to a veterinary dermatologist. These specific allergens are then diluted until they no longer cause an allergic response and the tiny amounts of the resulting solution are given regularly by injection. Though the efficacy of this treatment appears controversial, it has been claimed that this neutralizing dose can alleviate at least 75% of the symptoms of COPD in some cases.

What does the future hold?

If treated and controlled before permanent damage to the respiratory system occurs, your old horse will have every chance of resuming his previous level of work. However, where permanent damage limits gaseous exchange, your horse's workload will need to be reduced in accordance with the severity of the condition and he may need to be given corticosteroid treatment on a permanent basis. In the worst case, poor lung function may result in enforced retirement or euthanasia.

Respiratory Infections

What are they and how are they caused?

An age-related reduction in the efficiency of the immune system or prior damage to the lungs caused by COPD or PAPD can make your elderly horse particularly prone to both viral and bacterial infections, the effects of which within the airways are similar to that described under COPD.

Viral infections such as equine influenza or equine herpes (rhinopneumonitis) may be contracted by the inhalation of viral particles or by direct contact with contaminated water troughs, tack, clothing, infected horses, etc. Once in the body, a virus may bypass your elderly horse's initial defence systems as, unless trained to do so by vaccination or previous exposure to the same virus, his immune system may not initially recognise a virus as harmful. On reaching its target, a virus will penetrate your horse's cells and use the content of the cell to reproduce. As the viral particles multiply they disrupt and may eventually destroy and burst out of the host cell ready to infect neighbouring cells. However, as the virus spreads and is recognised as an invader, antibodies will respond and in most cases will eventually bring the virus under control within one to three weeks.

Bacteria, on the other hand, do not need to take over their host's cells in order to multiply but spread by division and subdivision of their own structure. They too can be inhaled or contracted from contaminated equipment but some will already be present within your elderly horse's body, lying dormant until conditions are suitable for them to move to, and multiply within, your horse's airways. Such opportunities often arise whilst his immune system is busy fighting off viral invasion or dealing with other allergens (*see* chronic obstructive pulmonary disease). Though easily recognised as a germ, bacteria can multiply so quickly that insufficient defences are available to overpower them, resulting in the development of a secondary infection.

What are the symptoms?

As his immune system attacks the invading organisms, your old horse will develop some or all of the following symptoms.

- Lethargy and depression
- Temperature may rise up to 106 °F (41 °C)
- Lack of appetite.
- Respiratory rate may increase to up to sixty breaths per minute.
- Initially a watery nasal discharge may be seen, which may eventually turn thick and yellow.
- A dry or moist cough may develop, the frequency of which will depend upon the severity of the infection.
- Swollen glands may be felt around the throat and the legs may fill.
- Though the effects of equine herpes virus (EHV) subtype 2 (known as EHV-4) are usually restricted to the respiratory system, EHV subtype 1 (EHV-1)) may also cause

neurological symptoms such as incoordination or paralysis. EHV-1 may also cause pregnant mares to abort or give birth to weak foals that die within ten days.

How are they diagnosed?

Initial diagnosis will be made on evidence of the above and a possible history of other horses on the yard showing similar symptoms. Confirmation and identification of the infection will then be made by blood testing and/or taking a nasopharyngeal swab (i.e. a sample of mucus taken from the very back of the nasal cavity).

Coping with respiratory infections

In general, if your elderly horse is showing symptoms of respiratory infection he should, as far as possible, be isolated from his stable companions and strict hygiene methods must be employed. Regrettably however, as many infectious particles are airborne and since your horse will have been harbouring and shedding the infection for anywhere between two and ten days before symptoms develop (depending upon the cause of the infection), it is highly unlikely that these measures will entirely prevent the infection of others. Nevertheless, such precautions should be taken as they will help limit the spread of infection in some cases. Since it is impossible to tell which horses are harbouring an infection and which are not, even apparently healthy horses on the same yard should not be allowed to go to shows or other equine gatherings for at least two or three weeks after the last case of infection has been diagnosed.

Medication

Unfortunately there are currently no viable drugs for horses which are capable of combating viral attack without also damaging the host cell. Antibiotics which are ineffective against viruses will therefore only be given if a bacterial infection is suspected. Irrespective of the cause of infection, supportive therapy may include the use of bronchodilators and mucolytics to help open up the airways and encourage the drainage of mucus. Depending upon the severity of the condition, intravenous fluids and anti-inflammatory drugs may also be recommended in some cases.

As your elderly horse recovers, a course of probiotics may prove useful in helping to repopulate the gut with beneficial bacteria, many of which may have been destroyed as a result of feverish temperatures or the administration of antibiotics.

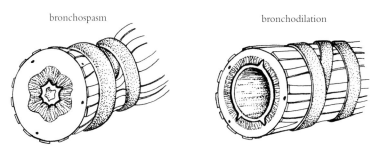

bronchospasm

bronchodilation

Bronchodilators can help relieve bronchospasm and make breathing easier.

General management

If an infection is suspected, veterinary advice must be sought and, if not already in place, a clean air regime must be implemented (*see* page 14). Initially your vet may recommend box rest within a well-ventilated stable combined with short periods of in-hand grazing. Thereafter, your old horse will benefit from being turned out in the field as much as possible, provided of course he is not going to become too cold as a result of wind and/or rain. Depending upon the severity of the condition, complete rest and plenty of fresh air may be required for several weeks following the initial infection as, even if the virus is defeated relatively quickly, the damage at a cellular level will take much longer to repair. Trying to work your horse too soon can permanently damage his airways and cause secondary problems such as heart disease, anaemia and liver damage.

Soaked or vacuum-packed hay should be fed from the ground to encourage free drainage of mucus from the nostrils. Supplementary B vitamins along with 10–20 g of vitamin C or an antioxidant supplement will prove beneficial. The feeding of echinacea or similar, to boost the efficiency of the immune system, may also help fight off bacterial or viral invasion.

What does the future hold?

Whilst infections can be secondary to COPD or PAPD, they can also be the initiating cause of such conditions. With adequate rest and prompt treatment, however, your elderly horse is likely to make a full recovery, though when rare complications such as heart and liver disease occur, euthanasia may be recommended depending upon the extent of the damage.

Obviously prevention is always better than cure and so you should ensure that your old horse and all his stable companions are vaccinated against both the equine influenza virus and the equine herpes virus (rhinopneumonitis) and that regular boosters are given in order to remind the immune system how to recognise a specific virus.

Chapter Eleven

EYE PROBLEMS

What are they and how are they caused?

The origin of the majority of eye problems seen in horses is more likely to be related to previous injury or infection than the process of ageing. Nevertheless by the time your horse reaches old age he may well suffer from one of the following common eye complaints.

- A **cataract** is an opaque area on the lens ranging from a small cloudy spot that has little effect on vision, to complete opacity of the lens causing blindness.
- **Keratitis** refers to inflammation of the cornea that can lead to secondary bacterial and fungal infections which may result in a blueish-white haze enveloping the cornea and the formation of ulcers. Eventually, adhesions may develop between the cornea and iris causing blindness as the eyeball collapses.
- **Recurrent uveitis** (also known as periodic ophthalmia and moon blindness) refers to inflammation of the uveal tract (i.e. the iris, ciliary body and choroid), repeated episodes of which may appear days, weeks, months or even years later causing more and more damage with each attack. The condition can cause degeneration of the retina, adhesions, damage to the cornea or cataract formation as well a shrinking of the eyeball.

Gavin, owned by Kathryn Farquharson, is twenty-four years old and quite a character and, as well as enjoying long hacks and participating in local shows, delights in finding mischievous ways to draw attention to himself.

The eye

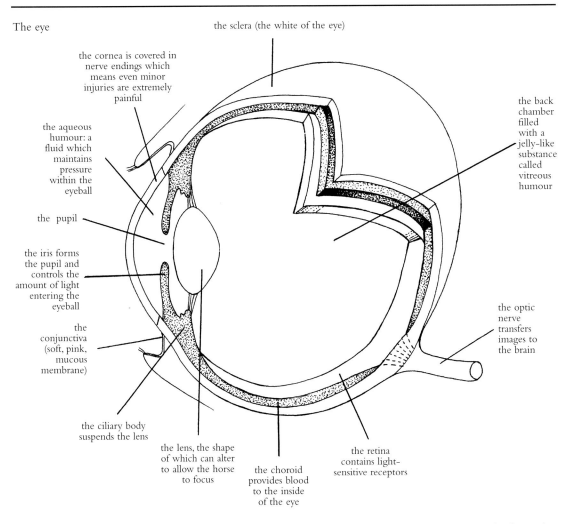

the sclera (the white of the eye)

the cornea is covered in nerve endings which means even minor injuries are extremely painful

the aqueous humour: a fluid which maintains pressure within the eyeball

the pupil

the iris forms the pupil and controls the amount of light entering the eyeball

the conjunctiva (soft, pink, mucous membrane)

the ciliary body suspends the lens

the lens, the shape of which can alter to allow the horse to focus

the choroid provides blood to the inside of the eye

the retina contains light-sensitive receptors

the back chamber filled with a jelly-like substance called vitreous humour

the optic nerve transfers images to the brain

There are numerous causes of such eye conditions including the following.

- Direct injury or blow, causing penetration or bruising of the eye.
- Irritation caused by foreign bodies such as hay seeds, pollen etc., all of which can lead to associated head shaking.
- Viral, bacterial or fungal infections such as equine influenza, equine herpes and leptospirosis bacteria (contracted from the infected urine of rats, cattle, swine and wildlife).
- Links have also been made between the development of recurrent uveitis and the onchocerca parasite. Believed to be transmitted by the culicoides midge, the worm lives in the tissues of a horse's neck, but travels throughout the body.

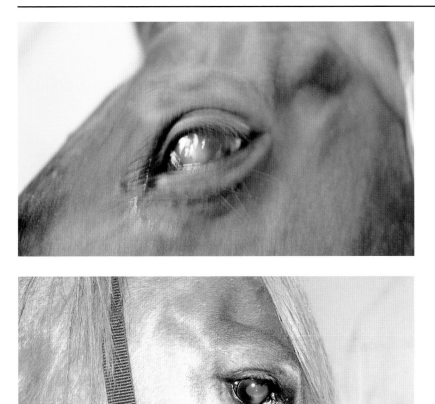

Keratitis

Recurrent uveitis

Whilst alive they cause little problem but, if present in the eye when killed by a wormer, they release allergens which cause inflammation.

- Tiny cataracts which are present at birth may degenerate very slowly until they cause serious visual impairment by the time a horse reaches old age.

What are the symptoms?

- Conjunctivitis, which is redness and inflammation of the thin membrane that joins the eyelid to the eyeball. This is a relatively common condition in itself (caused by trauma or irritation) and is not always indicative of more severe

227

problems, nevertheless veterinary advice should still be sought in all cases.

- Acute pain.
- Squinting or keeping the eyelids tightly closed.
- Blocked tear ducts and/or a watery discharge from the eye, which may turn thick and yellow if a secondary infection develops.
- Constant rubbing and increased blinking of the affected eye.
- Bright light seems to increase discomfort (known as photophobia).
- Constricted pupils.
- A change in colour of the cornea.
- Where vision is being impaired, your elderly horse may stumble and spook increasingly, refuse to jump, bump into objects etc.

How are they diagnosed?

If the affected eye is tightly shut, your vet will first apply a local anaesthetic and give a sedative to reduce pain and relax the lids. Once any obvious symptoms have been noted, your horse will be moved to a darkened box, where the absence of light will cause his pupils to dilate (open). This will make it easier for your vet to see the inner structures of the eye in detail using an ophthalmoscope, which is an instrument containing adjustable magnifying lenses and a single light source. A fluorescent dye may also be put into the eye to show up any wounds or ulcers on the cornea and to check that the tear duct drainage system is working properly. If an eye infection is suspected, a swab may be taken to help determine the choice of antibiotics.

It is actually extremely difficult for your vet to diagnose the extent of vision impairment. Typically, tests will include thrusting the flat of the hand towards the affected eye to see whether or not your old horse blinks, and making an obstacle course through which your horse is asked to manoeuvre with one eye blindfolded at a time in both brightly lit and semidark conditions.

Coping with eye problems

First aid

Any injury or apparent infection either of the eye or eyelid should be treated only by the veterinary surgeon. Never apply an ointment or give eye drops to your horse which were prescribed for another, and never try to force open tightly closed eyelids as this could cause severe damage and perhaps even a rupture of the eyeball. Instead, simply bathe the eye with previously boiled, lukewarm water and wait for your vet to arrive.

Medication

Cataracts are not affected by medication but prompt and aggressive therapy can help treat other problems and, in many cases may save your horse's eyesight or at least help to slow down degenerative changes.

- Atropine drops may need to be given between five and six times a day to help dilate the pupil and prevent adhesions forming between one part of the eye and another.
- NSAIDs (e.g. bute) may be given to help reduce pain and inflammation.
- Corticosteroid drops are excellent at reducing inflammation but can delay healing or cause fungal infections if ulcers or wounds are present on the cornea and must, therefore, be used with care. Conjunctival injections of long-acting steroids may sometimes be recommended.
- Antibiotics or antifungal treatment.

Note   As the eye washes out medication quickly, drops and ointments need to be placed into the corner of the eye on a frequent basis if they are to prove effective.

Surgical options

Surgical removal of cataracts is possible in some cases provided no other eye problems are present, but the cost and risks involved, for example the subsequent development of recurrent uveitis, make this operation a last resort. In some cases where chronic irritation is causing severe pain, your vet may recommend a damaged eye be surgically removed. Indeed, early reports suggest that this may prevent recurrent uveitis spreading from one eye to the other, however such a drastic approach still needs long-term scientific study.

General management

To reduce the risk of irritation to the eye from dust and mould spores, you should immediately employ a clean air regime (*see* page 14), and feed soaked or dust free hay from the ground. Your

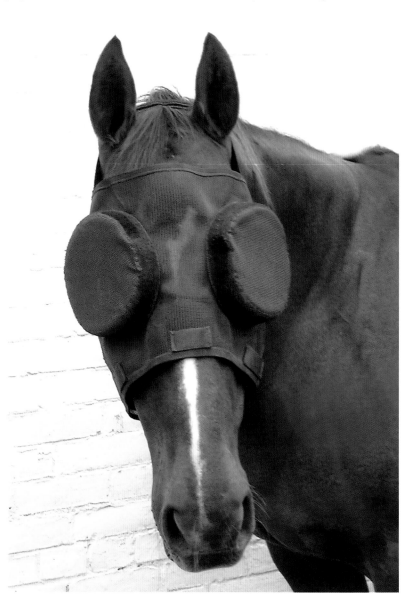

The Guardian Multipurpose Mask provides an alternative to having to keep those horses who are adversely affected by bright light, constantly stabled during the hours of daylight. Incorporating revolutionary sunshades, which offer 95% protection from ultra-violet light, the mask not only aids in the healing of eye injuries and in the veterinary treatment of many ocular diseases including uveitis, cataracts and cancer, but it also allows affected horses to be turned out in the field and ridden as normal, thus improving their quality of life and ability to work.

old horse should also wear a fly mask whenever he is turned out or ridden, not only to protect him from fly irritation, but to reduce the glare of the sun and also prevent foreign bodies such as pollen and grass seeds from entering his eyes. If, however, UV rays or wind still causes severe irritation, or if your horse is being given atropine drops, he may have to be kept stabled during daylight hours and on windy days.

Though blind in his left eye, 41-year-old Just William (known as Billy to his friends), owned by Sue Moorhouse, still successfully competes in ridden and in-hand classes throughout the summer with his young rider Daniel Priestley.

What does the future hold?

With prompt treatment, most minor eye injuries and infections will heal without causing permanent damage but if your old horse does not appear to be responding to treatment, do not be afraid to ask for a referral to an equine ophthalmologist for specialist advice on the most up-to-date treatment methods which may, in the future, even include the use of equine contact lenses.

When degenerative changes do occur, it is often impossible to predict the degree or even speed at which your elderly horse's sight may be lost and he should, therefore, have check-ups every three to six months in order to monitor his condition. In the meantime, you should get into the habit of talking to your horse whenever you are around him, so that, even if he eventually cannot see you, he will always be aware of your presence and will never be startled by a sudden and unexpected approach. You should also train him to respond to verbal commands and work on getting him used to being handled, mounted and lead from both sides. Allowing the sensory whiskers and guard hairs around his nostrils and eyes to grow naturally will also help prevent him from bumping into objects he may not be able to see clearly, thereby reducing the risk of injury.

Horses can, in fact, cope with the gradual loss of sight in one eye remarkably well, though the resultant loss of depth perception can cause them to stumble frequently on uneven ground. Extra lessons with your instructor will, therefore, prove invaluable for increasing your horse's balance and responsiveness to the aids on which he will become increasingly reliant for support and direction as his eyesight fails. The use of knee boots for ridden work will also prove a wise precaution.

Most of all you must be patient and sensitive to your elderly horse's changing needs but that does not mean that you should become overindulgent or make excuses for bad behaviour. Firm, fair handling is still essential if you are to be able to maintain his respect and give him confidence. You may also need to consider whether your horse will be happy being stabled on a busy yard where strange people, loud noises and constantly changing field companions can all take their toll. Many partially sighted or blind horses are much happier kept on a quiet yard, where they are guaranteed to be turned out in the same field every day with one or two special friends. Even blind horses can cope quite well in such situations provided neither the field boundaries nor the position of field amenities such as the water trough are suddenly changed.

Unfortunately, when the loss of sight in both eyes is very sudden, horses can become deeply distressed and in some cases, depending upon the temperament of the horse, the dedication of the owner and the facilities available, the kindest option may be to put your old horse to sleep.

Chapter Twelve

ORGAN FAILURE

Liver Disease

What is it and how is it caused?

The liver, which lies within the abdominal cavity, acts as a filter and has over one hundred different functions of which the following are the most important.

- The regulation of the concentration of protein (i.e. amino acids), carbohydrates (i.e. glucose) and fat within the bloodstream.
- The detoxification of drugs and poisons.
- The production of bile and vitamin C, as well as substances which aid blood clotting and protect the skin from the sun.
- The storage of fat-soluble vitamins A, D, E and K, together with B12 , iron and copper.

Damage to the liver may be caused by any of the following.

- Poisoning from plants (e.g. ragwort) and chemical toxins.
- Fat accumulation as a result of either obesity or conversely starvation (which causes the mobilisation of fat reserves).
- Bacterial or viral infections.
- Tumours or parasite infestations which block the flow of bile to the duodenum.

Blue Sombrero (Toby) a 26-year-old, 14.2 hh part bred Arab, often takes part in show jumping and cross-country events as well as showing classes and long-distance rides with his owner Andrea Beattie.

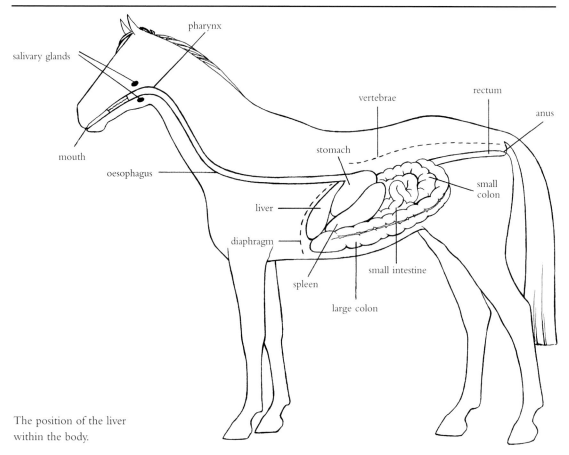

The position of the liver within the body.

- The excessive destruction of red blood cells, which leads to increased production of bile pigment (broken down from haemoglobin) that can overwhelm the liver.
- Stress: a sudden change of diet, infrequent feeding etc.

What are the symptoms?

Depending upon the cause, the initial symptoms of liver malfunction may be very slight. Your elderly horse may simply appear lethargic and depressed with a dull coat and little appetite, which eventually causes a gradual loss of weight. Areas of unpigmented skin may, gradually, become prone to sunburn (known as photosensitisation) and, as bile accumulates, he may look jaundiced as the whites of his eyes and the mucous membranes of his mouth and eyelids turn yellow. (**Note** Not all horses with sunburn have liver problems.) Diarrhoea, colic and fluid collection along the base of the belly may develop.

As the condition worsens and the liver is unable to filter out toxic substances, levels of ammonia (a byproduct of protein breakdown), may build up in the bloodstream. This may eventually be absorbed by brain tissue causing neurological signs such as incessant yawning, constant circling, head-pressing against solid objects, incoordination, blindness and dementia.

How is it diagnosed?

Initially, blood tests will be performed looking for elevated levels of liver enzymes after which liver function tests and the use of diagnostic ultrasound or a liver biopsy will help reveal the extent of the damage caused.

Coping with liver disease

If for no apparent reason your elderly horse seems 'off-colour' for more than a couple of days, ask your vet to take a blood test. There may be nothing seriously wrong but, if liver disease is discovered, early diagnosis will increase his chances of survival.

Medication

Where a bacterial infection or parasite infestation is thought to be involved, antibiotics or wormers may be given. Unfortunately, there is no specific medication that can help in cases of liver disease and treatment is simply aimed at supporting liver function.

General management

If your horse is refusing to eat, your vet may initially insist on him being tube-fed. Attempts to encourage him to eat voluntarily should however continue, and your old horse should be offered tiny amounts of whatever he finds tempting – be that grass, carrots, apples, chocolate or even jam sandwiches – in fact just about anything to try and restore his interest in food. This is particularly important in the case of the overweight horse or pony, as the body's reaction to starvation will be to mobilise fat reserves (a condition known as hyperlipaemia) which will cause yet further serious damage to the liver.

Once your horse's appetite returns it will be important to make certain changes to his overall diet in order to reduce the liver's workload.

- *Reduce protein levels.* Adequate, but low levels (i.e. a maximum of 8–10%) of good quality protein are required. Avoid high-protein feeds, which will include many of the compounds formulated for elderly horses. Choose late-cut hay (which is generally lower in protein) and do not allow your horse to graze on lush, quickly growing or newly fertilised pastures when protein levels in the grass are likely to be at their highest.

The 41-year-old Just William again: Billy has to be maintained on a low protein, low oil, high fibre diet after suffering from serious liver problems.

- *Keep fat and oil to a minimum.* Do not supplement your horse's normal feed with additional fat or oil.
- *Increase digestible energy levels.* To prevent the liver having to mobilise fat stores or convert glycogen into glucose to provide energy, feed a diet high in fibre and carbohydrates. As many compound feeds which are high in digestible energy are also high in protein and oil, you may need to choose those specifically designed for convalescing horses and/or straights such as micronized maize, sugar beet, etc. The need to increase carbohydrate levels can, however, make those who are also prone to laminitis particularly tricky to feed. If in doubt, therefore, maintain your horse on a solely high fibre diet and seek expert advise from a qualified equine nutritionist.
- *Give a good quality supplement.* Since vitamin storage and synthesis will be affected, dietary levels should be increased either by feeding a good quality supplement or a convalescent feed containing elevated vitamin and mineral levels. Additional B vitamins will prove helpful in increasing appetite and aiding the metabolism of protein, carbohydrate and fat, whilst an antioxidant will help to limit the damage caused by free radicals (*see* page 93). A daily dose of 10-20 g of vitamin C may also prove beneficial. Feeding the herb milk thistle is said to aid the rejuvenation of liver cells, increase bile production and lower fat deposits, and is therefore recommended in all cases. Echinacea is also frequently advocated, especially where blood tests show evidence of infection or indicate a depressed immune system.
- *Feed little and often.* Ad lib hay and small frequent feeds will help prevent overtaxing the liver.

What does the future hold?

If liver problems are discovered early, your elderly horse may make a full recovery as the liver has an amazing ability to rejuvenate. Subsequently, however, special attention will always need to be paid to his diet and stress levels. Occasional blood testing will be required to help monitor his condition. Unfortunately, if 70% or more of liver cells have been damaged by the time diagnosis is made, rejuvenation is impossible and the damaged cells will be replaced by fibrous tissue causing the liver to shrink in size. Once the brain has been damaged, and extensive neurological signs develop there is generally no turning back and putting your old horse out of his misery is then the kindest option.

Urinary Problems

What are they and how are they caused?

Urinary problems in horses are thankfully nowhere near as common as they are in ageing dogs and cats. Nevertheless, some old horses may experience an age-related reduction in kidney function, though this is rarely sufficient to cause clinical signs since the kidneys can continue to function even when some 70% of their tissue has been damaged.

The urinary system begins with the two kidneys which are protected by fatty tissue as they sit beneath the spine on either side of it, near the last ribs. From each kidney, a ureter then allows urine to flow into the bladder, which when full excretes urine via the urethra. The function of the kidneys is to:

- Filter excess water and waste products from the bloodstream for excretion as urine.
- Maintain fluid and electrolyte balance throughout the body.
- Maintain correct pH level of body fluid.
- Secrete certain hormones, e.g. those which are sent to the bone marrow to help stimulate the production of red blood cells.
- Convert vitamin D derived from sunlight into its active form, which aids the absorption of calcium and phosphorous.

Problems within the urinary system may be caused by any of the following.

- A decrease in blood supply to the kidneys (through dehydration, shock or haemorrhage, for example) reduces the production of urine.
- Damage to kidney tissue as a result of poisoning, drug

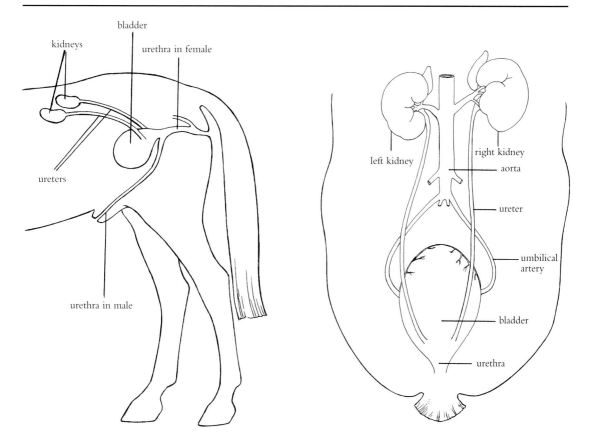

The urinary system

therapy, tumour formation, dehydration, shock, colic or a lack of fibre in the diet (which increases acidity in the gut)
- Infection.
- Though uncommon, the normal flow of urine can be obstructed by the development of stones (known as calculi), within either the kidney, bladder or urethra, which are normally made of calcium carbonate deposits around a nucleus such as dead bacteria or white blood cells.

Note The kidneys are well protected within your old horse's body and contrary to popular belief are highly unlikely to suffer from bruising.

What are the symptoms?

Signs of urinary problems will vary depending upon the cause of the condition, but may include any of the following.

- A change in the frequency, amount or colour of the urine.
- Pain, excessive grunting (a certain amount is normal) or continual straining when trying to urinate.
- Any otherwise unexplained increase or decrease in thirst.
- Depression, weakness, reduced appetite, weight loss, nervousness and other seemingly unrelated symptoms may be evident as a result of fluid imbalances throughout the body.
- Fluid swelling of the legs and underneath the belly.
- Mouth ulcers and gum inflammation may occasionally develop.
- Excessive accumulation of tartar on the teeth.
- Colic symptoms.

How are they diagnosed?

Taking into account your old horse's history and dietary management, your veterinary surgeon will recommend sending a blood test and urine sample for laboratory analysis. A catheter (i.e. a flexible tube) may be passed up the urethra to check for blockages caused by urethra stones, and a rectal examination may be performed to check whether or not the kidneys are tender and inflamed. Diagnostic ultrasound may also be used to visualise bladder stones.

Coping with urinary problems

If urinary problems are suspected, your old horse should be rested, kept warm and monitored closely until seen by your vet.

Medication
Fluid, electrolyte therapy and/or the administration of diuretics (which stimulate urine production and neutralise its acidity) may be recommended. Antibiotics may be given if there is evidence of a bacterial infection. If your vet suspects a blockage of the urethra, a muscle relaxant may be given to see if this will encourage the passage of stones along its length.

Surgical options
Where stones refuse to move from the urethra or have formed in the bladder, surgical extraction is the only option. Surgery on

the kidneys however is rarely attempted in anything other than extreme cases (such as those involving cancerous tumours) because of the difficulties in reaching the kidneys through the ribs and diaphragm.

General management

Impaired kidney function, reduces the body's ability to filter out waste products, particularly excess protein, calcium and phosphorous. Protein levels should therefore be reduced to between 8% and 10% of the overall diet (*see* page 236) and adequate, but low, levels of calcium and phosphorous should be provided. This is best achieved by feeding ad lib hay with either a good quality vitamin and mineral supplement, or suitable compound feed. Where extra energy is required, the addition of oil to the diet will prove useful. Avoid giving large quantities of feeds such as alfalfa (high in protein and calcium), sugar beet (high in calcium), or bran (high in phosphorous and protein). Supplementation of the water soluble vitamins B and C will prove beneficial. Anecdotal reports suggest that feeding a cupful (approx. 250 ml [$1\frac{1}{4}$ US cups]) of cider vinegar to horses twice a day (or half this amount to ponies) may help to increase the solubility of intestinal calculi. The herbs golden rod and echinacea may also prove helpful, whilst dandelion and nettle may be of use if a gentle diuretic is required. Free access to fresh water is also imperative for proper functioning of the urinary system. In some cases your vet may also recommend offering your horse electrolytes on a regular basis.

Where the constant dribbling of urine is a problem, rubbing petroleum jelly between a mare's upper thighs or on the insides of the hind legs of geldings and stallions will help reduce scalding.

What does the future hold?

Urinary tract problems can prove extremely serious and prompt treatment is vital. Survival rates vary depending upon the cause and severity of the problem and you must be guided by your veterinary surgeon. For instance, acute renal failure can be life threatening, especially if caused by toxic chemicals, and your elderly horse may not recover if fluid balance is lost and waste products and toxins are not filtered from the blood. However, those whose urine production increases within twenty-four to forty-eight hours of the administration of intravenous (IV) fluid treatment, generally have a more favourable prognosis.

Heart Problems

What are they and how are they caused?

Unlike people, elderly horses rarely suffer from heart attacks. In fact, research suggests that between 50% and 60% of all horses may have an abnormally beating heart and yet show no ill effect. However, an age-related scarring of the heart valves and a weakening and loss of elasticity of blood vessel walls, can place extra strain on an elderly horse's heart, particularly if his body is already under stress from other age-related problems such as parasite damage, illness or organ failure.

The heart is a pump made from muscle which is divided into four chambers. The upper chambers (the atria) contract together at the same time to push blood into the lower chambers (the ventricles). The valves of the heart then close to prevent the blood flowing back, and the ventricles contract together to push blood out of the heart and around the body. It is the contraction of the upper and lower chambers which produces the typical 'lubb dup' sound of the heartbeat that can be heard between thirty and forty times a minute in a healthy horse at rest, though the resting rate of a very fit horse may be lower.

An elderly horse with a heart murmur will produce an extra sound during a normally quiet period of the heart's cycle. Most commonly, murmurs are caused by a fairly harmless disturbance in the normal forward flow of blood through the heart. In a few cases, however, the cause may be attributed to valve disease which can compromise blood flow throughout the body. A thorough examination by an experienced veterinary surgeon is the only way to differentiate between the two.

Cardiac arrhythmia refers to irregular beating of the heart. This most commonly involves a 'drop' or 'skip' of a heartbeat which is caused when the ventricles occasionally fail to contract. This may simply be a way of regulating blood flow and is not considered a significant problem. However, a much more serious cause of arrhythmia occurs when the heart's pacemaker fails to regulate the heartbeat causing the atria to beat out of synchronization with the ventricles which, if not stimulated to contract, will not send sufficient blood through the body. This condition is known as atrial fibrillation and may be caused either by a brief interruption in electrical impulses in a large but otherwise healthy heart or, more seriously, by poor valve function or an infection which causes the heart muscle to become diseased and inflamed (known as myocarditis).

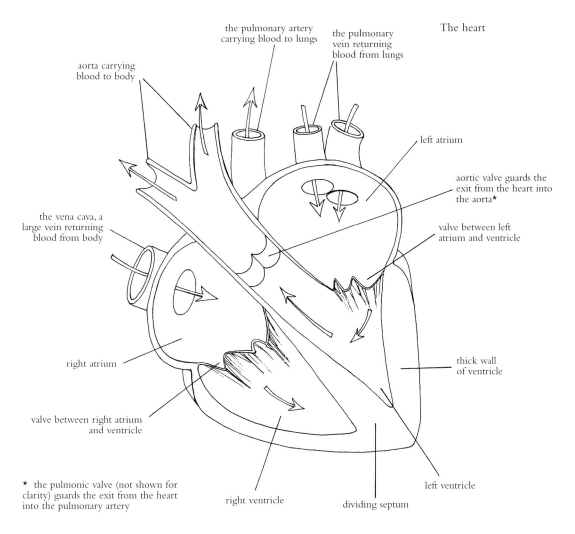

The heart

the pulmonary artery carrying blood to lungs

the pulmonary vein returning blood from lungs

aorta carrying blood to body

left atrium

aortic valve guards the exit from the heart into the aorta★

the vena cava, a large vein returning blood from body

valve between left atrium and ventricle

right atrium

thick wall of ventricle

valve between right atrium and ventricle

★ the pulmonic valve (not shown for clarity) guards the exit from the heart into the pulmonary artery

right ventricle

dividing septum

left ventricle

What are the symptoms?

Whilst abnormal sounds heard at rest which disappear on exercise are not considered serious, the symptoms of more significant heart problems vary greatly depending upon the severity of the condition but may include any of the following.

- Exercise intolerance, weakness and/or incoordination.
- Breathlessness and occasional coughing.
- Nose bleeds.
- Oedema between the front legs and along the underside of the belly.
- Poor appetite and subsequent weight loss.
- Colic.
- Collapse.

How are they diagnosed?

It is important for your old horse to be resting quietly whilst your vet takes his pulse and listens to his heart with a stethoscope because some murmurs may disappear if your horse's heart rate and blood flow have been increased by exercise, excitement or fear. A blood test will also be taken to help identify any pre-existing cause of the condition, such as liver or kidney failure, and show up any signs of anaemia or low blood protein levels, both of which can cause a thinning of the blood and therefore extra turbulence within the heart, causing a murmur that will in fact disappear once such problems are corrected. The loudness of a heart murmur, which is normally graded between one and six, will give some indication of its severity. An ultrasound scan will also prove helpful in determining the location and timing of the murmur as well as any changes in the size or functioning of the chambers or valves. If the rhythm of the heart has been altered, an electrocardiogram (ECG) will be performed to detect electrical activity within the heart. In both cases your elderly horse's heart will also be checked following exercise. If further evaluation is required, he may be referred to a veterinary hospital where he can be put on a treadmill so that functioning of the heart can be monitored at all gaits.

Coping with heart problems

Medication

There is no specific treatment for heart murmurs, though in some cases the digitalis group of drugs can help increase blood flow through the heart. In the case of atrial fibrillation, Quinidine may sometimes prove sufficient to restore a rhythmical heartbeat. However, the drug may have side effects in a few horses which can worsen the condition by making breathing more difficult, increasing fluid build-up, weakness and incoordination, as well as causing diarrhoea and colic. Since arrhythmia may sometimes correct itself, the drug will, therefore, only be used where poor rhythm of the heart is causing a serious problem. Where the heart is congested and oedema of the abdomen, sheath and legs is present, diuretics may also be recommended to reduce fluid accumulation. Whether or not drug treatment will have to continue for the rest of the horse's life depends upon the heart's response to treatment.

Surgical options

Due to the sheer size of a horse, open heart surgery is not possible.

General management

Depending upon the severity of the condition, box rest and in-hand walking may be initially recommended after which pasture turn-out will prove beneficial in encouraging circulation. Subsequently, an exercise programme should be devised in conjunction with your vet to ensure your elderly horse does not become overtired or stressed.

Salt intake should be kept to a minimum but if your horse has been placed on a diuretic, he should be given access to a salt lick so that he can compensate for the extra body salts excreted in his urine. Additional water-soluble B vitamins may prove beneficial and, where necessary, dandelion leaves will prove helpful in reducing fluid accumulation.

What does the future hold?

The discovery of a minor heart condition is not a sentence of death. Your elderly horse may live for many years without showing any ill effect, especially if he is employed in general riding club work such as hacking, dressage and low-level show jumping. However, stressful activities such as cross-country jumping should be avoided. Contrary to popular belief, horses with low-grade heart disease are no more likely to collapse whilst being ridden than any other. Sudden death is in fact more likely to be associated with the rupture of a major blood vessel which can occur even in extremely fit horses.

Unfortunately, not all horses with more serious heart problems will respond to drug therapy, particularly if arrhythmia is combined with signs of congestive heart failure or valvular disease. Retirement may be a possibility in some cases but, in others, where reduced blood flow throughout the body is causing seizures and the failure of other organs, euthanasia may be the kindest option.

Chapter Thirteen
TUMOURS

Cushing's Syndrome

What is it and how is it caused?

Cushing's syndrome is the term used to describe the effects of a slow-growing, benign tumour in the marble-sized pituitary gland which is positioned at the base of the brain and is responsible for regulating hormone secretion. As the tumour grows in size it presses on surrounding tissue and nerves and also produces abnormal levels of hormones which overstimulates the adrenal glands and triggers increased cortisol production. The condition may also be known as Cushing's disease, pituitary pars intermedia dysfunction (PPID – meaning dysfunction of a section of the intermediate lobe of the pituitary gland) or hyperadrenocorticism (meaning increased production of cortisol from the adrenal gland).

What are the symptoms?

The condition can cause a reduction in the ability to control body temperature, poor functioning of the immune system, anaemia, delayed wound healing, and even sight impediment. Commonly, any one or a combination of the following symptoms may appear.

- Excessive thirst and urination.

Monty, who was the prize in a *Horse & Hound* competition in 1984, has now been semi-retired from the show ring, and at the age of twenty-three is concentrating on long-distance rides with his owner Helen Seymour.

It is the overproduction of cortisol by the adrenal glands as a result of a pituitary gland tumour that is responsible for many of the symptoms which typify Cushing's syndrome.

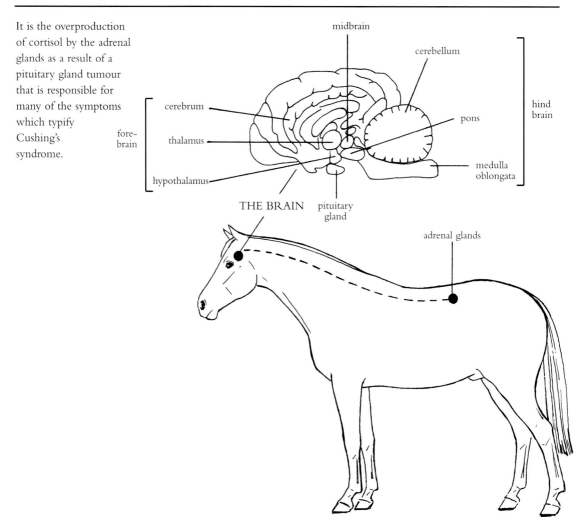

THE BRAIN

- A long, wavy coat or coarse hair that fails to shed and may cause heavy sweating in summer. The skin soon becomes irritated and persistent rubbing can lead to patchy hair loss.
- A combination of muscle loss over the top line and the weight of excessive fluid in the gut, can cause a sway-backed, pot-bellied appearance. Depressions normally seen above the eyes may become filled by fat deposits.
- Whilst your horse's appetite may increase, he will not gain any weight and may in fact start to lose condition.
- In most cases affected horses remain fairly bright and alert, though some may eventually become lethargic and weak, causing exercise intolerance.
- Chronic and recurrent bouts of crippling laminitis that prove

almost impossible to prevent and difficult to treat.

- The development of diabetes and an increased susceptibility to respiratory, skin and parasite infections, gum disease and mouth ulcers, joint infections and foot abscesses.

How is it diagnosed?

The aforementioned symptoms in an old horse are often sufficient indication to the veterinary surgeon of the presence of a pituitary tumour. However, blood tests showing high blood sugar levels, a reduced lymphocyte count, an electrolyte

A long wavy coat that fails to shed in summer is a typical sign of Cushing's syndrome.

At twenty years of age, The Englishman (Barnaby) owned by Jennifer A. George, came second out of seventy entries at his final cross-country event, which proves that old does not necessarily mean slow. Now twenty-one, Barnaby is still successfully shown and competes in show jumping and dressage events despite being diagnosed with Cushing's syndrome, arthritis, COPD and suffering his first ever attack of laminitis, all of which just goes to show how correct care and management can extend a horse's useful working life.

imbalance and anaemia can confirm diagnosis. High levels of glucose may also be found in the urine. If any doubt still remains the veterinary surgeon will look for increased levels of cortisol production in response to specific tests.

Coping with Cushing's syndrome

Medication
Pituitary tumours cannot be cured but, if diagnosed early, the use of the drugs cyproheptadine (e.g. Periactin [UK and USA]) and pergolide mesylate (Celance [UK], Permax [USA]) to inhibit the overproduction of cortisol, can prove very effective in controlling symptoms. Available in tablet or syrup form, the drugs will initially need to be administered on a daily basis and then gradually reduced to a maintenance level as the condition stabilises.

Surgical options
Pituitary tumours are virtually inaccessible and therefore cannot be removed.

General management
Since one of the most debilitating side effects of pituitary tumours is laminitis, your horse should be fed and cared for as

described under Laminitis. If, despite a tendency towards laminitis, weight loss is a particular problem, the addition of oil to the diet will help increase digestible energy (DE) levels, and will have the added benefit of helping to improve skin condition. Where mouth ulcers and gum disease are making chewing difficult, hay should be replaced with chaff, and soft mashes made from a combination of unmolassed sugar beet, soaked high-fibre or alfalfa cubes and/or cooked cereal meal, should be offered.

Cushinoid horses may continue to be ridden, though their workload may have to be reduced depending upon the severity of any associated ailments such as laminitis, joint and respiratory infections, sight impairment and loss of internal temperature control. During the summer months, your elderly horse may benefit from having his coat clipped in order to reduce sweating. Judicious rugging will be required throughout the year to prevent both the development of chills and overheating.

What does the future hold?

In the early stages, the use of drug therapy will enable your old horse to live normally for several years or more, though you should be aware that in order to control the disease, he will almost invariably have to remain on drug therapy for the rest of his life which, depending upon the drug used and the dosage required, can prove extremely expensive. Unfortunately, secondary problems such as blindness, dementia and laminitis may eventually claim your old horse's life.

Hypothyroidism

What is it and how is it caused?

True, or primary, hypothyroidism refers to an inadequate production of thyroid hormones which in the elderly horse is most commonly the result of a thyroid gland tumour. The thyroid gland, lies either side of the trachea, near the larynx and consists of two lobes connected together by a band of fibrous tissue. It produces the hormones thyroxine (T4 – which contains iodine), triiodothyronine (T3) and calcitonin which together

Position of the thyroid gland

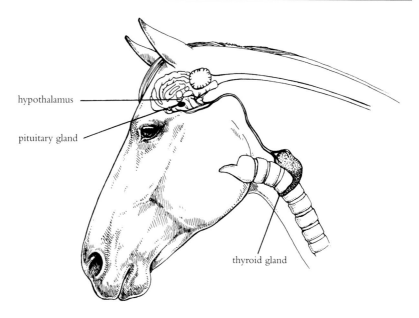

hypothalamus

pituitary gland

thyroid gland

help regulate and maintain many functions of the body including metabolism, sugar absorption, blood pressure, nerve function, heat production and calcium balance. A deficiency in these hormones can seriously compromise the internal environment of your elderly horse's body. (**Note** The opposite of hypothyroidism, hyperthyroidism, is caused by an overactive thyroid gland. Though common in other animals, equine cases of hyperthyroidism have never been recorded or proven.)

What are the symptoms?

The symptoms of hypothyroidism are very similar to those presented by Cushing's syndrome, i.e. a long, coarse coat that fails to shed, muscle loss, weakness, lethargy etc. The two conditions can, therefore, be easily confused. Unlike the cushinoid horse, however, hypothyroid horses tend to become cold easily and their appetite will generally decrease rather than increase. They will also frequently appear very dull and depressed rather than bright and alert and in some cases the thyroid gland may enlarge to such an extent that it is easily seen and felt in the throatlatch area. (**Note** Occasionally the thyroid gland may enlarge without causing any clinical effects.)

Whether or not hypothyroidism causes obesity or weight loss is, however, a matter of some debate. Many vets believe that the condition causes fat deposition, typified by the formation of a thick, cresty neck, and have in some relatively rare cases therefore tenuously linked hypothyroidism with the development of laminitis. In the USA however, experimentally induced hypothyroidism caused by complete removal of the thyroid gland, has suggested that hypothyroid horses are in fact more likely to appear thin and unthrifty. Veterinary opinion remains divided however, as many argue that since even low levels of thyroid hormones will influence the production of other hormones throughout the body, a true comparison cannot be made with the effects of the total removal of thyroid hormones from the circulation. Research is ongoing, as a definitive diagnosis can prove very difficult.

How is it diagnosed?

The problem in diagnosing hypothyroidism is that low blood levels of the thyroid hormones can be caused by many factors and is not on its own indicative of an inactive or diseased thyroid gland. For instance, the functioning of the gland is inextricably linked with the hypothalamus (a small area of the brain) and the pituitary gland, and problems in either of these areas can also lower the production of thyroid hormones. Similarly the utilisation of hormones T4 and T3 can be affected by managerial factors such as the feeding of a diet which contains inadequate/excessive levels of iodine. Stress, pregnancy, starvation, poor appetite, high-protein diets or the administration of pain-relieving drugs, such as bute, can also affect hormone levels. Your vet may, therefore, suggest that your old horse is put on a low-protein, high-fibre diet and is taken off any drug therapy for some ten days or more before blood samples are taken. Your vet may also suggest monitoring the response of the thyroid gland to an injection of thyroid-stimulating hormone (TSH). In a normal horse this would increase the production of thyroid hormones but, in a truly hypothyroid horse, would have little effect.

Coping with hypothyroidism

Medication
Most hypothyroid horses respond well to the daily addition of a

powdered thyroid supplement to the diet. The effective dosage will be determined initially by the severity of your old horse's condition and, thereafter, monitored on a regular basis for the rest of his life. Your vet will only prescribe this treatment, however, if he is sure that your horse is truly hypothyroid because, if given to a horse with a normally functioning thyroid gland, such supplementation can result in excessive levels of thyroid hormones in the bloodstream. This will be recognised by the pituitary gland which will subsequently stop manufacturing TSH causing the thyroid gland to reduce hormone production, thus creating the very problem you were trying to treat.

Though unlikely, if your veterinary surgeon believes that a deficiency in iodine is thought to be a contributing cause, adding cod liver oil or a seaweed supplement to your old horse's feed may prove beneficial.

Surgical options

Tumours of the thyroid gland are generally benign and slow growing. In rare cases when a thyroid tumour proves to be malignant or is severely interfering with swallowing and/or breathing, it can be surgically removed. However, as the gland has a rich blood supply, there can be substantial blood loss during surgery. This factor combined with the complete loss of hormone production means that operations are to be avoided whenever possible.

What does the future hold?

With appropriate care, hypothyroid horses can live a virtually normal life for many years, though they will have to stay on medication for the rest of their days.

Melanomas

What are they and how are they caused?

Melanomas are tumours of the cells which produce skin pigment. It is estimated that some 80% of grey horses over the age of fifteen have one or more of these growths, though the exact

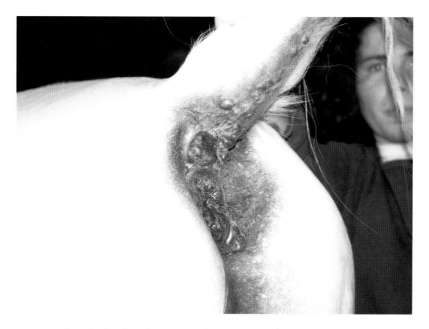

Melanomas

reason for their development is as yet unknown. In most cases the tumours are benign and slow growing, and are un-likely to cause any problems unless they become large, ulcerated and/or infected. Whilst melanomas may remain inactive for months or years, they can become malignant at any time, spread-ing and growing quickly. Occasionally melanomas may develop which are malignant and aggressive from the outset. In severe cases the tumours may spread internally.

Depending upon the size and proliferation of the tumours they may interfere with the functioning of the urinary tract, cause impactive colic or problems during breeding and foaling. Tumours located around the head can make it difficult for the horse to flex at the poll, can interfere with breathing and make swallowing uncomfortable.

What are the symptoms?

Melanomas may appear singly, or in clusters of unsightly black or brown nodules. They may develop anywhere on the body, but are most commonly seen on the underside of the tail, around the anus and genitals or at the margins of the ears and around the parotid salivary glands or jugular region.

How are they diagnosed?

On clinical signs.

Coping with melanomas

Melanomas cannot be cured, therefore treatment is aimed at controlling their development. Tumours which are not causing any specific problems are best left alone because if disturbed they have a tendency to regrow and become more aggressive. Melanomas must however be monitored carefully for any change in their appearance, size or number. There is no single course of treatment that will offer effective control in all cases, therefore if tumours are affecting your horse's quality of life, various combinations of drug therapy and/or surgical treatments may be necessary.

Medication

Oral doses of a drug called cimetidine can in some 30–50% of cases reduce both the size and number of active melanomas by stimulating the body's own antitumour defence mechanism. Although the drug is expensive, if effective it could extend your old horse's life by slowing down, and in some cases even halting, the development of the tumours for many years. Some reports have also suggested that antioxident supplements may be of benefit.

Small to medium-sized tumours may be treated by injecting a chemotherapy drug into the tumour itself. A few months after chemotherapy treatment stops, the tumours do have a tendency to regrow, but the treatment may be repeated as necessary.

Surgical options

Small melanomas can be removed surgically, though it is extremely difficult for your vet to remove all the abnormal cells from the site of the tumour and regrowth is likely to occur. However, the chances of a successful outcome can be increased by combining surgery with other treatments, including the aforementioned drugs, cryosurgery and radiation therapy.

What does the future hold?

Some melanomas may remain benign for ten to twenty years and have no harmful effect but if they become aggressive and either fail to respond to treatment or spread internally, they may cause sufficient distress and damage to warrant euthanasia.

Sarcoids

What are they and how are they caused?

Sarcoids are one of the most common forms of skin tumour and whilst the vast majority are benign and slow growing, others may develop and grow rapidly within a matter of days or weeks. They tend to become increasingly problematic as a horse ages and if knocked or rubbed can become ulcerated and infected. There are in fact six types of sarcoid, each differing somewhat in their appearance, though not all are easily recognisable. All sarcoids, however, are considered to be a form of skin cancer.

Though the exact reason for the development of sarcoids is unknown, particular genetic characteristics are thought to play a role. Whilst biopsies of sarcoid tissue have frequently revealed a virus-like genetic material, no actual virus particle has yet been discovered and at present there is no evidence to suggest that sarcoids can be passed from one horse to another.

Sarcoid

What are the symptoms?

An individual sarcoid may remain static for many years, however others may multiply rapidly or develop to the size of a tennis ball and have either a broad base or hang from a stalk. Sarcoids may appear anywhere on the body, though they most commonly develop around the mouth, eyes and ears, on the chest, underneath the belly (particularly around the sheath and udder) and on the inside of the thighs. Sarcoids may also develop at the site of previous skin injuries.

How are they diagnosed?

Most sarcoids can be diagnosed on clinical signs by an experienced veterinary surgeon. Biopsies will not be taken unless absolutely necessary as they can actually stimulate sarcoid growth.

Coping with sarcoids

General management

As with any form of cancer, the earlier treatment begins, the more effective it may be. Any suspected sarcoid lesions should, therefore, be evaluated by your veterinary surgeon as soon as possible to enable him to choose the best form of treatment available for the particular type, size and location of the sarcoid. Any subsequent change in the shape, size or number of sarcoids should be closely monitored.

Extra care must also be taken to ensure that the sarcoids are not aggravated by tack or rugs rubbing up against them and, in the summer months, when sarcoids will frequently crack and bleed, fly repellent should be applied liberally to help prevent infection. Since susceptible horses can develop sarcoids at the site of any skin damage, the prompt hygienic management of wounds also becomes especially important.

Medication

Drug therapy may consist of a course of injections of a vaccine containing the bacterium bacille Calmette Guérin (BCG), which is normally used to help combat tuberculosis in humans.

Injected directly into a small tumour, the vaccine can draw the immune system's attention to the sarcoid and stimulate it to reject the abnormal cells, though the site may appear to get worse before it gets better. BCG injections can also prove successful in the treatment of larger sarcoids if combined with surgery. However, the vaccine is difficult to get hold of in the UK and in some cases can cause anaphylactic shock.

Chemotherapy injections of cytotoxic drugs, such as Cisplatin, directly into the centre of a sarcoid lesion has proved helpful in some cases, though such drugs are difficult to obtain in the UK. Where appropriate, the preferred treatment by many vets is the topical application of a cytotoxic cream which has proved particularly effective in controlling both the size and number of certain types of sarcoid tumours.

There have been some reports of sarcoids treated successfully by homeopathic remedies such as thuja (either given orally or applied externally as an ointment) or by making a remedy known as a nosode from a sample of your horse's own sarcoid tissue. However, such remedies must be used with great caution and only in consultation with an experienced veterinary surgeon, as in some cases they may simply aggravate a sarcoid and make matters worse.

Surgical options

The removal of sarcoids using cryosurgery, laser treatment or constriction (which involves the application of a tight elastic band around the stalk of a single tumour to cut off its blood supply), is best used in conjunction with other treatments, as the tumours have a tendency to regrow (often more aggressively) somewhere between six months and three years after the operation. Radiation therapy is a particularly effective form of treatment in some cases but is very expensive and restricted to specialist veterinary hospitals.

What does the future hold?

In some cases sarcoids are simply a blemish, and affected horses can live for many years without any associated problems. However, as with the development of any form of skin cancer, sarcoids can have serious implications. In fact, in some cases they can be potentially life threatening, for whilst a sarcoid will not actually kill a horse, a number of affected horses will be put to sleep if the size or location of the sarcoid means they can no longer be ridden. In fact, sarcoid development is taken so seriously that insurance companies may refuse to cover afflicted horses or will at the very least apply an exclusion clause to cover skin disease.

Squamous Cell Carcinomas

What are they and how are they caused?

Like sarcoids, squamous cell carcinomas (SCC) are another form of skin cancer that spread very slowly but which can cause a good deal of local damage. The cauliflower-like growths most commonly affect horses over the age of ten and, though they can appear in any colour of horse, they seem to most frequently affect light-skinned horses such as Appaloosas. Researchers believe that this is because SCC develop as a result of overexposure of unpigmented skin to ultraviolet rays.

What are the symptoms?

The tumours, which tend to ulcerate and bleed easily, generally appear around the membranes of the anus, vulva, penis, mouth, nose and eyes where little or no hair or skin pigment is available to offer protection from sunlight. However SCC have also been found in the stomach, where their effects on the digestive system can cause weight loss, colic etc.

How are they diagnosed?

To be certain of diagnosis a biopsy should be performed.

Coping with squamous cell carcinomas

Surgical options
Effective treatment usually involves surgical removal of the growth followed by radiation therapy or cryosurgery. If the

tumour regrows the same procedure can be performed again without any reduction in effectiveness.

Medication

Injection of a chemotherapy drug directly into the tumour has also proved successful in some cases.

General management

To help prevent recurrence, your elderly horse should wear a fly mask which will help reduce the penetration of ultraviolet rays around his eyes, whilst a sun block can be applied around other unprotected areas such as the mouth and nose.

What does the future hold?

Prompt and aggressive treatment is usually successful.

Appendix One

Veterinary Emergency Authorisation Form

If you ever intend to leave your horse in the care of someone else, whilst you go on holiday, for example, you should complete and sign a veterinary care authorisation form similar to that shown here. In our seemingly litigation-happy society, this will give the carer and the attending veterinary surgeon confidence to act on your behalf in your absence, and will help prevent delays that could otherwise cause needless suffering.

Horse's name: .... Age: ....
(Attach identification certificate e.g. flu/tetanus vaccination card)

Owner's name: ....
Address:..
....
Home tel. no: .... Work tel. no: .... Mobile no: ....

In my absence, I hereby give permission to the person(s) named below to call out a veterinary surgeon and to act on my behalf based on the information provided on this form.

Name: ....**Name:** ....
Tel: .... **Tel:** ....

VETERINARY DETAILS
Name of practice: ....
Address:..
....
Surgery tel. no. ....Emergency tel. no. ....
Current medication/known allergic reactions: ....

INSURANCE (if applicable)
Insurance company name: ....Policy no: ....
Address: ....
Tel. no: ....Fax no: ....

Insurance is provided against:

All veterinary fees incurred either through accident or illness YES NO Limit: £/$ ....

External, accidental injuries only   YES NO Limit: £/$...

If treatment costs are likely to exceed the above insurance limit/or would not be covered by my policy I would/would not wish to proceed with treatment up to a financial limit of £/$..

My horse is NOT INSURED

I would/would not be prepared to proceed with veterinary treatment up to a financial limit of £/$.........................

GENERAL GUIDELINES

1)   If my horse required surgery (e.g. for colic, tendon injury, fracture repair etc.) I would/would not want to proceed with an operation, depending upon the following (circle as appropriate).

a) Chance of success:

80% or above, 70-80%, 60-70%, 50-60%, 40-50%, 30-40%, 20-30%, 20% or lower.

b) Based on my veterinary surgeon's opinion as to what would be fair on my horse.   YES   NO

c) Even if following treatment my horse could no longer be ridden.   YES   NO

2)   Preferred method of euthanasia: a) Lethal injection   b) Gun   c) Captive bolt pistol

3)   If my horse died for an unknown reason I would want a post mortem carried out:

a) YES   b) NO   c) Only if required by insurance company.

4)   I would prefer my horse's body to be:

a) Taken away to be used by hunt/slaughterhouse (only applicable if horse has not received drug treatment).

b) Taken away to be cremated by slaughterhouse.

c) Cremated at a pet crematorium: i) With other animals   ii) Individually

d) In memory of my horse I would like: i) A section of mane or tail.   ii) His/her shoes removed.

iii) Some/all of his/her ashes returned

I hereby agree to be responsible for any veterinary fees and associated costs incurred in relation to the care of my horse, in my absence. I undertake to abide by any decision made by the above named persons in consultation with the attending veterinary surgeon. I will not pursue any claim against those persons or the veterinary practice in relation to any action taken in the best interests of my horse in the circumstances envisaged above.

Signed: ....   Date: ....

Appendix Two

Useful Addresses

The Classical Riding Club
Eden Hall
Kelso
Roxburghshire
TD5 7QD

Flair Air Bag Systems
First Thought (Equine) Ltd
Little Duskin Farm
Covet Lane
Kingston
Canterbury
Kent
CT4 6JS

A. J. Foster Saddlemakers
22-23 Station Street
Walsall
West Midlands
WS2 9JZ

Guardian Multipurpose Mask Company
PO Box 431
Carney
Oklahoma 74832
USA

The Internatonal League for the
   Protection of Horses
Anne Colvin House
Snetterton
Norwich
NR16 2YX

The National Foaling Bank
c/o Meretown Stud
Newport
Shropshire
TF10 8BX

The REACT Equine Allergy Clinic
PO Box 261
Dorking
Surrey
RH5 4YJ

Super Solvitax Veteran Horse Classes
Seven Seas Pet and Animal Health Care
Hedon Road
Hull
HU9 5NJ

The Veteran Horse Society
Office 9, Kenilworth Business Centre
131 Warwick Road
Kenilworth
Warwickshire
CV8 1HY

INDEX

Note: Page numbers in **bold** refer to illustrations; those in *italic* to tables or boxed text

Owned by Sara Willsdon, 19-year-old Fella, pictured at the National Veteran Championships in Wythenshaw Park, Manchester, is in excellent condition and a regular participant in dressage and riding club team events.